# HOSEA
# LOVE'S
# COMPLAINT

### HERMAN VELDKAMP

# HOSEA
# *LOVE'S COMPLAINT*

HERMAN VELDKAMP

www.cantaroinstitute.org

*Hosea: Love's Complaint*
First published in Dutch.
Translated by Theodore Plantinga.

This English edition is a publication of Paideia Press (3248 Twenty First St., Jordan Station, Ontario, Canada L0R 1S0). Copyright ©2024 by Paideia Press. All rights reserved.

Except for brief quotations in critical publications or reviews, no part of this book may be reproduced in any manner without prior written permission from Paideia Press at the address above.

Copy-editing: Paul Aurich
Cover design: Steven R. Martins
Interior book design: Martin Avila

ISBN 978-1-990771-93-4

Printed in the United States of America

# Table of Contents

| | | |
|---|---|---|
| 1. | Beeri's Son | 7 |
| 2. | Forgotten Greatness | 17 |
| 3. | Love's Complaint | 27 |
| 4. | Love's Anger: The First Child | 37 |
| 5. | Love's Anger: The Other Two Children | 47 |
| 6. | Love's Victory | 57 |
| 7. | Holy Rebellion | 65 |
| 8. | Where All That Silver Came From | 75 |
| 9. | Lured into the Wilderness | 85 |
| 10. | From a Valley to a Door | 95 |
| 11. | Harmonious Prayers | 105 |
| 12. | Trembling at God's Goodness | 115 |
| 13. | Criticizing Priests and Criticizing Ourselves | 125 |
| 14. | Feeding Sin | 133 |
| 15. | Piety with a Flavor | 143 |
| 16. | What We Deserve | 153 |
| 17. | Noblesse Oblige | 163 |
| 18. | God's Knowledge and Our Knowledge | 173 |
| 19. | The Stumbling Block | 183 |
| 20. | Convincing Proof | 193 |

| | | |
|---|---|---|
| 21. | Attack from the Rear | 203 |
| 22. | Inheritance and the Rich Man | 213 |
| 23. | General or Physicians? | 223 |
| 24. | The Prodigal Son | 233 |
| 25. | Of Sunshine and Rain | 245 |
| 26. | God's Predicament | 255 |
| 27. | Conforming to the World | 265 |
| 28. | The Sleeping Baker | 275 |
| 29. | One-Sidedness | 285 |
| 30. | Unheard Prayers | 293 |
| 31. | Sensible Asses | 303 |
| 32. | Sowing and Reaping | 313 |
| 33. | A Hostile Audience | 323 |
| 34. | A Horrible Prayer | 333 |
| 35. | The Love of Monuments | 343 |
| 36. | Standing Firm | 351 |
| 37. | Favorite Activities | 361 |
| 38. | Exodus | 369 |
| 39. | Paying Attention | 377 |
| 40. | Like Doves | 385 |
| 41. | Our Forefathers | 395 |
| 42. | Sins on Record | 403 |
| 43. | The Lily and the Poplar | 411 |

# 1

## Beeri's Son

*The chief eunuch gave them other names, calling Daniel Belteshazzar, Hananiah Shadrach, Mishael Meshach, and Azariah Abednego (1:7 JB). The word of the Lord came to Hosea the son of Beeri, in the days of Uzziah, Jotham, Ahaz, and Hezekiah, kings of Judah, and in the days of Jeroboam the son of Joash, king of Israel (1:1).*

IT WAS A STIRRING AGE when Hosea, the son of Beeri, made his voice heard in the Kingdom of the ten tribes. Israel was enjoying a golden age under Jeroboam II, the king who occupied the throne in Samaria at that time. Many thought it was a great time to be alive, for never had the authority of Israel's kings extended further, and never had the Israelites lived in greater luxury.

When Hosea raised his voice in *such* a time and spoke of judgment to come, all indications suggested that he was wrong–completely wrong. To his contemporaries, therefore, Hosea was a narrow-minded bigot who refused to look at the facts. At best, he was an arch-pessimist, as all prophets seem to be.

Nevertheless, Hosea turned out to be right. With his own eyes, he witnessed the fulfillment of those somber prophecies. It is highly probable that he lived to see the dark day when Samaria fell, and the ten tribes were deported to Assyria. If prophets took any pleasure in the misfortune, they foresee– and they don't–Hosea could well have said to those who had laughed at him earlier: "I told you so!"

According to the first verse of the book, Hosea was still prophesying during the days of Hezekiah, king of Judah, whose rule certainly did not begin before 727 B.C., that is, five years before the start of the period that ended in Israel's total defeat and exile. Thus, this prophet certainly lived through a great deal! He witnessed the *foreign* enemies getting closer and closer to his country until the kings of Israel became vassals of the Assyrian conquerors. He also witnessed boundless political confusion *within* his own country: it was a time of blood and tears. In a period of twenty years, there were no fewer than six new kings.

How was this possible? The one "king" murdered the other and became king in his place. Zechariah, Shallum, Menahem,

Pekahiah, Pekah, and Hoshea were the usurpers who seized the throne in turn. It was a hopeless battle of faction against faction, one group favoring Egypt and another Assyria, while no one favored the Lord. It was a struggle in which the dagger had the last word, and assassination was the order of the day.

And while Israel was torn internally and the land was consumed by armed conflicts, the damage was made even greater through a war with Judah, Israel's brother nation. Thus, it should come as no surprise that Israel easily fell prey to the world power Assyria.

The chaos in political life was equaled–if not exceeded–by the degeneration in religious, social, and moral respects. We have already heard Amos, Hosea's contemporary, denouncing Israel's decline.[1] Beeri's son sings the same tune–but in his own way. A prophet is not a parrot who simply repeats what God tells him but a person of flesh and blood. Just as the song a bird sings is rooted in its anatomy, each prophet's way of speaking depends on his nature.

Amos sees Israel's sin as *injustice*–especially social injustice! Hosea points to the same sin when he speaks of *faithlessness*. The Lord's people are unfaithful to their husband just as an adulterous wife is unfaithful. Worshipping calves means abandoning the service of the Lord; it is spiritual adultery, faithlessness! Relying on Assyria, and then Egypt, and then Assyria again is also faithless conduct. The Lord

---

1. See my book *The Farmer from Tekoa* (Paideia Press, 1977).

becomes very, very jealous when His people fail to ask Him for help in times of need.

But it makes little difference whether Amos accuses the Israelites of *injustice* or Hosea accuses them of *faithlessness*. The two charges boil down to the same thing. The farmer from Tekoa is angry because God's *righteousness* is dishonored by Israel's conduct, while Beeri's son is just as angry–or perhaps even angrier–because God's *love* is spurned and scorned.

It's fine to call Amos the prophet of God's righteousness and Hosea the prophet of God's love–as long as we do not think in terms of a *tension* or *contradiction* between these two, for with God there is no conflict between love and righteousness. In Him, they are one. Thus, we should not declare that Amos is a straightforward, crude, unbending farmer who keeps repeating the same uncompromising prophecies of doom, while Hosea is a charming musician playing gentle music on his flute. No, that's not the way it is at all!

True, Amos is the prophet of divine *righteousness*, and Hosea is the prophet of divine love. This is even reflected in their names. The name Amos means *burden-bearer*, and Amos was, in fact, burdened with the awful task of announcing God's judgment to his people. But the name *Hosea* means *salvation-bearer*. Hosea actually bears the same name as Jesus, in whom God's love reaches its climax. Love could go no further. Thus, we need not look to Amos for this stirring account of God's love that we find in Hosea, who tells us that Israel is God's bride whom He will lure into the wilderness where He will speak tenderly to her so that she will remain His bride forever (2:14, 19).

Love is not all sweetness and light. Love can also manifest itself in *anger*. A love that is scorned arouses God's wrath just as much as righteousness that is violated. Amos says that Israel does wrong, and Hosea complains that Israel is unfaithful. This gives us some variation. Yet, there is no variation in meaning, for these are two different ways of expressing the same idea. Both Amos and Hosea are leading up to the same conclusion: wrath, judgment, and punishment! The one bases his anger on God's righteousness, while the other bases it on God's love.

Actually, the wrath of which Hosea speaks (i.e., the anger of a jealous man, the anger resulting from a scorning of divine love in callous disregard of God's feelings) is much more frightening than the wrath voiced by Amos. Can you think of anything worse than being consumed by the flames of love? Isn't it much more horrible to be cursed by the mother who loves you than by some stranger? Isn't it heartbreaking to be told that we have paid no attention whatsoever to such great mercy and love?

Hosea was given the unpleasant task of announcing that if we do not allow the flame of love to *warm* our hearts, it will *consume* us instead. When we view Hosea in light of this, we can see why Amos gives us neither the moving sound of wounded love that we hear from Hosea's harp nor the overwhelming outburst of wrath that comes from Hosea's mouth. Hosea makes us tremble! Only those who know how painful faithfulness can be and how angry a wounded lover can become will understand how the prophet of divine love could say:

> I will be fierce as a panther to Ephraim,
> fierce as a lion to Judah–
> I will maul the prey and go,
> carry it off beyond hope of rescue–I, the Lord
> (5:14 NEB).

Hosea's way of expressing himself reminds us of Jesus, his namesake, whose spirit was present in Hosea. (Jesus Himself was prophesying through Hosea.) The same mouth that spoke of *love* also spoke of unquenchable fire! Thus, we shouldn't waste our time looking for a contradiction between justice and love, choosing Hosea or Amos over Jesus, for to do so would be to admit that we know nothing of God's righteousness and even less of His love!

We know virtually nothing about Hosea as a person. The little that we do know can be summed up quickly enough. We already noted that his name has the same meaning as Jesus' name. But that was not unusual in itself. Such names as Hosea and Joshua and Josiah were as common among the Israelites as John and James and Robert in our country. There are more people in the Bible whom we could call namesakes of Jesus.

We also know that Hosea, unlike Amos, was not of the Kingdom of Judah but came from Israel itself, which led him to speak of the king of Israel as "*our* king" (see 7:5). Finally, Hosea introduces himself to us as "the son of Beeri," but who Beeri was and what sort of man he was is also unknown to us. Thus, Hosea emerges from the darkness of history like Melchizedek without father or mother or genealogy.

Some commentators believe that Hosea came from a family of priests. Others argue that he came from a farming family, since his use of metaphors testifies to an extensive knowledge of farming. Yet, these are suppositions that cannot be proven. Hosea's *person* is completely concealed behind his *office*.

We do learn a few things about Hosea's *marriage* in the first chapter. We read that at God's command, Hosea married a woman named Gomer, the daughter of Diblaim, who is also an unknown figure. We are told that Gomer bore three children, and we discover that the marriage brought much pain and unhappiness to the prophet (see chapters one and three of Hosea).[2*]

---

2  * I choose for a realistic understanding of Hosea's marriage as opposed to any idealized view. I will return to this matter later, in chapter 3.

But the story of this marriage is not passed on to us to reveal some interesting and more intimate aspects of Hosea's life. Rather, this marriage served to reinforce the *Word of the Lord* which Hosea proclaimed. Hosea was *ordered* by God to marry, just as Jeremiah was ordered *not* to marry and Ezekiel was ordered not to mourn the death of his wife.[3]

Through his unhappy marriage, Hosea was to give Israel a vivid lesson about the sorry relationship between God and His people. The faithlessness of his wife was to make him feel the same kind of pain in his own life that God felt because of the unfaithfulness of His people. Hosea was to preach not only through words but also through *deeds*. With body and soul, he was to be God's slave and say, "Here I am, Lord."

Even Hosea's marriage was subordinated to his *office* and to the *message* he was commissioned to bring. The personality of Hosea recedes into the background, for the important thing is the message he preaches!

At the very beginning of this book, there are two things that must be made clear. The first is that the Word of the Lord comes at a time of *political instability* and *tumult*, a time when the nation is *unfaithful* to the Lord. In such circumstances, all personal questions become secondary. The things going on

---

3    See my book on Ezekiel, *entitled De balling van de Kabaroe*, 235–6.

are too serious and consequential for us to worry about some scandal in the life of the unimportant preacher.

Once we realize that Hosea's time is much like ours, we will be deeply ashamed of our intense interest in *personal* trivia, our quest for the minor details of theological and non-theological quarrels, and our boundless appetite for spicy stories. We will no longer ask whether Rev. A is a more entertaining preacher than Rev. B. Instead, we'll listen in holy fear to the Word of the Lord as it came to Hosea, the son of Beeri, and ask what that Word means for us in the second half of the twentieth century. In short, the important thing is to *listen*.

Second, let those who are called to bring God's word remember that God asks His prophets—and He has made us all prophets—to convey His message in *all* that they do. God asks His messengers to preach through their *deeds!*

If God's church echoes with the beautiful words and the voices of the prophets predicting nothing but prosperity, while those who sit in the pew fail to set the seal of God's word on their homes and marriages and business affairs, the sun will set on both the church and the world.

# 2

# Forgotten Greatness

*The word of the Lord that came to Hosea the son of Beeri, in the days of Uzziah, Jotham, Ahaz, and Hezekiah, kings of Judah, and in the days of Jeroboam the son of Joash, king of Israel (1:1).*

LET'S NOW TAKE ANOTHER look at the verse with which Hosea introduces his book. This text is surprisingly important, for it casts light on the *dates* of Hosea's career as a prophet. Knowing these dates enables us to understand this man of God better. Although it is not true that every person is a product of his environment and times, and although prophets cannot be *explained* on the basis of historical circumstances, we do get a better perspective on what prophets have to say if we are familiar with the historical background of their words and deeds.

Thus, we can and may look at the prophet Hosea in the context of his time. We should be thankful that the scriptures give us some information about when he lived. If we knew *nothing* about the dates, much of what the prophet says would seem as mysterious to us as the incomprehensible language of an oracle. Yet, God's word was not meant to puzzle us.

This is not the only reason why the first verse is important. Equally important as the information it contains–and even eloquent–is its *silence* on certain points. Sometimes silence is more eloquent than words.

What Hosea is silent about is a whole series of kings of Israel during whose reign he lived and prophesied–the kings I mentioned in the previous chapter. We know their names from the historical books of the Bible: Zechariah, Shallum, Menahem, Pekahiah, Pekah, and Hoshea. There are six of them, but Hosea doesn't say a word about them. They are of no importance to him. Like the psalmist, Hosea seems to be saying, "I will not take their names upon my lips."

This is a thought-provoking omission. It's all the more puzzling because Hosea came not from Judea but from Israel. Thus, he is silent about the names of his *own* kings and dates in his book by making reference to "foreign" rulers! He names all those foreign rulers (the kings of Judah) in order: Uzziah, Jotham, Ahaz, and Hezekiah. Not one is missing! But when he turns to the rulers of his own country, six of the kings who ruled during his time are left out. Apparently, Hosea regards it as sufficient to mention one of Israel's kings—Jeroboam, the son of Joash.

This is not something for Israel to be proud of. On the surface, it seems as strange as hearing a Dutchman declare that he lives in the days of Queen Elizabeth of England rather than Queen Juliana of the Netherlands!

Why this strange omission? We should not try to explain it as an unintentional oversight, for the Holy Spirit was guiding Hosea just as much when he wrote the very first verse as when he wrote the moving promises and severe threats later on. Nor should we consider the possibility that Hosea was unacquainted with these names. Anyone who takes an interest in public affairs—and public life was a special concern of the prophets—would know the names of his famous contemporaries, especially those who succeeded in becoming king. No, such explanations will not do.

A more promising explanation is the following. The kings of Judah, as descendants of David, were the only legitimate royal house. The royal house of the kingdom of Israel did not form a continuous line. (Especially after Jeroboam II, many usurpers came to the throne.)

But this suggested solution leaves it unexplained why the name of Jeroboam was not omitted by Hosea as well. If Hosea only wanted to mention the "pious" kings, why would he mention Jeroboam, the son of Jotham? Jeroboam was certainly no servant of the Lord. Furthermore, King Ahaz of Judah, whom Hosea did mention, was known mainly for his *godlessness*.

Could it be that Hosea was too ashamed of these kings to mention them? People who dishonor their families are spoken of as "black sheep." Their names are rarely mentioned in the home, especially when visitors are present. Yet these lost sons and daughters are not forgotten, for not a day passes–or should pass–when their names are not mentioned before the throne of grace in earnest prayer. Their parents don't like to talk about them in conversation; they're too ashamed.

This could be Hosea's reason for not taking the names of these kings on his lips. The unmentioned kings represent an exceedingly dark chapter in Israel's history. Almost all of them were depraved murderers who did not shrink from regicide, men who climbed onto the throne over the dead bodies of their predecessors!

One of the psalmists gives us a beautiful picture of God's throne when he declares that righteousness and justice are its foundation. This throne is pictured as resting on the ark containing the two tablets of the law. This means that God's throne is based on law, in which the purest justice is manifested. But these kings of Israel, who, as theocratic kings, were supposed to bear the stamp of God's kingship, represented the exact opposite; their shaky thrones stood on ground drenched with human blood.

This may well be the reason why Hosea failed to mention the names of these men of might. He was ashamed of them, for they were not genuine kings. Yet, there is another point to bear in mind: the prophets did not normally shrink from openly denouncing the sins of their own people–and even their rulers.

The ultimate reason for Hosea's silence was that he did not consider these men worth mentioning since their deeds were completely useless for God's kingdom. As we consider this explanation, we must remember that you do not have to be a God-fearing person to do something useful for God's kingdom. The Lord can use avowed enemies of the church– and He has often used them for His purposes. Although such enemies think they are breaking the church down, they are in fact building it up. The king of Persia certainly cannot be counted among those who were born in Zion. Yet the Lord said to Cyrus: "You shall be my shepherd to carry out all my purpose, so that Jerusalem may be rebuilt, and the foundations of the temple may be laid" (Isa. 44:28 NEB).

It can be said of all the kings mentioned by Hosea in the first verse of his book that they "served" God in some way or other, that is, that they served some divine purpose or other. This even applies to unfaithful Jeroboam II, the only king of Israel mentioned by Hosea. Jeroboam did not fear God– which was definitely an evil in the eyes of the Lord–but he carried out the task assigned to him. He was the *deliverer* appointed by God and spoken of by Jonah; he was the one who would free Israel from the domination of Damascus. "He restored the border of Israel from the entrance of Hamath as far as the Sea of Arabah, according to the word of the Lord, the God of Israel, which he spoke by his servant Jonah the son of Amittai, the prophet, who was from Gath-hepher" (II Kings 14:25).

Even godless Ahaz, who is also mentioned in the first verse, served God's purposes. The beautiful prophecy in Isaiah 7:14 is the result of his unbelieving attitude. When Ahaz, in his imprudent unbelief, refused to even ask for a sign, the Lord spoke to him through Isaiah to tell him that there would be a sign anyway: "Behold, a young woman shall conceive and bear a son, and shall call his name Immanuel." Isaiah hangs a lantern on the back of godless Ahaz, so to speak; Ahaz himself does not walk in the light, but he casts light on the paths of all who live in humble fear of the Lord. It is certainly not a joyful or glorious task to serve as a torchbearer for others while you remain in the dark yourself, but it is a task, nevertheless.

Thus, the Lord says to all Ahaz-figures, to all preachers of the word who let the light shine for others but not for themselves, to all Jeroboams who work actively for God's cause without themselves sharing in God's treasures: "You shall be my shepherd to carry out all my purpose, so that Jerusalem may be rebuilt, and the foundations of the temple may be laid."

But the Lord does not and will not use people like Shallum and Menahem and Pekah and Pekahiah and Zechariah and Hoshea even in this "negative" way. Such people are completely useless to Him, and therefore they fade away in the mist. Their names are not even mentioned by God's prophet.

Doubtless these "kings" surrounded themselves with great splendor. All of them were ambitious men. They tried to make "names" for themselves and wanted to elevate Israel to the status of a world power. But they lived only for themselves and for their *own glory*. Therefore, their fame has faded, and their greatness is forgotten. They are not important enough for a prophet to date the years of his career by referring to them. They would love to have seen the years of their reign given a prominent place in the history books, but the prophet Hosea obliterates them with his silence. He doesn't even mention their names–just as though they had never existed!

These kings of Israel were members of the covenant people–in fact, very prominent members. Yet, they are nameless in God's eyes. They are nameless because they never learned to devote their lives to the service of God. Instead, they spent their lives solely pursuing their *own* interests.

This pitiful sight is still with us in our time. Just look carefully through the ranks of those who call themselves "children of Zion."

No, you need not be guilty of assassination or adultery or theft to be without a name in God's eyes and to be missing from the book of life. Many make the fatal mistake of supposing that only recognized scoundrels and open sinners will be excluded from the kingdom of God. That's certainly not what the Bible teaches us. What is the sin that makes us fit for nothing but the fires of hell? Being *fruitless* and *useless!* One may be a refined person and a respected member of the church and enjoy an excellent reputation among men, but still be without a name in the eyes of God. The question is simply whether we have lived *for ourselves* or *for the Lord.*

Unfortunately, being concerned exclusively with oneself and one's own interest has become a way of life for many people. Therefore, we must take a careful look at our own lives to see how often we have deliberately chosen *not* to seek ourselves and have instead *denied* ourselves. The result of this examination will doubtless be painful. The somber testimony of the Scriptures that sinners all look out for themselves does not, unfortunately, apply to the "world" only. It is even possible to be very zealous on behalf of the Lord of hosts in the hope of gaining *personal* fame and glory. There is nothing more devious than the human heart!

Remember the warning of Jesus: "Do not rejoice that the spirits submit to you, but rejoice that your names are written in heaven" (Luke 10:20 NIV). But if our names are *not* in the book of life, our greatness will soon be *forgotten*. Our names may be mentioned in reverent tones among men and may appear on the list of those who have served in the church council or perhaps even be included in our denomination's directory among the ordained ministers, but if the fruit of a renewed life was not visible in our lives, we will not be mentioned in the book of life.

That fruit, of course, is not *our* work, just as the vine does not produce fruit by itself but depends on the *root*. "If you abide in me," Christ has promised, "you will bear much fruit."

Is Christ living in you? That's the question!

# 3

## Love's Complaint

*Go, marry a whore, and get children with a whore,*
*for the country itself has become nothing but a*
*whore by abandoning Yahweh (1:2 JB).*

MUCH HAS BEEN WRITTEN about Hosea's strange marriage. Some interpreters cling stubbornly to the view that the marriage between Hosea the prophet and Gomer, the daughter of Diblaim, never actually took place. They maintain that the story is to be understood in a figurative sense. Some regard it as an *allegory*, like the story Nathan told David about the rich man who took the poor man's only lamb. Others argue that it is to be understood as a *vision*, that Hosea was only married to Gomer in a dream, just as Peter saw the "unclean" animals on a great sheet in his trance.

Then there are interpreters who argue just as persistently that everything in the first chapter of Hosea must be understood *literally*, that the prophet really did enter into an unhappy marriage with a worthless woman. The advocates of the literal interpretation are divided, however, on particular questions. This shouldn't surprise us, for engagement and marriage always give people a lot to talk about. Sometimes there's nothing wrong with talking about a marriage, but it does become dangerous if our thinking about the scriptures makes us forget to listen to God's word as it speaks to us *through* the Scriptures.

I do not propose to elevate all arguments that have arisen in connection with the question of Hosea's marriage. Suffice to say that I agree with the interpreters who think in terms of a *real marriage*.

The time had come when the word as preached no longer made an impression upon Israel. Therefore, the *spoken Word* would have to be reinforced by a proclamation through deeds. The Israelites would have paid little or no attention if Hosea had spoken to them in allegorical terms and had told them what he saw in a vision. After all, everyone has dreams! But a marriage between a prophet of the Lord and a wanton woman who ran away from her husband would surely draw their attention. Everyone would be buzzing with gossip; it would soon become their favorite topic of conversation.

That was exactly God's purpose. Once everyone was talking about the scandal and had a chance to express their sanctimonious opinion about the slut whom the prophet had chosen as his wife, Hosea would speak up and say, "You people are just like that wife of mine!"

The marriage officially recorded between Hosea, the son of Beeri, and Gomer, the daughter of Diblaim, was a *forced marriage*. It was not forced in the ordinary sense, for Gomer was not pregnant before the ceremony took place. It was forced in that God *ordered* Hosea to marry Gomer. He had no choice in the matter.

If Hosea had been allowed to choose, he would certainly not have taken as his life's partner a woman with a reputation for lewdness. But his was not to reason why: his was to subject himself to the will of God, who commanded him to marry a whore. This was a command from the Lord God Himself, and there was nothing for Hosea to do but obey. If it pleased God that Hosea should marry this woman, he would do so, however painful it might be–and painful it was!

Who could help but be moved by the agony of the marriage drama sketched for us here in such realistic terms? Is there a marriage story in our time that can equal it? Just look at Hosea, and then at his wife. Don't you see that a head-on collision was inevitable?

The entire personality of Hosea can be summed up in two words–*faithfulness* and *love.* How faithful he was is apparent from the series of kings mentioned in the first verse of the book. These kings cover a period of 60 years. During all those years, Hosea struggled to serve God faithfully. That he was a sensitive and considerate man with a heart full of love is apparent from the fact that there is virtually no other prophet able to tell of the Lord's love for his unfaithful people in such a fervent way as Hosea.

The tragedy of Hosea's life was that God decreed that he *must* marry a woman with a character the complete opposite of his own. Gomer was simply unacquainted with love and faithfulness. She turned her love of life into an empty and contemptible game. She threw herself into the arms of other men, causing her beloved husband the greatest pain. She certainly earned her reputation as a worthless woman!

We should not assume that Gomer was already a "woman with a past" when Hosea asked for her hand in marriage. She was certainly a lewd and frivolous person–in that sense she was already a "wanton woman"–and Hosea felt immediately that they were not a good match. Perhaps he hoped for the best all the same.

At the outset everything appeared to be going well. Before long there was parental joy in the home of Hosea and Gomer, for Gomer gave birth to a son (1:3). But the happiness did not last long. Serious trouble came more quickly than Hosea expected, although he must have realized that things were bound to go wrong. His wife Gomer gave birth to two more children (first a daughter and then another son), but the birth of these children was not a reason for delirious joy: Hosea, to his sorrow, could not testify that he was the father, as he had been able to do in the case of Gomer's first child. The father would have to be sought among Gomer's lovers.

The discovery that Gomer was unfaithful must have been painful to Hosea. Yet, although he made his pain known in the names, he gave the two children (i.e., *Lo-ruhamah*, which means not pitied, and Lo-ammi, which means *not my people*), he did love and accept them as if they were his own, which they were not.

The conflict became even more painful when Gomer ran away from him. (That she did so is apparent from chapter 3.) Now the problems in their relationship were out in the open. Hosea, whose love seems inexhaustible, went after her, for according to the command he received from God, he must not only marry her but *love her* (3:1). This makes the tragedy all the greater.

If only Hosea were free of that woman! If only he could let her go! But that's just what he couldn't do. He had to love her, and he did love her with the self-surrendering love in his tender heart. Despite all that had happened, he must have loved his unfaithful, runaway wife passionately!

But why should we speak of Hosea's pain? The real pain was in *God's* wounded heart. God had to watch His people, the bride He had chosen for Himself, become unfaithful and desert Him to chase after Baals: "The land commits great harlotry by forsaking the Lord" (1:2).

If only God could free Himself from that unfaithful bride! If only He could hate her and repudiate her! But that's just what He couldn't do. Freely He had chosen to love Israel, and now He *had* to love her through thick and thin.

Yet things should not and could not continue the way they were. Thus, in Hosea's marriage, we are given a vivid picture of the tragedy, the fearful conflict, the lovers' quarrel between God and His people.

By forcing His prophet to marry the adulterous Gomer, the Lord made Hosea feel something of the pain He Himself suffered because of His unfaithful people. Through the events in his own life, Hosea was made to feel and understand the complaint of God's wounded love–if only in a weak way. Prophecy and life become one for him. Hosea was not a parrot repeating God's word but a living, animated witness. He spoke not just through his mouth but out of a broken heart. That's an important lesson for all who speak for God and about Him.

A second lesson taught by the story of Hosea is that the Lord wants to make *total* use of His servants. He doesn't just ask for their services as spokesmen but claims all the aspects of their lives, making demands even on their marriage and their most intimate feelings.

Because Hosea serves God in all that he is and does, he is like his great namesake Jesus. When we encounter Hosea in the Scriptures as someone who has come to do God's will, we are really encountering Christ. God has given us an example in the person of Hosea, in the hope that we will walk in Hosea's footsteps. The Lord does not need servants who are willing to do *something* for Him: He needs people who are willing to give themselves *totally*.

Now we turn to the unhappy marriage of Hosea and Gomer, which is an illustration, a vivid picture of what had happened to the relationship between God and His people. Just as a man and woman get married, the Lord chose Israel as His bride. He loved her in a manner that defies description and demonstrated that love in all sorts of ways. He pampered her. Indeed, one could say that He "spoiled" His wife with His generosity.

And what did Israel do? How did she respond to God's love? Listen to the Lord's complaint: "The land commits great harlotry by forsaking the Lord."

Israel did just what Gomer did, even though she was quick to express dismay at Gomer's unfaithfulness. And that's usually how it goes. We have a sharp eye for the sins of others–

especially if we are the victims–but we don't seem to notice that we do the same thing ourselves to God.

Israel was completely blind to her own sin. Yet, sin she did. She chased after the Baals and sought assistance from foreign kings instead of the Lord. Her worship became an external show. These offenses were not just individual sins but manifestations of the one great sin of Israel's life–spiritual adultery. The Israelites were faithless covenant breakers!

The Lord is not angry about this: He's just deeply hurt. His wounded love, which gets no response from Israel, complains over and over: "The land commits great harlotry by forsaking the Lord."

Are we any better than the Israel of Hosea's time? I trust that you and I are not guilty of open adultery. However, much we may denounce "whores and drunks," do we realize that our life with God is a continually flawed relationship?

In a good marriage, the husband and wife are supposed to live *with* each other and not just sleep beside each other. But there are thousands who live *beside* God instead of *with* Him. They are busy looking in all directions, but they do not look at God. They never get around to *responding* to God's love by deeds of gratitude and love. They live for themselves–that's all there is to it!

In the midst of the church's secularized life, a life in which there is no heart full of love, I hear the monotonous complaint of God's unanswered love: "The land commits great harlotry by forsaking the Lord."

Did you know that for God's love to complain about you is just about the worst thing that could ever happen to you? Do you know what's worst of all? That you don't even *hear* the complaint!

# 4

# Love's Anger: The First Child

*And the Lord said to him, "Call his name Jezreel; for yet a little while, and I will punish the house of Jehu for the blood of Jezreel, and I will put an end to the kingdom of the house of Israel. And on that day, I will break the bow of Israel in the valley of Jezreel (1:4–5).*

GOD'S LOVE WILL NOT go on complaining forever. If His love was not capable of anger, it would not be worthy of the name love. God's love is like a flame that warms us but burns us if we spurn its warmth and show no interest in its blessing.

Love's anger is already visible in the name which Hosea, acting on God's command, gave the first child born to Gomer. That child was named *Jezreel*. This was hardly a beautiful name, for it does not have a positive meaning, as we shall soon see.

The reason for this name, of course, was that the boy would walk around among the people with a name that spelled trouble for Israel. He, too, would be a walking proclamation. His threatening name would remind people continually of the *judgment to come*, for *Jezreel* means God *sows*. This son of Gomer and Hosea was a representative or embodiment of the entire nation, as it were, and his name meant that his people would no longer stand recorded in God's book as *Israel*. They would be called *Jezreel* instead.

As you can see, this change in name was a fairly small one, for the two names have similar sounds. In the Bible, we read about more such small changes in names: Sarai became Sarah, and Abram became Abraham. Now it was the turn of the grandson of Abraham and Sarah, but this time the change in name was not to be for the better but for the worse. The grandson's name had already been changed once before from *Jacob* to *Israel*. That was a promotion. But now comes a demotion! The name Israel makes us think of struggle and conquest—your conduct has been that of a prince! But the name *Jezreel*, by contrast, makes us think of dispersion and defeat.

By way of explanation, the Lord tells us: "On that day, I will break the bow of Israel in the valley of Jezreel." Whether Israel's final defeat actually included a battle in the valley of Jezreel, we do not know. It may be that the "valley of Jezreel" is mentioned here as a symbol. In any event, it makes no difference, for we are told that Israel's bow, its most important weapon—today we would speak of missiles instead—will be broken. Israel's army will be smashed, and its glory will fade. The Lord will intervene in the battle and make *His own people* moan: they will be scattered far and wide and be hunted down. This faithless people will be reduced to ashes and will melt away before His eyes as wax melts before fire.

Thus, Israel will be humbled after the height of Peniel. Israel has become Jezreel! Do you understand what this awful judgment, the change of name, implies?

Suppose the Lord were to come to us and say that our Reformed churches are really Deformed churches! Well, that's the sort of thing Hosea had to tell his contemporaries. Reformed Israel, you are so deformed that although you hold your head high in pride and maintain that you are the greatest of all nations and boast of your glory, all your fame and glory will soon evaporate like a morning mist! "I will break the bow of Israel in the valley of Jezreel."

Israel will become Jezreel! How quickly things change! How the mighty have fallen!

The reason for this judgment to come is this: "I will punish the House of Jehu for the blood of Jezreel." Clearly, this is an allusion to the guilt Jehu took upon himself when he seized the throne at the cost of the blood of Jehoram, Ahaziah and his brothers, Jezebel, and all the royal seed of Ahab's house.

This royal blood that had been spilled still cries out to be avenged. There was still blood guilt to be dealt with, according to Hosea, and the punishing anger would soon be unleashed.

This is worthy of special attention, for two reasons. First, it appears here that the children are made to pay for the sins of their fathers. Jehu had died long before Hosea wrote these words. The royal dynasty in power (descendants of Jehu living in the time of Hosea) would have to pay for wrong done by their forefather, King Jehu, so many years earlier.

God goes far into the past to find grievances. Is that fair on His part? Of course it is, for Jehu's descendants were not innocent young princes unacquainted with evil. We could say that in this case, too, the sons continue in the sins of their fathers. We know that the Lord visits the unrighteousness of the fathers upon the children, unto the third and fourth generation of those who hate Him.

The children do not escape unpunished, but neither do the fathers. This miserable business really started with the fathers. That's one of the disturbing realities of the unity of generations. No one sins all by himself, for his sin drags his family and descendants down with him, just as knocking over the first of a neatly arranged row of dominoes causes all the rest of them to topple over too. We see our own sins magnified in our children. Like father, like son! The blood guilt of our fathers is a force in our lives. Do you see the implications?

Each time I sin, I am sinning against God, against myself, and against my children!

There is a second reason why this judgment should draw our attention. Jehu's guilt calls for punishment, as we have seen. The blood that has been shed cries out to be avenged. "But was Jehu really guilty?" we ask ourselves in surprise. The blood shed by Jehu was far from innocent. Wasn't Jehu speaking the truth when he asked Jehoram: "What peace can there be, so long as the harlotries and the sorceries of your mother Jezebel are so many? (II Kings 9:22).

What makes the matter even stranger is that Jehu undertook this bloodbath not on his own initiative but at the command of the Lord Himself. Through a servant of Elisha, he was told: "Thus says the Lord!" These words he could not ignore. The divine "Thou shalt" rang in Jehu's ears as God told him: "You are to strike down the family of Ahab your master, and I will avenge the blood of my servants the prophets and all of the servants of Yahweh on Jezebel and the whole family of Ahab. I will wipe out every male belonging to the family of Ahab, fettered or free in Israel" (II Kings 9:7-8 JB).

What a puzzle! We hardly know what to think of God any longer. At one point He says one thing, and a little later He says the opposite. He declares that the blood of the Lord's prophets must be avenged on Jezebel, but when Jehu obediently carries out this command and does exactly as he is told, his children are informed that the blood of Jezebel and her clique cries out to be avenged!

It must be very dangerous to be around God, for He is a consuming fire, and you can never be sure that you will not somehow get burned. Had Jehu refused to carry out the assignment given him by God, he would have been in trouble for disobeying. Now that he has carried out his odious duty, he's in trouble anyway, for the blood he has shed cries out to be avenged!

This matter looks still stranger when we recall that God is threatening Jehu's *descendants* with punishment due for misdeeds of long ago, while He never said anything about those misdeeds to Jehu himself but on the contrary praised him for what he had done and even *rewarded* him: "Since you have done properly what was pleasing in my sight, and have achieved all I have set my heart on against Ahab's family, your sons shall sit on the throne of Israel down to the fourth generation" (II Kings 10:30 JB).

I'm about ready to give up and say, "I just can't fathom it!" But I stop short of saying this because the Scriptures teach us that the Lord sees what is in our hearts. This casts some revealing light on the complicated story of Jehu.

Consider this. Things look so frightfully *difficult* in God's Kingdom. It looks as though even the righteous can hardly expect a blessing! I may be very zealous on behalf of the Lord of hosts–just as Jehu was zealous–and do what is pleasing in God's sight, but what if I am seeking glory and praise for *myself* through all this zeal, so that people will consider me an exemplary Christian? That turns my zeal into sin, for whatever is not a fruit of faith is sin! If I'm a member of a church and attend church for some reason other than a desire to hear the word of God and to commune with His people, my church attendance is sin! Thus, it's not hard to become guilty in God's eyes, for He sees what's in our hearts.

It's not a question of *what* we do but *how* and *why* we do it. If I give some money to a poor beggar because I know I will be praised for it, then my act of charity, however large the gift, is a sin. Even if I were to give *all* my goods to the poor, it would still mean nothing if there was not love in my heart. Thus, the deeds of which we are most proud turn out to be sinful. We need forgiveness especially for those acts we consider the most saintly of all.

This was Jehu's problem. He did just what God had commanded, but not in a spirit pleasing to God. From an *external* point of view, he had carried out the Lord's commands scrupulously, but it is clear from his later actions that there was no piety in his heart.

If the Lord had *not* commanded him to undertake the bloodbath, he would have done so anyway, for it suited his own purposes to slaughter all his rivals. As Jehu saw it, God's command coincided perfectly with his own interests. Yet he was not above ignoring God's commands when it suited him:

"Jehu was not careful to walk in the law of the Lord the God of Israel with all his heart" (II Kings 10:31). He was looking out for *himself*, and he was not interested in serving the Lord, although in his own eyes and in the eyes of men he appeared to be a capable servant of the Lord.

Appearances are deceptive. But the Lord sees what's going on in our hearts, and He bases His decision on what He finds there. He also rewards us faithfully for outward, formal obedience, and therefore Jehu's sons did indeed rule Israel unto the fourth generation. But as soon as the fourth generation had passed, the unavenged blood again cries out for justice. The important thing is not to forget about Jehu's inner guilt, for in his heart, Jehu was a murderer who was happy to use God's commands to achieve his own ends.

Thus, there was guilt on the part of both the rulers and the subjects. The people chased after idols, and the rulers were interested only in their own welfare. The House of Israel had abandoned the Lord and turned to the vilest harlotry. Nevertheless, both the rulers and their subjects declared: "We are servants of the Most High God."

Does this judgment stemming from love's anger, the judgment that Israel had become Jezreel, that the Reformed churches have become the Deformed churches, apply to us as well? If we are interested only in *ourselves*, if life for us is just a matter of "every man for himself," we can rest assured that it does. The bow may still be in our hand, and our outward glory may still be visible to the entire church, just as the days of Hosea and Jeroboam were glorious, but the foundations were already decayed and rotten, and it will only be a matter of time before disaster strikes. "I will break the bow of Israel in the valley of Jezreel."

Then everyone who fears God will realize just how far things have gone that God must take away our glory and break our bow. But this is not the worst thing that could happen to us. Even if we have to be called Jezreel from now on and go into exile, we can survive–as long as we are not called Lo-ruhamah (not pitied) or Lo-ammi (not my people). Even if we are stripped of all our glory and power, let's hope that we are never left without God.

Our prayer should be: "Lord, make me repent and believe, so that I'm no longer in myself but You alone."

# 5

# Love's Anger: The Other Two Children

*She conceived again and bore a daughter, and the Lord said to him, 'Call her Lo-ruhamah; for I will never again show love to Israel, never again forgive them.' After weaning Lo-ruhamah, she conceived and bore a son; and the Lord said, 'Call him Lo-ammi, for you are not my people, and I will not be your God' (1:6, 8-9 NEB).*

GOMER'S SECOND BABY WAS A GIRL. Under normal circumstances, this would be a reason for great rejoicing, wouldn't it? The first baby was a son, and then came a daughter. What more could any father and mother ask for?

But the birth of this daughter did not bring joy into the home of Hosea and Gomer. The birth was anticipated not with joy and eagerness but with gloom and unhappiness. Gomer's unfaithfulness had destroyed their initial happiness, and the beauty of marriage had vanished from their lives. Therefore, Hosea, acting on God's command, named this baby girl *Lo-ruhamah*, which means *she will not find mercy*.

This was not to say that *Hosea* would not be merciful to this baby fathered by someone else. With a love that moves and stirs us, he adopted her as his own child. She was given a place in Hosea's home alongside her brother Jezreel.

What her name signified was that God would no longer pity the house of Israel, as He explained in His command to Hosea, and that Israel would definitely be carried off into exile. That horrible name by which people would address her and refer to her would be a continual reminder of the judgment to come. Lo-ruhamah would be a living proclamation!

As we read this, we feel like saying, "Something has gone wrong here!" The marriage of Hosea and Gomer was supposed to reflect the relationship between God and His people. It was supposed to be a concrete and visible message about the relationship. Hosea now has pity on this child and on her mother, but the Lord declares that He will not have pity on His people!

Is the Lord less merciful than His prophet? No, of course not! The Lord had *repeatedly* done just what Hosea did when he adopted the baby girl. Again and again, He had taken His faithless daughter Israel into His arms. Everything was then forgiven and forgotten. Thus, what *Hosea* did was an accurate reflection of what God had done in history.

But this could not go on forever. Love demands a response; it cannot remain one-sided. "I will *no more* have pity on the House of Israel," says the Lord (1:6). Thus, it is not yet an accomplished fact. God's mercy still surrounds Israel, despite the unfaithfulness that is so painfully obvious. The name *Lo-ruhamah* does not mean that the bond is already severed, never to be restored. It reflects God's mercy as well as His judgment.

But the name is certainly a warning, a signal to all that something is very, very wrong. It is a warning to Israel's sons as well as her daughters, for the alternation between son and daughter is probably intended to indicate that all have gone astray and have become useless. The name is a serious admonition: "See to it that I don't have to warn you again, for I will no more have pity on the House of Israel."

Love is patient. Love is kind. Love does not act thoughtlessly. But love can certainly become angry if it is repeatedly scorned: "I will no more have pity on the House of Israel, to forgive them at all."

The worst thing that could happen to the people of the Lord is for the Lord to refuse to be their merciful God any longer. Let

Him take away my health, my possessions, even my children–as long as He does not withdraw His love and mercy from me, for that would make everything so horribly dark. Therefore, *Lo-ruhamah*, the name of the second child, represents an even heavier judgment than the name of the first child. The name *Jezreel* meant no more than that the Lord would break Israel's *bow* and its *spea*r, but the name *Lo-ruhamah* means that He will *hide His face* from Israel.

Some regard the former judgment as worse than the latter, believing that they would rather do without God's favor than without their riches and power. The name Jezreel, which speaks of the fading of outward glory, scares them much more than the name *Lo-ruhamah* which points ahead to the loss of the source of Israel's glory.

The wisest among the people of Israel have always understood perfectly well that God's *mercy* was Israel's most valuable possession and the backbone of its national existence. Israel's prophets, psalmists, and historians have always sung the praises of God's mercy in poetry and prose. "As a father pities his children, so the Lord pities those who fear Him," David had written (Ps. 103:13). To this description of God as a merciful *father*, Isaiah adds a description of God's mercy that reminds us of a mother:

> Does a woman forget her baby at the breast,
> or fail to cherish the son of her womb?

Yet even if these forget,
I will never forget you (Is. 49:15 JB)

That this mercy of the Lord was not a matter of some poet's imagination or some prophet's ecstasy is clear from the factual testimony given by Israel's prose writers. The man who wrote the dry chronicles of the kings of Israel tells us: "But the Lord was gracious and took pity on them; because of His covenant with Abraham, Isaac, and Jacob, He looked on them with favor and was unwilling to destroy them; nor has He even yet banished them from His sight" (II Kings 13:23 NEB). Right up to the days of the prophet Hosea and his godless royal contemporaries this continued: "For the Lord had seen how very bitter the affliction of Israel was, with no one, neither fettered nor free, to come to the help of Israel. But Yahweh had resolved not to blot out the name of Israel from under heaven" (II Kings 14:26 JB).

Now He finally did say that He would blot out Israel's name. He said this through the mouth of Beeri's son and the name of Gomer's daughter. Her name was Lo-ruhamah, and the message contained in this name was that the Lord would not continue to be merciful.

There would come a time, the Lord warned them, when no one would sing Psalm 103 anymore, a time when the Jews sitting in the temple listening to the forty-ninth chapter of Isaiah's book of prophecy would grumble: "That's how it used to be. Those were the good old days." There would come a time when the harps would be hung in the willow trees and the many beautiful songs of earlier ages would no longer be sung.

The Lord will not continue to be merciful *if* Israel goes on being unfaithful to Him. There is a condition, and therefore the door of hope is still open: God is talking about what He will do *unless* Israel repents.

The repentance did not come about. The people laughed at all those prophetic warnings and actually turned the strange name of Gomer's children into a joke. This is clear from the name given to the third child–Lo-ammi. Hosea writes: "After weaning Lo-ruhamah, she conceived and bore a son; and the Lord said, 'Call him Lo-ammi; for you are not my people, and I will not be your God.'"

Of course, everyone knew that *Lo-ammi* means *not my people*, but the deeper meaning of the name borne by the third child apparently escaped Hosea's contemporaries. In all likelihood, they just made fun of it and assumed that Hosea gave the baby this name because he was not its father. Therefore, Hosea adds an explanation of the name. He reveals that the time had now come when Israel would no longer be called God's people. Israel had always been known as God's people and had taken great pride in this honor, but now it was over.

That the end had come should not be a surprise to the Israelites. They had shown clearly enough through their conduct that they did not belong to God, and hence God drew the obvious conclusion: "I will not be your God." This punishment was a simple consequence of Israel's sin, just as punishment so often follows sin.

The name *Lo-ammi* contained a much harsher judgment than the other two names. *Lo-ammi* (not my people) meant rejection. It meant a final dissolution of the marriage. Everything would be over between Israel and God, and the final ties would be severed!

The name *Jezreel* only meant that God would break the bow and strip Israel of its glory. Love had not yet vanished, for He still spoke out of love. He decided to take things from His child not because He hated her but because He loved her.

But His people did not want to listen to His voice. Then Lo-ruhamah was born. God withdrew His mercy, and things got worse. Still, Israel did not cry out, "Have mercy on us!" Israel abandoned God and His commandments and ran after other gods instead.

Yet, all was not lost. The bow had indeed been broken, and God's face no longer radiated His favor and light. All the same, there was still something left–the covenant bond. Israel was a child that had been repudiated, a child that no longer found mercy in her father's eyes. Still, she was a child.

But now came the finale. God cut the last of the ties, and there was nothing left of the relationship. "You are not my people, and I will not be your God." What a tragedy that it should come to this!

We cannot say that the Lord acted in the heat of passion and failed to be patient with His people. Hosea shows this in a simple and effective way. He tells us that Lo-ammi was born after Gomer had "weaned" Lo-ruhamah, who was probably about three years old by then. Of Isaac we read: "The child grew and was weaned" (Gen. 21:8). It took quite a long time in the ancient Near East before a child was weaned. This simple dating of Lo-ammi's birth, this implicit indication of how much time had passed between the birth of these two children, the comment that Lo-ammi with his awful name did not follow Lo-ruhamah into the world within a year, is again a silent testimony to God's patience.

The Lord waited a long time before announcing His mature judgment. He waited a year, and then another year, and then a third year! Here in the Old Testament, we already see a reflection of the story of the fig tree that did not bear fruit: the master told his servant to let the tree stand for one more year and to cut it down if it still had not borne fruit by then.

Will it come to this with us as well? The name of the triune God was pronounced over us when we were baptized. Let's look now to see what name applies to us. Could it be Jezreel, Lo-ruhamah, or Lo-ammi?

Let's make sure that we are never called Lo-ammi! Let's repent of our faithlessness. God is love–but His love can turn to wrath. We must be sure not to forget that!

It seems to me that I see children with strange names running around in the streets of our ecclesiastical Jerusalem.

# 6

## Love's Victory

*The Israelites shall become countless*
*as the sands of the sea*
*which can neither be measured nor numbered;*
*it shall no longer be said, 'They are not my people,'*
*they shall be called Sons of the living God*
*(1:10 NEB)*

IT DOESN'T MAKE SENSE! Through Hosea, the Lord has just said to Israel: "You are not my people, and I will not be your God." Thus, the relationship between God and Israel has come to a radical end! This was the decree of God's unanswered love, which turned into wrath. It's all over, and that's all there is to it.

But now we encounter a wonderful, surprising, paradoxical reversal: "Yet the number of the people of Israel shall be like the sand of the sea, which can neither be measured nor numbered" (1:10). Lo-ammi will be told: "You are sons of the living God."

It just doesn't make sense! We begin to wonder what God is up to. Does this "yet" mean that He will withdraw all the threats made earlier? Has God repented of what He just said? Is He a passionate father who is immediately sorry that He uttered such angry words? Is He soothing wounded feelings here?

No, none of these explanations are acceptable. They are unworthy of God! His yes *means* yes, and His no means no. God cannot say both yes and no. The words that proceed from His mouth are firm and unshakable.

There must have been some people in Hosea's audience who first trembled when they heard the frightening announcement that Israel was no longer God's people but thought to themselves when the sermon took this unexpected turn: "Good! We aren't in such trouble after all!" There are such people to be found in all ages, and they're still around today. They are eager to sin—so that grace may abound. They tell each other that God is love and He will be glad to forgive them! They are eager to lay claim to God's promises, but they don't take His threats seriously. "Surely He can't mean that," they think.

I'm sure all of us are aware that the Bible gives no support to such an attitude. Therefore, this can't be what this "yet" means. But what does it mean then?

We are stuck, for it cannot be denied that what God says here is the complete opposite of what He said earlier. First, God spoke of *rejection*, and now He speaks of *election*. First, there was a *threat*, and now we have a *promise*. Which are we to believe–the threat or the promise? Which are we to depend on? Which will be fulfilled? Will Israel be God's people or not? Both statements are equally absolute. "I *will not* be your God," He declares, but He also says, "The Israelites *shall* become countless as the sands of the sea." The one seems to cancel out the other. It seems impossible that both could be true. Which one is true, then, and which one is false? Or are both false? There seems to be no answer to the problem.

I have already made it sufficiently clear that I do not go along with those who seek to play off one truth against the other or prefer to follow the safe route by choosing the promise. Yet I also refuse to take the side of those who maintain that the threat bound up in the name *Lo-ammi* is not *absolute*. They argue that the judgment that Israel will not be called God's people is only temporarily true, that it applies mainly to the time of the exile, and that Israel's God does not forget to be merciful even when He is angry. This explanation will not do, for it doesn't take the element of judgment seriously enough.

The key to the puzzle is this: we must not assume that the people to whom the "yet" of the promise is addressed are the very same ones who are doomed to no longer being God's people. In fact, different people are meant in the promise than in the threat.

We could hardly ask for a better exegete of Hosea than Paul. Paul applies the *promise* directly to the *heathens*–and not to Israel. Israel remains *Lo-ammi* (not my people), but of the heathens, the book of Hosea teaches: "Those who were not my people I will call My people, and the unloved nation I will call My Beloved" (Rom. 9:25 NEB). Peter sees it exactly the same way. Of those who were called out of *darkness*, he says: "Once you were no people, but now you are God's people; Once you had not received mercy, but now you have received mercy" (1 Peter 2:10).

Thus, there is no contradiction. Because we have been given this New Testament light, we don't have to ask whether the threat is true or the promise, for both are true. The threat is certainly true, for the Kingdom of the ten tribes did go into exile. The promise is also true, for when the children of the king are cast out, God issues a call to the east and the west for others to take their places as children at His table. Now that Abraham's children of the flesh have become "not my people" (Lo-ammi), God seeks new children for Abraham among the heathens.

In this, we see love's victory, for love needs something to love! Over the heads of the degenerate covenant people, God's love cries out in triumph as it catches sight of another Israel, a *spiritual* Israel: "Yet the number of the people of Israel shall be like the sand of the sea which can neither be measured nor numbered." God will see to it that those who despise Him are replaced by the despised heathens, by heathen brothers and sisters: "Say to your brother, 'My people' (*Ammi*), and to your sister, 'She has obtained pity' (*Ruhamah*)" (2:1).[4*]

In this, God did not break faith with Abraham but rather fulfilled His promise to him. Abraham had been promised a seed as numerous as the "sand of the sea." When the name *Lo-ammi* tells us of the judgment of God's angry love, we may think, "But what happened to God's faithfulness and His honor?" Here we have one answer. God will not break His word: "the number of the (spiritual) people of Israel shall be like the sand of the sea." This is love's victory!

This "yet" of divine love, then, is in no way to be regarded as a reprieve for Hosea's audience. In fact, there is no hope whatsoever for those who live according to the flesh–at least, not in God's Word. Hosea's statement that the people of Israel will be as numerous as the grains of sand on the seashore is so sharp and uncompromising that we would hardly expect to hear such a thing from his mouth. It is as though Hosea

---

4    *Of course, it is true that Israel did not perish completely, as is also apparent from the fact that Anna was from the tribe of Asher (Luke 2:26). A "holy remnant" was left. Therefore, we really should not say that the heathens replaced Israel: they were added to this holy remnant.

were saying to the people: "God will see to it that He always has children–many children–but you sinful people will not be seated at His table."

The feast will go on, but with different guests, for those who were originally invited are not worthy. Even if all of Israel decides not to come, the guests at the feast will be as numerous as the sands of the sea. God will gather them from the east and the west, from all nations, tongues, and races. This is the "yet" of God's love.

It's awful to be passed over this way, especially if you are as quick to feel left out as Israel was and live in the illusion that you alone are "chosen."

Even if all of Zion's sons and daughters are deported, then, we need not worry about empty places in Zion. Yet sometimes this fear does take hold of us. We are deeply concerned–and rightly so–that so many who were baptized have fallen away from the faith, and that so many of the church's "members in good standing" who have not fallen away and are still scrupulous about doing their duty and keeping the Sabbath are in fact lost because they have not become new people. God does not tell us to be unconcerned about these things and to simply forget about them. But He does assure us that He will find replacements. The empty places will be filled–by others!

This makes us rejoice, but it also makes us very sad. We rejoice over the new members of Christ's body, but we grieve over those who have been lost. It's certainly a frightening thought that the *number* of the chosen will be reached, although you and I–children of the covenant–might not be among those who make up the total!

We must read the promise in this personal and concrete way. It also applies to us as individuals. For too long our souls have slumbered because of a false sense of security, sustained by the idea that although we are sinners and will remain sinners until the day of our death, the Lord still grants us the "yet" of His love–fortunately! Therefore, all will be well in the end: the drama will have a happy ending.

This is an illusion, for it is not what the Scripture teaches us. There is indeed an all-encompassing love of the Lord that makes hearts melt like wax and places the most contemptible sinners next to princes and the mighty of this world. That's what we learn from Hosea, who bears the same name as Joshua and Jesus. Hosanna! Blessed be the one who comes in the name of the Lord!

But He also makes these sinners *children* of the living God. He makes *new people* of them. These new people are living contradictions of the old saying that you can't change human nature. In what they say and do, they prove that man can be changed.

But this change does not come about through our own strength. It comes about through a miracle–the miracle of regeneration and the wonder of daily conversion. This miracle must be explained not on the basis of our love for God but on the basis of *His* love for us. *His* love is victorious!

It is a love that conquers the pleasures of sin! It is a love that finds a heart full of hate inside us but declares nevertheless: "Yet I shall give you a new heart so that you will love Me and keep My commandments."

Is this love victorious in your life and my life? That's the question!

# 7

# Holy Rebellion

*Denounce your mother, denounce her,*
*for she is not my wife*
*nor am I her husband.*
*Let her rid her face of whoring,*
*and her breasts of her adultery (2:2 JB).*

HONOR YOUR FATHER and your mother! This time-honored commandment hardly seems to fit in with the pressing appeal which the servant of the Lord makes here. He asks his children to denounce their *mother*. This isn't exactly revolutionary rhetoric, but it certainly opens the door to rebellion.

Hosea is asking for trouble here, for his words will lead to disobedience. He asks his children to stop keeping silent about what their mother does and stop resigning themselves to it. They must not shrink from criticizing their mother. They must come right out with it and tell her off in no uncertain terms. Denounce your mother!

Of course, we are not to take this passage literally. Here again the prophet is speaking in figurative language. The mother of whom he speaks is the mother who is no longer the Lord's wife, that is, Israel as a nation. Perhaps we could speak of this mother as the (Old Testament) Church. Thus, the family we're dealing with is the church. But that doesn't make the picture look any better.

Arguments and quarrels in the home are deplorable but fighting within the church is just as bad! We know all about that in our time. We would like the church to be a place of peace and pleasant rest and blessing, so that it may become a stronghold where we are assured of happiness and enjoyment. That's what we would like, and so would Hosea. But when the rest becomes a false rest and the peace is abused in all sorts of ways, then the children of the church must come out of their corner and make their criticisms heard. In such a situation, silence is dangerous. They must dare to raise their voices in protest against what's going on. That–and nothing else–is what Beeri's son means as he seeks to create a spirit of resistance. Denounce your mother!

It was not without good reason that the prophet lit the holy fires of dispute. His first purpose in doing so was to admonish the Israelites earnestly to examine *their own lives*. His second purpose was to bring about a thoroughgoing *reformation*.

Hosea was interested in self-criticism because the appeal to "denounce" their mother was first of all an appeal to these children to direct their complaints and objections to the proper address. Let me make this clearer by reminding you that there was a real danger that the children would accuse God, their father, instead. There is no reason whatsoever for pointing the finger at God, Hosea informs them. If things have gone wrong with the Israelites, it is not the fault of their Father in heaven. The guilty party should be sought closer to home–indeed, in their own home. The guilty party is their mother on earth.

Unfortunately, it is by no means unusual for us to denounce God and throw our complaints at Him. The children of Gomer walked around with judgment in their very names, as we saw earlier. And when the judgments were finally carried out, they would act just as if they had no idea what they might have done to offend God. God would instead be *blamed* for everything. Rather than criticize themselves and examine their own lives, they would cry out, "The Lord has forsaken our land!"

Isn't that how things usually go? If for some reason something goes wrong in our lives, if we start going downhill, if we are tormented by the thorns and thistles, if one misfortune follows another, then we complain bitterly about God. We cannot understand how it all fits in with God's love. We criticize our father. That's why Hosea comes along to straighten us out. He appeals to us to examine our own lives critically. Denounce your *mother*–and not your Father!

I have spoken of this appeal as an invitation to self-criticism. You might want to argue that when children reproach their mother, when the members of the church criticize their "mother" (the church), their words don't count as self-criticism. And I would have to admit that self-criticism usually does not mean accusing your mother.

In our time children are bold in accusing their mother. The criticisms of the mother church made by the members, especially the younger members, are not gentle. The one accuses the church of this, and the other makes the opposite accusation. Here the church is too broad, and there it is too narrow. The one finds the mother church too old-fashioned, and the other finds her too much in step with the times.

We feel like saying: "Hosea is no longer relevant on this point, for we don't need a prophetic appeal to get the critics going. It may be that the children of Israel in Hosea's time were not yet sufficiently mature in this respect, but we are certainly not afraid to speak out. Perhaps Hosea's contemporaries approved of everything the church did, but we're far beyond that stage!"

But I have a question for you: do you hear any self-criticism in all these complaints made today? And what do people hope to achieve through all the criticism of our "mother," the church?

Fair criticism is always valuable, and that's just what the prophet calls for. It's a great sin to remain silent when it's time to say something. Therefore, we should not assume that the prophet wants us to withhold our criticism. On the contrary!

But there's one thing we must not forget. The people to whom Hosea referred once by way of the metaphor of the mother are the same people he referred to as children. The church is not a vague and undetermined something far away from us. You and I are the church. Therefore, someone who hurls unjust criticisms at the church is only hurting himself. There's no getting around it. But someone who rightly believes that the church needs to be reprimanded will also be aware that *he* is the one in need of a reprimand in the first place. Good and useful criticism of the church begins and ends with self-criticism.

If we believe that the church must change its conduct, then we must begin by changing our own conduct. We should not fix our attention on things so far away that we can't see them clearly; we should look first at the same things right around us. The Reformation of the church must begin with the Reformation of our hearts. Conversely, the deformation of the church begins with our own spiritual sickness.

If it is really true that the mother church and the children in Hosea's metaphor represent the same people, and if it is true that Hosea wants us to look first at our own shortcomings, this distinction between the mother and the children, the church, and its individual members, has a still deeper meaning. What the prophet has in mind, as I mentioned earlier, is a thoroughgoing *reformation*.

Naturally, he will not be satisfied as soon as he sees that there is a disturbance in the church. The complaints about the mother and the accusations which the children make are supposed to have the effect of forcing the mother to listen. The children are to plead *so that* she will mend her ways, *so that* she will "rid her face of her whoring, and her breasts of her adultery." The goal is repentance and conversion.

To reach this goal, Hosea makes an appeal to the "conscience of the individual." No doubt he was appealing to the best among the Israelites, those who had not yet been affected by the spirit prevalent at that time. He bases his appeal on the office of the believer. These faithful believers were called upon to register a protest against the sinful direction in which the nation as a whole (their mother) was moving. It was in this way that Hosea wanted reformation to take place. This is the proper way.

There is such a thing as a mass mind, even in the church. If the wrong spirit and outlook become dominant in the church, virtually everyone will succumb to it in time, regardless of what this spirit may represent. It may be a spirit of self-sufficiency, of worldliness, or of dead orthodoxy. It could be anything. "My name is legion, for we are many." The danger is great that such a spirit will carry the day everywhere. People will accommodate themselves to it or give up fighting it. The protests and criticisms will come to an end. With an eye to this danger, the prophet now shakes some *individuals* out of their slumber, exhorting them not to spare their mother and not to stop criticizing and admonishing.

Fortunately, there have always been individuals ready to respond to Hosea's call. Such individuals are often pitied by others. They are called dreamers and idealists. But it is thanks to the quarrels with their mother that the church was reformed in the past and will be reformed in our time.

What are we to argue and quarrel with our mother about? Within what framework is mutual censure not only permitted within the church's family but required?

Hosea explains this to us clearly. Not only does he maintain that there must be arguments, but he also tells us just what the children are to say to their mother, just what complaints they are to raise. They must say, "She is not his wife, and he is not her husband."

The accusation which the children of God are asked to make is that the marriage bond has been broken. The complaint is that although the intimate fellowship and secret contact with God has not disappeared entirely, there is all too little of it left. The problem is that a worm is gnawing away at the roots of this relationship; its life, its communion with Christ, has been damaged. That's what the church's great unfaithfulness consists of. The children are to tell the church that she must return to her intimate communion with Christ, her Head and Savior. That's the main thing: that's what needs to be discussed. On that point we must admonish and reprimand one another in a friendly way. Therefore, we must even be willing to quarrel with each other in holy indignation.

The more the debate about the church moves in this direction and concentrates on the main issues, the better. And the "children" must not stop accusing and protesting as long as their "mother" rejects these and other such concerns as a false form of mysticism.

Anyone who studies the ecclesiastical quarrels of our time will see that this appeal of the prophet does not mean bringing coals to Newcastle. The prophet's words are not superfluous. On the contrary, Hosea is highly relevant to our time. He calls for criticism and dispute–but he is very concerned about what the issue in the debate will be.

Abraham Kuyper understood Hosea very well on this point. One of Kuyper's friends wrote: "he did not rest until he knew that our hearts were the property of the Savior. Once I presented him with a long argument about 'Christian principles,' and to my shame he asked me, 'But is everything in order between you and God? Has Jesus brought you to God?"

# 8

# Where All That Silver Comes From

*And she did not know
that it was I who gave her
the grain, the wine, and the oil,
and who lavished upon her silver
and gold which they used for Baal (2:8).*

THE LORD'S EARNEST COMPLAINT is based not on a "horrible misunderstanding" but on a complete *lack of understanding* on the part of His people, His "wife," as Israel is still called here. Israel doesn't realize it was God "who gave her the grain, the wine, and the oil, and who lavished upon her silver and gold."

That was *sinful* ignorance. No nation was in a better position than Israel to know that God is not only the creator of heaven and earth but also one who upholds and governs everything in His Providence. God Himself had revealed this to Israel. The psalmists had pointed it out repeatedly:

> The earth is the Lord's and all that is in it,
> the world and those who dwell therein.
> For it was He who founded it upon the seas and
> planted it firm upon the waters beneath (Ps. 24:1-2 NEB)

> For every beast of the forest is mine,
> the cattle on a thousand hills.
> I know all the birds of the air,
> and all that moves in the field is mine (Ps. 50:10-11).

> All creatures depend on you
> to feed them throughout the year;
> You provide the food they eat,
> with generous hands You satisfy their hunger (Ps. 104:27-28 JB)

The faithful in Israel had confessed this from generation to generation, fully aware of what it meant. These psalms had been sung countless times in the temple services. Yet Israel no longer knew anything of this. The very first principle of the "knowledge of God" had been lost.

If only that was all there was to it! But Israel's ignorance went much further. In a certain sense, it is true of all creatures that they receive good things from God the Lord in heaven, that He fills their mouths with food and their hearts with joy. But Israel had a special advantage above all others, for God had entered into a *covenant* with Israel. Because of this covenant, Israel was the object of His special attention and care. The Lord looked after His people just as a husband looks after his wife, for the covenant was like a marriage bond.

And the Lord had indeed taken good care of Israel. He had spoiled Israel, so to speak. She had become a woman living in luxury. Tenderly, He gave her things she didn't even think of asking for, until she had much more than she needed. He saw to it that all the pure desires of her heart were satisfied.

Because she trusted in Him, He put a crown of the finest gold on her head. She was His princess! Because she had been treated royally, the Lord's prophet sums up not the everyday gifts received by Israel but the luxuries. It was not just bread and water, wool and flax, food, and clothing that she received from the Lord; Hosea tells us that the Lord gave her *grain* and *wine* and *oil* and lavished *silver* and *gold* upon her.

Thus, Israel was indulged and spoiled by her husband and merciful provider. But she forgot completely who gave her those gifts. She thought and even dared to say that her fruitfulness and wealth came from the Baals, the agricultural gods of Canaan, and the forces of nature! Israel believed that she could get along without God–but not without the sun (the sun-god Baal, who gives warmth to the earth) or without Astarte (who sends dew from heaven).

And what did this faithless woman do now? Not only did she chase after another man, abandoning her husband and forgetting the God of life who had performed so many miracles, but she also took along the precious gifts which her husband had given her in his tender love. The gold and silver and wine and oil were now given to Baal. With her filthy hands, she placed those treasures at *his* feet.

Was this adulteress really unaware that she was giving to Baal the gifts she had received from her husband, the gifts that rightfully belonged to Him? Not really. But she didn't want to think about that, for it was much nicer to give these things to Baal!

Baal wasn't as firm and strict and austere as her husband. At home, she always had to be careful and think about what she was doing, but in Baal's house, she could really be herself and do what she had always wanted to do. And that's what life is all about, after all! Make the most of each day! Eat, drink, and be merry!

While Israel is dancing in the woods and devouring Baal with her adulterous eyes, her husband is left at home alone.

He complains. He is forced to watch all of this, as she leaves the home where she has already been well treated and takes everything with her. The lament of his unrequited love can be heard over Israel's fruitful hills: "For she does not know that it is I who gave her corn, new wine, and oil, I who lavished upon her silver and gold which they spent on the Baal" (2:8 NEB).

What about us? Do we know where all that silver comes from? We claim that we do! It has been impressed upon us from childhood that harvest and sunshine and rain, corn, and wine and oil, silver, and gold do not come to us by chance but from the hand of God our Father. This is one of our church's doctrines. Of course, we know where all that silver comes from! We know it in theory!

But is this awareness a heartfelt understanding and is it reflected in how we live? Or could it be that the Lord's unrequited love has a similar complaint to make about His people in the twentieth century, who claim to know where all that silver comes from but often act as though they don't?

An investigation of the *idols* in our homes already gives us reason to worry. Of course, we don't call them "Baals," and we're not so primitive that we believe in gods of nature, agriculture, money, or trade. All the same, there are idols present in our lives, and we pay them high honors!

When we're concerned about increasing our wealth and we have to take risks, we look to "Lady Luck" as the powerful goddess who controls the wheel of fortune. We try to gain her favor by way of rabbit's feet and four-leaf clovers.

A farmer looks at his strong, calloused hands and asks, "How much will *I* take in this year through all *my* crops?" In the depth of my own mind, *I* am a god.

And there are so many who seek their security and welfare–especially their welfare–in what they regard as *holy*, whether it be themselves or someone or something else. They erect altars to their idols and burn holy candles in the corners of their homes. They burn a candle to gain a blessing for their business ventures and then burn another to ask the goddess of reason for a "clear mind." In the way they live their lives, they deny the only savior and husband and father in heaven–and not just by failing to pray. They may praise Him with their mouths–at least, they do so when things are going well, and their wealth is increasing–but when they suffer a setback their praise turns to something else.

As Protestants, we like to point the finger at the Roman Catholics with their candles and their alleged idolatry, and we shake our wise heads at those Israelites who kept chasing after nature gods and Baals. We tell each other that it is God who gives us grain and wine and oil and lavishes silver and gold upon us. But who are we trying to fool?

I have another question: What happens to all that silver and gold? Let's think about it carefully. The Lord gave Israel everything, just as a husband provides for his wife. That's the comparison. What is the "wife" supposed to do with what she has been given? She is not supposed to use it to show off and adorn her body with the most beautiful clothes and jewels. The Lord doesn't want us to show off! Nor does the Lord want us to waste anything of what He has given us, for He hates waste. He is even more set against devoting His gifts to idols.

Carrying our comparison further, we could say that the husband gives his wife silver and gold so that she will be able to look after her family and take good care of the household. In other words, God's gifts to us are intended to enable us to serve *Him* and serving Him means helping the needy.

Well, what happens to all that silver and gold? Are you aware that the Lord did not give it to you so that you could play the role of a man of means, of a property owner? He gave it to you so that you could serve *Him* with it by caring for His house and helping provide for the needs of His people. Did you realize that when you claim that your money is yours to do with as you please, you are showing that you have not understood where all that rain and wine and oil and silver and gold came from?

Is there no reason for God to complain about today's Israel on this score? When Israel was still small and nothing to look at, when she was still a child in the wilderness, she willingly brought decorations and gold and silver to adorn the Tabernacle. But when she grew up, when things went well during the prosperous years of Jeroboam II, the Lord had to complain that *His*–that's right, God's–gold and silver were being brought to the temples of idols! Is there a corresponding difference between the time when our church formed an insignificant little group and the time when the rich and powerful began to join us in the pew?

The beauty of this whole story is that God does not air the complaint of His unrequited love without reason. He has a definite purpose in mind. Of course, He does! But what is that purpose? His purpose is not to hurt His unfaithful "wife" once more or to tell her off in front of all the neighbors. He wants His unfaithful wife back!

Isn't it amazing that God wants His unfaithful, runaway wife back and almost begs for her love? He actually wants her back! And if He doesn't accomplish His goal through complaints, His love is ingenious enough to think of another way to get her back. Her Baal will let her down so completely that she will wind up a pauper and will have to go into miserable exile. Then, driven by need, she will turn to the Lord for help. In her misery, she will say: "I will go back to my husband again; I was better off with him than I am now" (2:7 NEB).

That's hardly a noble motive. It would be a shame if she were driven back to God by *need* alone. There is something impure and egotistic in the thought that in the final analysis we're better off with God than with the world.

Hence, we must assume that mixed with the impure motives of this chastened Israel returning to God was an awareness of guilt, just as there was in the story of the prodigal son. It's fortunate for us that God forgives the impure motives that play a role in our repentance and does not pay much attention to our calculations of how much better our father's servants have it. Let's be thankful that He focuses instead on the confession that issues from our broken hearts, the confession that we have sinned.

God also wants us back. Whether we are driven to Him by need or by the thought of His generosity is not of primary importance–as long as we do go back to Him. The main thing for us is to be kissed awake and disarmed by the sunshine of His goodness and to become aware that the gold and silver come from Him. Otherwise, we will have to learn our lesson by following the dark path of rough and bitter resistance.

Has God achieved His purpose with you and me? That's the question!

# 9

# Lured into the Wilderness

*That is why I am going to lure her and lead her out
into the wilderness and speak to her heart (2:14 JB).*

THIS TEXT TALKS ABOUT *judgment*. That's what the word *why* in the first line indicates. Why will God lead his people into the wilderness? Because "she"–Israel, is still spoken of as the Lord's "wife" "forgot Me," says the Lord (2:13). That's why. We couldn't ask God to make Himself any clearer, and we need not bother God later, when the judgment is actually being carried out, by asking why.

This judgment will mean suffering, for the "wilderness" into which God will lead Israel is nothing but the unspeakable misery of *exile*. That Israel should suffer such a fate simply doesn't seem possible under the successful rule of Jeroboam II, but it is already inevitable.

This "wilderness" must be thought of not in a literal sense but in a figurative sense. When Israel went into exile, she didn't literally live in a wilderness. What Hosea meant is that Israel would become just as poor in exile as she was when she entered Canaan.

Once she was an impoverished child living in the wilderness, and that's what she will become again. All the blessings and treasures which the Lord *gave* Israel, he will *take away*. Israel will be just as poor as she was before. "I will lead her out into the wilderness." This judgment is just as severe as an earlier judgment from Hosea's mouth:

> Or I will strip her and expose her
> naked as the day she was born;
> I will make her bare as the wilderness,
> parched as the desert,
> and leave her to die of thirst (2:3 NEB)

That's what she deserves!

Anyone who turns the Lord's gifts over to idols and then forgets and abandons God can expect pain and more pain. Here, O Israel, the Lord your God is a jealous God. "That is why I am going to lead her out into the wilderness."

All this would be easy to interpret and would create no problem whatsoever if Hosea had limited himself to saying that the Lord will *lead* Israel into the wilderness. But that's not all he said. He also added something very strange–at God's command, of course.

What he added was strange because of the context, the other things he said in this passage. He talks not only of God leading Israel into the wilderness but also of *luring* her: "I am going to lure her and lead her into the wilderness." He actually speaks of God's sending Israel into exile as "luring"!

The word *luring* calls entirely different thoughts to mind than *leading*. We think of an invitation presented in a loving way, as when we speak of the voice of the gospel luring us. And this raises questions. What does God have in mind–judgment or favor? Does the journey into the wilderness of exile mean destruction or construction? Does it mean annihilation or restoration? Does it mean a blessing or a curse? Is Israel to rejoice that God is luring her into the wilderness, or must she weep at being led into exile? When Hosea mentioned "luring" and being led away in the same breath, his simultaneous Yes and no must have confused his hearers thoroughly. Were they supposed to cry or laugh?

The same inconsistency is apparent in what follows: "And I am going to speak to her heart." God will send her out to wander in the wilderness of a miserable exile. Is that speaking to her heart? Surely there must be some sort of mistake,

Hosea! Don't you mean instead that He will be silent in His anger? Or is this bitter sarcasm on God's part?

It gets harder and harder to understand what Hosea means, for his words seem to conflict with each other. First, he speaks both of luring and being led, and now we see that his *conclusion* is also inconsistent: send her away and speak to her heart!

Exegetes who listen to God's mouth and not to His heart will shake their heads and wonder what to do. These dry biblical scholars will start arguing that something has been added to the original text to corrupt it, for this doesn't fit and that doesn't make sense! It wouldn't be hard to find more of these "inconsistencies." Someone might argue that Hosea's talk of God "luring" Israel into the wilderness is in conflict with the historical facts. God did not *lure* Israel into exile: *throw* would be a better word to describe what actually happened.

The alluring voice of the prophet did *not* bring about change in Israel. And therefore, Israel had to be driven out of its rut, just as Lot, who didn't want to listen either, had to be driven out of his beautiful city of Sodom. Are we any different? Aren't we shown time and again that if we don't listen, we'll have to learn the hard way? And then we wind up feeling miserable as we live in the loneliness of the wilderness. Were we lured into the wilderness? No, we were dumped there!

But–and here we come to an even more serious objection–isn't *luring* someone into the wilderness in conflict with God's nature? The cunning bird-catcher *lures* the poor birds when he uses bait to get them to enter his net. The devil *lures* people when he promises them a paradise (which turns out, of course, to be a wilderness) and when he promises them heaven by telling them they will become like God–and then leaves them in the wilderness of a cursed earth. Surely that couldn't be what God was doing! We could say that the Lord *lures* us into heaven and invites us to his table so that his house will be full, but surely, we wouldn't say that God lures us into the wilderness.

It's time to stop listing the inconsistencies, for this line of reasoning will not get us anywhere. The proper explanation will make sense only to those who have learned through secret fellowship with God that the wilderness can mean a blessing, that the valley of mulberry trees can become a fountain of salvation, and that life's adversity and loneliness can be turned to our advantage. Those who have understood this no longer *complain* but *thank* God for his incomprehensible and seemingly inconsistent ways. God lures men into the wilderness in order to give them *paradise,* and he makes them *lose* everything so that they will *gain* everything. Even the time spent in the wilderness is for the good of those who are called according to his purposes. That's what our text means!

There is no getting around the fact that Israel was *driven* into the wilderness of exile, but God lets his prophet use the word *lure* to indicate that the *love* of His divine heart was operative in and behind the misery. Israel had forgotten the Lord, but the Lord had not forgotten her! The Lord was eager to get His bride back! Therefore, He resolved to go after her and lure her, in order to win her love again.

The Lord's love is indeed amazing. It leads Him to lure Israel into the *wilderness*. There was no better way for the Lord to achieve His purpose with Israel.

That's what *history* taught. God had lured Israel into the wilderness once before when she was Egypt's slave. That time He *liberated* her and chose her as His wife–in the wilderness! She had to go into the wilderness, and she went willingly. The desert with its endless sand and loneliness and heat then became a true place of feasting. Israel was recreated through the wedding. The wedding and the celebration afterward were held in the wilderness. The Lord received her festively and provided her with honey out of the rock. He held her in His loving embrace and spoke to her heart–in the wilderness, of all places!

Now Israel has run away from God and has again become a slave. This time she is a slave not of Egypt but of Baal; she is caught in *Baal's* net. Thus, Israel must go into the wilderness again. May she go, or must she go? The judgment is irrevocable. Or will it turn out to be a blessing in disguise?

Will God send her into exile? Or will he invite her to be His bride again? Yes, that's what He'll do! He will send her into exile by luring her. The wilderness will become a place of celebration, and its loneliness will give way to fellowship. The judgment will become a blessing. What was Israel to do when she heard these words of Hosea? Was she to laugh, or cry, or do both at once?

"That's why I am going to lure her and lead her into the wilderness." The point is that the Lord wants to be alone with His people for once. It's quiet in the wilderness. There the Lord and Israel will be undisturbed. There He will not be distracted by the tumult of the feasts of Baal, and His voice will not be drowned out by all the noise. There He can speak to Israel quietly, and she will be able to ponder what she has done. The time spent in the wilderness will be for Israel what the time spent feeding the swine was for the prodigal son.

Not all the people of Israel will come to their senses in the wilderness, but some of them will. In the midst of so much misery, they will come to faith's conclusion: "I have sinned, and I shall repent!" In their fear, they will call upon the Lord, and he will answer them by "speaking to their heart." Then the barren wilderness will become a place of unspeakable blessing.

The wilderness really isn't such a bad place after all. In some ways it's better than being in a banquet hall, and it's certainly better than having full barns and saying to yourself: "Relax, my soul. Take it easy, eat, drink and be merry."

It may be that your wilderness is a lonely sickbed on which you lie for years, where people seem to forget about you. The wilderness may be the sorrow of a broken-hearted widow or widower whose spouse has been taken away by God. Or the wilderness may be financial hardship when unemployment and other setbacks make your situation look as somber and fruitless as a desert. There are so many wildernesses in the world and so many lonely people living in them. Yet no such wilderness is a complete evil, provided that we keep the proper perspective.

It's not easy for us to see how a wilderness can prove to be a blessing. There's certainly nothing charming or enticing about living in a desert, for a desert means heat, drought, thirst, and sand! Milk and honey look better to us! Yet, throughout the ages, the wilderness has been God's great forge, where He prepares instruments for His service.

*Before* the years in Midian's wilderness, Moses believed he could do anything–but all he was really capable of was destruction and killing. *In* the wilderness, he learned that he could do nothing on his own but had to rely on God. In Gilead's wilderness, Elijah became the leader of Israel. In the wilderness of Judah, John the Baptist became a herald of Christ's coming, and it was in the wilderness that Jesus won His first great battle. In his blind solitude on the road to

Damascus, Paul became God's chosen instrument. And in the wilderness of exile, Israel was to find her God again.

Many have found God in the wilderness and have learned that the wilderness can be a festive place. It is not an easy place to live, but it is worry-free insofar as God sends manna every day and makes water flow from the rock. The wilderness is a horrible place, but it's also a blessed and glorious place!

In addition to being a glorious place, the wilderness is a place where the truth comes out. For this reason, many do not regard it as a desirable place to be.

Anyone who travels from Jerusalem to Jericho passes through the wilderness of Judah, where there are no people around to watch you. Therefore, neither the priest nor the Levite hesitated before passing by the poor man lying half-dead at the side of the road. If this scene had taken place in Jerusalem, they would have played the philanthropist, of course. That's how the solitude of the wilderness brings out the truth. It unmasks us and shows what we're like inside.

Maybe this is the reason why almost everyone avoids being alone, why people so often pass up the opportunity to be alone with God, why people don't like private, person-to-person conversations, why people throw themselves so completely into the hustle and bustle of everyday life. If this is indeed the reason, may God lure all of us into the wilderness.

# 10

# From a Valley to a Door

*I will make the Valley of Achor a door of hope*
*(2:15).*

THE VALLEY OF ACHOR, which is southwest of Jericho, has always called thoughts of trouble to the minds of the people of Israel. An Israelite father telling his children about the Valley of Achor would automatically speak of a whisper, for the name *Achor* means *valley of turmoil, misfortune, trouble!*

I'm sure you know what happened there. Just as God wanted the first fruits of the harvest, He also wanted the first of the cities of Canaan for Himself. All the riches of Jericho were to be devoted to Him in a great bonfire. But there was one man, Achan, who thought it was a shame to throw all those precious things into the fire. With his greedy hands, he seized some of the valuables and hid them secretly in his tent. No one would know!

That was a *hidden sin* on Achan's part. It was a serious offense not because anyone was hurt by it but because he was stealing from *God*. This is the most common–and at the same time the most serious–form of theft within the camp of God's people. It's certainly not unheard of for the chosen ones whom God loves to steal from each other–think of the Heidelberg Catechism's condemnation of false weights and measures in Lord's Day 42–but stealing what belongs to God is much more widespread.

Over here we have someone who deprives God of what he owes Him by claiming he has "no time" for work in God's Kingdom. Over there is someone who robs God of the money he owes Him, for he considers it a shame to give so much of his hard-earned money to the church, the Christian School, evangelism, and the poor. He seems unaware that he is a "steward" but instead acts as though the earth and everything on it were his own property instead of God's property.

All this takes place in secret, of course. Neither of these thieves will wind up in prison. Those who say they have no time to serve in the church council are not arrested by the police, any more than those who can't be bothered with evangelism or those who refuse to contribute to Christian causes and can't spare more than a dime for the poor. Such people may even be honored and respected members of the church, freely criticizing those who do all the work. Achan remained a soldier in good standing in God's army as long as his sin was a secret.

In the meantime, Israel could *not* move ahead as a victorious army as long as the hidden evil continued, and Achan lived on among the people as a hidden source of corruption. Therefore, although the mighty fortress of Jericho had fallen without a battle, a stunning defeat was suffered when the weak city of Ai was attacked.

The reason for this defeat is obvious to us. The church of the Lord will never win any battles as long as it is consumed from within by an evil that festers like an infected wound. The defeats of the church are due to its *hidden sins*.

It makes no difference what *name* we give to the evil we fail to combat and root out. It could be anything. Whether we call it Achan or Mammon or Maltus or name it after the devil himself–for the devil specializes in slander and quarreling–doesn't matter. As long as there is an outlaw left in the army, the church will suffer defeat after defeat. The church will have no victories over the *world* to boast about as long as it has no victories of its *own flesh* to report. No one can be a sanctifying influence on anyone else if he is unholy himself.

The church will have no power if she harbors an Achan in her midst. She will not march victorious behind her King. She will be defeated and scorned, and no one will take her seriously.

It is fortunate that the Lord himself opens the eyes of the church to the offenders in her midst, and that he does not let his people go on blindly believing they can handle everything themselves. Thus, He intervened when Israel was stuck between Jericho and Ai. Through the casting of lots, he pointed the finger at the guilty party. The sinner was unmasked, and the Israelites were given the opportunity to get rid of the outlaw in their midst.

The people did not hesitate for a moment in rooting out the evil. The Reformation was radical! "And Joshua and all Israelites with him took Achan the son of Zerah, and the silver and the mantle and the bar of gold, and his sons and daughters, and his oxen and asses and sheep, and his tent, and all that he had; and they brought him up to the Valley of Achor" (Josh. 7:24). There Achan was stoned together with all his family and possessions. Afterward, the entire household and all its members were burned, so that nothing–absolutely nothing–was left. This reminds us of the radical demand made by the Heidelberg Catechism, namely, that our old self must be crucified, put to death, and buried (Answer 43). That's just what happened in the Valley of Achor.

For the sinner and his household, the man who confessed his sin only when he was forced to, the Valley of Achor became a *place of despair*. Screaming and gasping in fear, Achan and his family were plunged into eternity. For them, the Valley of

Achor became a door to hell. "Abandon all hope, ye who enter here." It was truly a valley of turmoil and trouble.

But for those who had been "reformed" and purified, the Valley of Achor became a *door of hope*. They had already given up hope of ever conquering the promised land. Joshua grumbled: "Alas, O Lord, why didst thou bring this people across the Jordan only to hand us over to the Amorites to be destroyed?" (Josh. 7:7 NEB). But now that the cause of Israel's setback had been pointed out and the evil nipped in the bud, the spirits of the Israelites rose again, and hope was reborn in their hearts.

The Valley of Achor was not a dark pit in which all of Israel was to be slaughtered. The valley of trouble turned out to be a door: the Lord opened a door through which Israel could enter Canaan. Now that the evil had been removed from their midst, God's blessing again rested on Israel's army. Once more it became powerful. The people of Israel emerged from the courtroom purified. Israel was now like the church in Philadelphia, which was the only one of seven churches of Asia Minor that did not have to hear the threatening words "But I have this *against* you." God promised this church that he would make "those in the synagogue of satan... come and bow down before your feet" (Rev. 3:9).

A church that calls itself reformed but is not, will enter the valley of defeat. But a church that roots out the evil in its own midst will move in triumph through the victory gate. The Valley of Achor becomes a door of hope.

Now we understand why the prophet Hosea once more drags out this unhappy story of the valley of trouble named Achor. His time was like Achan's time in that there was great evil in Israel. It's the same old story: the Israelites were stealing from God Himself. The wine and oil and gold and silver that the Lord had given Israel had been turned over to Baal.

Sin enters human life with depressing regularity, but punishment is just as regular–to the Valley of Achor! The entire nation of Israel had to appear in court, to be sentenced to *exile* in the valley of unhappiness. God pronounced judgment on the people that reminded him of Achan.

But now comes a miracle! Exile in the Valley of Achor will not mean total destruction. God just can't put His people out of His mind. He will not make the Valley of Achor a dark pit in which the people perish forever. Instead, he makes it a door, a gate, a passageway! The exile will not mean death but rather a purifying fire. It will mean a transition, with the people entering the valley at one end and emerging at the other end chastened, renewed, and purified.

But this doesn't include everyone–or even almost everyone. More than half the children of Israel will die Achan's death. For those who refuse to repent, there is no door and no hope.

But there will be some who say, "Now I see what a sinner I am." In exile they will break radically with the evil of serving Baal and will banish this evil from their lives. They will have nothing more to do with it. For them the place of lamentation will become a gateway to salvation and a door of hope.

The apparent destruction will turn out to be a purification. A rejuvenated and renewed Israel will pass singing through the door of exile on its way back to the land of Canaan "as in the days of her youth, as at the time when she came out of the land of Egypt" (2:15).

In His covenant faithfulness, God turns things inside out. He turns the valley of despair into a door of hope. What seemed to be Israel's grave turns out to be a gateway to resurrection. What appeared to lead to destruction results in the unlocking of a new future.

Who is that figure emerging from the grave of Babylon, this valley where Achan was stoned? It was Jacob, who broke with his sinful ways and turned to the Lord!

Those who entered the Valley of Achor with tears and lamentation now *sing* of the valley which, through God's grace, has become a door of hope. For them it is the Lord's gateway. His upright people passed through it in order to honor God in a humble way and enjoy His blessing!

This Valley of Achor makes us think of both the *present* and the *future*. When we think of the present, we note that the church of the Lord in our day is trapped in a *valley* and can hardly be said to be moving through an *open door*. It is trapped in the valley of vilification, where stones are thrown at it. It is trapped in a valley of scorn, where its enemies laugh at its powerlessness. There are many who do not care to enter the door of the church because they believe they would wind up in a valley of death where they would quickly succumb to the cold.

How long will it be before the church moves forward in triumph over this valley and throws its doors wide open? How long will it be before God's holy warriors march out of their barracks to annex the world for their King and make those who sit in satan's synagogues come and bow down to them? When will the Valley of Achor become a door of hope–an open door?

It won't happen as long as the church stands in the corner where all the blows fall. It will only happen when we *repent* and *remove the evil* in our midst–the evil of being like the world, the evil of a defeatist attitude, the evil of egoism! Removing the evil comes first. Otherwise, we will suffer one defeat after another, and there will be no door of hope before us.

We also think of the *future*. This valley of misfortune then becomes the valley of the shadow of death. Because of our sin, *all of us* are sent into that valley. But the Heidelberg Catechism assures us that even this valley has become a door, a gateway. *Our* death is not a punishment for sin but a dying to sin and gateway to eternal life (Answer 42). In this way, too, the Valley of Achor becomes a door of hope.

What is our ground for believing that the valley of the shadow of death will turn out to be the gateway to eternal life? Christ is that ground! Because He has taken our transgressions upon Himself, He was wounded on our account. He suffered like a criminal. He suffered just as Achan suffered. He was not stoned but crucified. He had to endure the punishment that brings us peace. The valley in which He was crushed became our door, our gateway to eternal life.

If this hope is well founded, we must make use of His power to nail our old, sinful nature to the cross with Him. Only if we die to sin before we die will we *really* escape death. Then the Valley of Achor will be a door of hope for us.

It is not enough to confess that we are sinners. We must also combat our sins. The evil must be removed from our lives. The quiet, hidden sin of Achan—you know what it is in your life—must not be allowed to continue, for if it does, not only will you suffer defeats in your *life*, but your *death* will be a complete defeat. The Valley of Achor will become the gateway to hell.

Don't delay, then, in removing the evil from your life. Listen carefully to Him, and your soul shall live. Listen to his promise:

And there I will give her vineyards,
and make the Valley of Achor a door of hope.
And there she shall answer as in the days of her youth,
as at the time when she came out of the land of Egypt.

# 11

# Harmonious Prayers

*And in that day, says the Lord,*
*I will answer the heavens*
*and they shall answer the earth;*
*And the earth shall answer the grain,*
*the wine, and the oil,*
*and they shall answer Jezreel (2:21–22)*

THE END OF HOSEA 2 is full of the sights and sounds of a glorious future. In the most beautiful of colors, the prophet sketches a time to come. So lovely is the picture that it has never been *fully* fulfilled in this world–and never will be. Beeri's son soars high on the wings of prophetic vision and catches a glimpse of the *new earth* beneath the new heaven.

The blessings listed by Hosea are first all *external*. In verse 18 we read that the Lord, acting on behalf of His people, will make a covenant with the wild beasts of the field. The Lord will *bind* these wild animals and make them give up their violent ways.

Among these wild animals are not only the lion, who tears his prey limb from limb, and the venomous snake but also the worm, who gnaws away at the roots of the crops, and the locust, who devours the harvest. There will be no crop failure on the new earth. There will be no discordant sounds to spoil nature's song. There will be no one and nothing to cause suffering or decay–neither man nor beast.

In his quest for destruction, man is much more refined and sophisticated than the wild animals, for he can do what the animals cannot do–hate. There will be no place for such a creature on the new earth. "And I will abolish the bow, the sword, and war from the land; I will make you lie down in safety" (2:18). That will be true peace on earth!

Even more important than the safety of God's people is the prophecy that the inhabitants of the new earth will be *holy*. The Lord promises: "I shall betroth you to me forever" (2:19). What could this promise of a "betrothal" mean but purity? As a holy, unspotted bride without blemish or flaw, God's people will be led into His dwelling place in a stately way. The sin of Israel's adultery will be relegated to a forgotten past.

It is this marriage relationship that makes heaven what it is. The prosperity and peace of which I spoke are not what heaven is all about. Heaven is not first and foremost a place with gates of pearl and streets of gold but rather a place where we live in intimate communion with God. What does a wife who truly *loves* her husband care about his gold and silver if she does not possess *him?* Anyone who is not gripped by the Pauline idea of "always being with the Lord" (I Thess. 4:17) will not enjoy heaven's climate.

The most beautiful thing of all, Hosea tells us, is that there will never be an end to this intimate communion. This marriage is eternal: "I will betroth you to me *forever*." He then adds: "I will betroth you to me in righteousness and in justice, in steadfast love, and in mercy. I will betroth you to me in faithfulness."

Here we see revealed the qualities of God which guarantee His people's future glory. The first of these qualities is His righteousness, for in virtue of the covenant of grace, the Lord–and not satan–has a right to His people and they have a right to Him. This righteousness is manifested through Jesus Christ. "Zion shall be redeemed by justice." Of course, this righteousness means that God's enemies will be judged. The Heidelberg Catechism tells us: "All His enemies and mine He will condemn to everlasting punishment; but me and all His chosen ones He will take along with Him into the joy and the glory of heaven" (Answer 52).

The second quality guaranteeing our salvation is God's mercy and *loving-kindness*. This comes to beautiful expression here. We remember that it is the *adulterous wife* to whom all these beautiful things will happen. According to the law, such an adulterous wife would have to be *stoned*. The only sensible "I will" will then be "I will put you to death!" But a miracle happens! To our surprise, the "I will" turns out to be: "I will betroth you to me."

God doesn't say, "Let's get married." He says, "*I* will betroth you to me." The One who says this is the One to whom and through whom all things are. Thus, there is no place for boasting since the blessings we enjoy are entirely undeserved. We glory only in God's free grace. Instead of being lost as a prostitute, Israel is chosen as a bride!

The third of the virtues of God on which the salvation of His people is founded is His *faithfulness*. Because of His faithfulness, our salvation is eternal. Not a single inhabitant of the new paradise need fear that the sword of the cherubs will drive him away from the tree of life–thanks to God's unshakable faithfulness to Israel.

It is in the context of this sketch of the future state of salvation that the prophet introduces his amazing words about the harmony of prayers:

> I will answer the heavens
> and they shall answer the earth;
> and the earth shall answer the grain,
> the wine, and the oil,
> and they shall answer Jezreel.

"I will answer," says God. This presupposes that the prayers are raised. The picture the prophet paints of these prayers is poetic but simple. He sees the prayers as a chain with many links. Jezreel–or Israel–wants grain and wine and oil–that's the first prayer. But the grain in turn needs something from the earth–that's the second prayer. Yet the earth can bring forth nothing without rain from heaven, and therefore the earth stretches out its arms to heaven–the third prayer. Now, the heavens can pour rain on the earth only if God opens up the floodgates, and so the heavens cry out to the God of heaven–the fourth prayer.

All these prayers are heard. God hears the heavens, and the heavens hear the earth, the earth hears the grain, and the grain hears Jezreel. God is the first link in this chain, and Jezreel is the last. The ultimate issue is how the Lord provides His people with all they need.

Of course, the prophet could have said that God will always hear the prayers of His people. That would have been a more ordinary and prosaic way of speaking.

Why does Hosea call on this flight of poetic fancy, in which grain, the earth, and the heavens are represented as praying? His purpose was not to give free rein to his imagination. Nor does he express himself in such terms because he loves poetic language. What this poet and prophet wants to convince us of first and foremost is that the new world, which we wait eagerly for, will be a world of *prayer*.

When the curse is removed, everything in the new creation will be caught up in prayer and supplication. The heavens pray, and the earth prays. The grain prays, and the wine and oil pray. In fact, the entirety of the new creation will be one great prayer. No one will curse and no one will sigh, for everyone will bow before the great Creator of all things.

There will be an amazing and beautiful *harmony* in these prayers. The prayers of all creatures will be joined and integrated. All will be harmonized in powerful agreement–the grain with the earth and the earth with the heavens.

It would not be fair to say that there is no prayer in the creation at present. On the contrary, the creatures without souls are engaged in a protracted, non-verbal prayer. For the present, this praying is really a *sighing*. The Scriptures teach that the entire creation sighs together and yearns for the day when the children of God will be redeemed.

You can hear that sighing in the sounds of the fields scorched by the sun, in the moaning of dumb cattle, in the howling of the wind, in the plaintive sounds of the woods. Those sounds represent nature's Advent prayer. In this longing for Christ's return, nature is often ahead of the children of re-creation, for so often they cannot force the word *Maranatha* from their lips.

These creatures without souls are not the only ones praying. People also pray–when they are not cursing. Yet there's something missing in their prayers–harmony. Their prayers conflict with each other. One prays for rain, and another prays for dry weather. Two men seek the same position, and both ask for that position in prayer. "Answering" the prayer of one means disappointing the other. In our holiest moment, that of prayer, we so often shove ourselves forward and push others away from God's throne. When a war breaks out, both sides pray for the blessing of the Almighty on their weapons. These prayers collide, and we search in vain for harmony.

Since there is little agreement between our prayers, God cannot "answer" each prayer that reaches Him. Thus, someone who asks for grain may receive thorns instead, and someone who asks for grain and oil may wind up with nothing. The earth asks the heavens for rain but is sometimes answered with cyclones and hailstorms. The heavens do not hear the earth, and the earth does not hear the grain, and the grain does not hear Jezreel. We become confused and struggle with the difficult problem of "unanswered prayer." Finally, we give up on prayer and mutter, "It's no use anyway." We wind up sighing along with the rest of creation.

A beautiful prophecy that I find very appealing is Hosea's assurance that one day the riddle of unanswered prayer will no longer disturb us. All prayers will be part of a chain; they will be linked and will fit together. My blessing will no longer mean a curse for someone else. The prayers in the new world will be joined in one melodious whole. Together we will sing in mighty harmony, and our song will be followed by an incalculable series of answers to our prayers.

Since I already feel the beginning of eternal joy in my heart, since the joy of heaven is not a totally new element but in principle is already a familiar part of my experience, I must now be much more *careful* about what I ask for in prayer. Am I perhaps praying selfishly? Am I prepared for the possibility that my request will not be granted since I know that there is someone else who is much more in need of what I requested for myself than I am? Am I prepared to pray for my enemies? When we exercise this necessary self-control, the problem of "unanswered prayer" becomes much simpler for us.

The ideal of the harmony of prayer is coming closer. We see the heavens reaching out to the earth.

Once we have come to see how many discordant sounds are present in our prayers, we will be ready to change the petition "Forgive us our debts" to "Forgive us our *prayers*."

# 12

# Trembling at God's Goodness

*They shall come in fear to the Lord and to His goodness (3:15).*

ONE OF HOSEA'S WAYS of describing Israel's future conversion is his statement that Israel will come in fear to the Lord and to His goodness. What an amazing thing to say! We can all imagine that someone might tremble at God's *greatness* or His *holiness* or might be afraid of His *anger*. Trembling is understandable in the face of such "virtues" of God, and it is proper for sinners to tremble. But would anyone actually tremble at God's *goodness?* That's just what the converted do, the Bible tells us here.

This is one of the essential characteristics of God's converted people. As long as a person is still unrepentant, he can fear God's mighty majesty if need be and can cringe at the thought of punishment from God's hand. This doesn't seem at all strange. We remember Cain's fear and Saul's fear. But would such a person tremble at the *goodness* of the Lord? He's most familiar with that goodness. He sings about it and rejoices in it, but never does he fear it. He's just like Israel when she still turned her back on God and ran into the arms of her lovers. Israel was abusing God's favor and goodness. At best, she accepted that goodness as something to be taken for granted. It was normal and it made sense: the Lord is good to Israel!

That's the attitude towards God's goodness that we find among the unconverted. They are not afraid to take hold of God's goodness with their filthy fingers. They don't hesitate at all. They even speak from time to time of the "blessings of the Lord" and give thanks in church on their 25th wedding anniversary, despite the fact that they have used the mercy and favor of their Lord only for their own advantage. They can talk about the Lord's goodness in a charming and touching way, yet they have never trembled at that goodness. Only the converted do that!

Someone who has repented and turned to God trembles when he thinks of God's goodness. He doesn't know where to hide. He is deeply ashamed that the Lord is so good to him.

When this small ship of his life almost sinks under the weight of God's surprising blessing, he does not draw attention to himself proudly but cries out, "Lord, turn Your face from me, for I am a sinner." Thus Hosea, with his sensitive soul, could portray the conversion of Israel in a beautiful and tender way by saying, "They shall come in fear to the Lord and to His goodness."

Someone who has never trembled at God's goodness knows little about conversion, however much he may have trembled for other reasons.

The Lord had been especially good to Israel. For the second time, the tender love of God for His people was illustrated concretely in what Hosea had to do with his unfaithful wife. Obediently, he carried out God's command.

Apparently, Gomer, of whom we hear in the first chapter, had lived such a shameful life that she wound up running away from her husband. Hosea was now ordered to bring her back. Not only that, he was also to "love" her.

His love for her, however, was not born out of duty or a divine command. When the Lord gave this order, He planted in Hosea's heart an unextinguishable love for the ungrateful, unfaithful, sinful Gomer. This love was so deeply rooted that we are moved and touched as we watch Hosea running after his wife. There is one thing he desires and one thing that fills his soul: to get back the wife that ran away from him.[5]

But it was no simple matter to get her back. Gomer was certainly in a bad way: she had become a *slave!* That's how blind sin makes us. She had thought her new life would be all fun and frolic, but it turned out to be the exact opposite. She found out, to her dismay, that the man she was living with was not a husband to her but a tyrant. She was forced to do the most humiliating work as a slave.

Gomer's condition was a pitiful reflection of Israel's condition as a nation. Israel believed she would find freedom in serving Baal, but she became a slave to sin. Here we could apply Paul's claim that when we sin, we become slaves to sin.

However, it came about, Gomer was indeed a slave. Therefore, Hosea couldn't just take her back; he had to *buy* her back from her master. "So I bought her back for fifteen shekels of silver and a homer and a lethech of barley" (3:2). All in all, this added up to 30 pieces of silver, which is the price one would normally pay for a slave.

In this way, Gomer again becomes Hosea's lawful wife. Hosea could return to his home with the wife he had bought

---

5. I take it that the "woman loved by another man, an adulterous" (3:1 NEB), whom Hosea was to go and love, was not some other woman but the same woman mentioned in chapter 1, i.e., Gomer.

back. Gomer was restored to her position of honor as a free woman and wife.

To make sure of her love from then on, Hosea resolved to discipline her. He said to her: "For many days you must keep yourself quietly for me, not playing the whore or offering yourself to others; and I will do the same for you" (3:3 JB). This was a stern measure, but it was animated by love.

Gomer would have to "remain quiet" for a certain period of time and live in strict isolation. Hosea assumed that in her solitude she would reflect on her life, and a desire for her own husband would begin to grow within her. It was not at all his intention to torment her. Rather, he wanted to repair the relationship. Meanwhile, he was impatient himself for the time of isolation to pass, as the conclusion of verse three makes clear. Hosea planned to wait for her!

The "goodness" of God shines through in all of this. Hosea's amazing way of dealing with Gomer was intended as a vivid illustration of a message, namely, that the Lord deals with His people in exactly this way. Thus, in verse one the prophet adds: "... even as the Lord loves the people of Israel, though they turn to other gods."

Here, everything is placed under the heading of God's "goodness," whether He blesses Israel or disciplines her. It is because of the Lord's goodness that He goes after His runaway people, so to speak. It is because of His goodness that He follows Israel in His love and cannot abide the thought of His people being trapped in the snares of sin and becoming slaves of Baal. The goodness of the Lord is likewise present in the threatening judgment of *exile*. The exile was intended not as a destruction of Israel but as a disciplinary measure. Thus, Hosea's disciplinary measure (i.e., isolating Gomer) is also applied to Israel: "For the children of Israel shall dwell many days without king or prince, without sacrifice or pillar, without ephod or teraphim" (3:4).

Hosea speaks here of the loneliness and isolation of exile. Israel's existence as an independent nation will come to an end: she will be "without king or prince." Worse still, there will be an end to her communion with the Lord when she lives in miserable exile far from the Holy Land: she will be "without sacrifice or pillar, without ephod or teraphim."

God's goodness comes through most richly in that He *waits* all this time. Like Hosea, He refuses to choose another wife during the period of waiting. He continues to wait for His people.

There is nothing more moving than the idea of God waiting for man. In the parable of the prodigal son, the New Testament shows us something of this waiting on God's part. When the son was still far away, his father saw him. Thus, the father was waiting for him, looking for him. Every day he climbed up on the roof of his house to see if his son was coming. Each morning again he asked himself, "Will he come home today?"

God is waiting for you, sinner. The question is not whether the Lord will come. The question is whether the sinner will show up. That's heaven's concern. God is waiting.

This time God will not be disappointed as He waits. Israel's isolation in exile will bring about a growing desire for communion with God. "Afterward the children of Israel shall return and seek the Lord their God, and David their king; and they shall come in fear to the Lord and to His goodness in the latter days" (3:5).

They shall seek the Lord. That's the first aspect of their conversion. They shall seek not the things of the Lord but the Lord Himself. And they shall seek David their king. That's the second aspect of their conversion. The Kingdom of the 10 tribes, which had turned away from David's royal house, will again be subject to its scepter. The communion with God will again reveal itself in *obedience* to the king anointed by God. In the fullness of time, the king will be Jesus Christ, the Son of David.

The final aspect of their conversion, which I already mentioned at the beginning of this chapter, is their trembling at God's goodness. Israel will recognize God's goodness in punishment and will marvel at that goodness in God's love, which seeks Israel out. No longer will Israel play games with that love. Instead, she will accept it with trembling hands. Now she will say—for love is not verbose— "Thou art my God" (2:23).

Have we learned to tremble at God's goodness? That goodness, of course, is not reflected only in our success in life. Sometimes there is more of God's goodness present in our *failures* than in our success.

That "goodness" is manifested especially in the ordinary things of life, in every piece of bread, in every glass of water, in every ray of sunshine. It is manifested in the health of our children, in the fact that we have been baptized, and in the fact that we may attend church each Sunday. That goodness is present in our lives in a thousand different ways.

There are many who disregard this fact. They take it for granted. That's how they expect things to be. It's only normal, after all. Because they have no eyes for God's goodness in "ordinary" things and see even less of His goodness in His chastisement, they're always full of complaints.

The child of God sees things differently. He is amazed, first of all, that God's goodness continues day after day. He does not regard his daily bread, his income, his meager weekly wages, and his good health as things to take for granted, as things to which he has a right. He is uneasy about them. He doesn't quite understand them. He trembles when he thinks, "Who am I, and what is my house?" Trembling, he stands before the goodness of the Lord and stammers, "Lord, is all of this for me?"

Have we reached the point in our conversion that our grabbing greedily at God's blessings, our taking His goodness for granted, and our whining to gain His favor have been replaced by fear? Can it be said of us, "They shall come in fear to the Lord and to His goodness"?

# 13

# Criticizing Priests and Criticizing Ourselves

*Yet let no one contend,*
*and let none accuse,*
*for with you is my contention,*
*O priest (4:4).*

CRITICISM OF "THE NATION'S LEADERS" is a very old phenomenon: Hosea already reproached the Israelites for their complaints and threats about their leaders. But the interesting thing is that Hosea, who reproves the people for criticizing the priests, proceeds to do the same thing himself. When we read what Hosea goes on to say (4:6-10), this becomes very clear. The prophet throws the book at the priests, as it were. His accusations are sharply worded: "They feed on the sins of my people; they are greedy for their iniquity" (4:8). His indictment is devastating: "Because you have rejected knowledge, I reject you from being a priest to me" (4:6).

What was Hosea up to? Certainly, a great deal could be said about those leaders. Why weren't the people allowed to express their criticisms? Hosea went ahead and said his piece, after all, and he certainly didn't pull any punches!

What Hosea did was something completely different from the usual grumbling. Hosea spoke out against sin as such. Whether the guilty were leaders or followers was of no concern to him. None who took the wrong path in doctrine and life were spared–not even the priests.

If the people had agreed with Hosea in his criticism that spared no one and nothing, Hosea would have praised them rather than admonished them, for when office bearers go astray, the people need not remain silent. In fact, because of the office of believer, they *may* not remain silent. They *must* protest with words–and even with deeds if need be.

But that's not what was happening in Israel. No one paid any attention to how the priests lived. The people had no objections at all to the participation of the priests in the calf worship in Dan and Bethel. Everyone was silent about it; everyone seemed to think it was fine. After all, it was a beautiful excuse for their own sins. What better way is there to declare yourself innocent than to point out that the leaders do it too?

No, the criticisms made by the people went in an entirely different direction than Hosea's criticism. According to the law, the priest also served as judges. No one was allowed to be his own judge. If two men in Israel were locked in a dispute, they were to go "to the Levitical priests, and to the judge who is in office in those days...and they shall declare to you the decision" (Deut. 17:9). There was no higher calling possible. Refusal to abide by this law was punishable by death: "Anyone who presumes to reject the decision either of the priest who ministers there to the Lord your God, or of the judge, shall die; thus, you will rid Israel of wickedness" (Deut. 17:12 NEB).

In Hosea's days, the decree was no longer taken seriously. Time and again, the binding decisions of the priests were resisted. People refused to abide by them. The governmental authority was simply set aside. The people did not listen to what was said in God's name.

Meanwhile, those who were so quick to criticize the priests were not critical of themselves in the slightest. Perhaps it's not so strange that they failed to criticize themselves, for they also refused to put up with criticisms from others. That's what Hosea meant by the words: "It is not for a man to bring a charge" (4:4 NEB). When they did wrong, they didn't want anyone to point it out to the judge; they didn't want to hear a complaint or a gentle admonition or a reference to their sin from anyone. If anyone did dare to say something, he would quickly be dealt with in a less than pleasant way.

Yet, there was enough to criticize. The picture Hosea paints of the covenant people in his day is a sad one indeed: "There is swearing, lying, killing, stealing, and committing adultery; they break all bounds and murder follows murder" (4:2). This declaration is hard to believe: murder, robbery, and adultery were the order of the day, according to Hosea. And woe to anyone who dared to say anything about it! If a judge dared to punish such a robber or murderer, the whole gang would denounce his ruling in threatening, abusive language.

We might be inclined to suppose that those awful conditions were a result of the fact that one revolution followed another after the time of Jeroboam II. But Hosea tells us simply that the cause is to be sought elsewhere: "There is no knowledge of God in the land" (4:1). This undermined two pillars on which society rests, namely, faithfulness and love. Thus, knowledge of God (doctrine) and what we do (conduct) are more closely connected than many people are inclined to suppose. It's the same old story: where God is not feared, human life is not respected.

Even if no one will tolerate anyone else pointing a finger at him in criticism, *God* will not keep his criticism to Himself. His criticism comes to expression in the facts:

> Therefore the land mourns,
> and all who dwell in it languish,

and also the beasts of the field,
and the birds of the air;
and even the fish of the sea are taken away (4:3).

Thus, the Lord steps forward directly as the accuser of his people,[6] without relying on any such metaphor as the unfaithful wife of the earlier chapters. In unequivocal terms, he makes his judgment known. The words to pronounce judgment point to the final judgment.

No one will dare to oppose this judgment handed down by the highest judge. All will remain silent, for even if they were to ask a thousand questions, they would not receive an answer.

This is how God criticizes those who criticize the priests but refuse to listen to a word of criticism themselves.

Are things any better in our time? Don't Hosea's words rip open some wounds in the life of the church today?

Let's admit, first of all, that we, too, like to "criticize the priests." I'm not referring to our criticism of what the churches' office bearers do and fail to do. When these office bearers work their hearts out day and night, sacrificing all their strength in the service of the church, no one ever says a word about it. But as soon as something goes wrong in the church, people

---

6. This is apparent from the word: "the Lord has a charge to bring against the people of the land" (4:1 NEB).

are quick to open their mouths and set off the alarm bells. But that's not really the point that concerns me right now, for that's not what Israel's criticism was about either. No doubt there are enough things about the church to criticize, but let's not forget that faithful office bearers also think to themselves, "I wish they would stop. I'm well aware of the problem."

Neither is my intention to talk about our criticism of sermons, our eagerness to point out that this one is too long and that one too short, that this one is too dry and that one too emotional, that this one is too doctrinal and that one too moralistic. No doubt there are enough criticisms of this sort that could be made, provided–and this is the decisive issue–we also realize that complaining about the sermon is the best and most effective way of closing our hearts to *God's Word*. And closing our hearts to the Word represents the most outrageous and dangerous kind of criticism we could imagine.

The real danger is this: "criticism of priests" can all too easily become criticism of the Bible. Now, the term *Biblical criticism* is almost a dirty word in our Reformed ears. In the ordinary sense of the term, *we* are not guilty of any such thing. After all, who would dare to remove as much as one page from the Bible or even drop a single letter?

Yet the Reformed believer can be the greatest of biblical critics! He becomes a biblical critic when he compares different parts of the Bible in a calm way and studies them.

But we are no more interested in bowing to the decision of God's Word for our lives than the Israelites were willing to bow to the judicial decisions made by the priests. We simply refuse to abide by the Bible's rulings. We declare that we will not bow down before the Bible.

Of course, we bow our heads in church when we hear familiar and well-known biblical texts to the effect that we are deeply corrupt sinners. We don't object to those words. We're far too Calvinistic to try to appeal that judgment.

But what do we do when the Word of God is applied to us in a very concrete and personal way, when we are commanded to break with certain specific sins? What do we do when a preacher or an elder of the church comes to visit us and reminds us of the ruling made by the highest Judge, telling us that we must be subject to this brother or that sister, that we must be more humble and not consider ourselves so important? Then protest wells up inside us, and we demand that the decision be changed. We declare that we are being done an injustice. We just don't understand why *we* should always have to regard ourselves as of lesser importance.

We're the kind of people who get involved in such quarrels with priests. It's in our blood. The confession that a man must humble himself utterly has greater implications than we realized, for we thought the one who must be humbled is our neighbor. We don't realize it applies to us as well.

Hand in hand with this criticism of priests goes the refusal to listen to any criticism of our own lives. It's as though we were saying, "I don't want anyone to reprimand me, and I'm not about to reprimand myself."

Self-criticism is almost unheard of in our time. Therefore, there are many rich young rulers wandering freely and cheerfully through the streets of our Calvinistic Jerusalem. Like the augurs in the streets of ancient Rome, they cannot face each other without breaking into laughter. They are well aware that they–unlike the Israelites of Hosea's time–are not guilty of theft, murder, robbery, or adultery, but they know just as well that they do not begin to approach the *love* that represents the fulfillment of the law. The first of these rich young rulers was unmasked by Jesus, and the others are no better. They still act as though they don't know what Jesus asks of us, and they can't contain their laughter when they meet each other.

Meanwhile, the Lord has some devastating criticism for these people who criticize priests freely but refuse to be critical of themselves. *They* will say to the Lord, "We know you! Of course, we do! We know you very well, for we've heard a lot about you. You used to teach in our streets." Then *the Lord* will say, "I never knew *you*."

# 14

# Feeding on Sin

*They feed on the sin of my people (4:8).*

WHEN PROPHETS HAVE SOMETHING to say, they don't put it in familiar and beloved phrases well known to all, phrases that are likely to lull people to sleep. Their purpose is to wake people up and put the fear of the Lord into them. Therefore, they often talk in a strange, unpolished way.

Hosea, for example, does not shrink from accusing the priests (the "they" in verses 7 and 8) of *feeding on sin*. Instead of manifesting an *aversion* to sin, which is what we would expect of priests, they enjoy it and eat it up. They lick their lips at the thought of sin. It makes their mouths water.

Was Hosea slipping into hyperbole of the pulpit here? Not at all. Hosea didn't strive to speak in pulpit language. Carefully written sermons and beautiful orations may smooth out the soul's creases somewhat, while leaving most of the audience unmoved, but Beeri's son was not interested in such things. His words hit both the people and the priests like the lash of a whip.

Hosea addressed himself to *both* of these groups. He was certainly not the type to tell the little man some hard and bitter truths while sparing the feelings of the rich and powerful. When he sees sins that cried out for reprimand, he spares no one. He even said that the people and the priests will be treated alike (4:9). First, he addresses himself to the followers (4:1–5) and then he turns to the leaders.

After rejecting the criticism of the priests that the people offered, he proceeded to criticize the priests himself. His criticism was far from mild, and it culminated in the accusation: "They feed on the sin of my people."

What were these priests of Israel doing that was so wrong? Let's pause for a moment to find out.

Things looked pretty bad in Israel at that time, as we have seen. Theft, murder, and adultery were the (dis)order of the day. The prophet was angry at the priests in particular because this ethical degeneration was in large measure their fault. It was the task and calling of the priests to instruct the people in the law, but they failed to do so. They neglected their responsibilities in a shameful way.

A people that no longer has any knowledge of God's law and Word, a people that knows nothing of His directives for faith and life, is hastening to its destruction. This is a fixed law. Such a people will be lost and destroyed—because they have no *knowledge* (4:6). It is the fault of their leaders.

That was only a sin of *omission!* I said "only," but that does not mean that sins of omission are to be taken lightly. On the contrary, they are to be taken very seriously. There are many who labor under the illusion that *neglecting* what God commanded us to do is not as serious as actually *doing* what God told us not to do. They believe that someone who takes advantage of his neighbor is guiltier than someone who refuses to help his neighbor. This is an illusion. Sins of omission result from a lack of love, for love is always reliable. Love forgets nothing and is not slothful. Love is the fulfillment of the law and the hardest thing about the law. Therefore, Jesus reminds us about the eternal fire waiting for those who failed to clothe the naked and feed the hungry, those who claim that they "forgot."

The failure of the priests to give instruction in the law was a very serious matter. That failure had pushed an entire people to the brink of destruction. Who is to say we may excuse our conscience because of our sin of omission?

But Hosea has much more to say about the priests! They do not only neglect the law but also disobey it. In addition to their *negative* guilt, there is *positive* guilt. Listen to what Hosea says: "The more priests there are, the more they sin against me" (4:7 NEB).

Of course, it was fine with the people that the priests no longer admonished them. In fact, they thought more highly of the priests because of it. But as the priests increased in honor and esteem, their sin also increased. It's the same old story that we see repeated so often in human history.

Just how much their sin had increased is apparent from what Hosea says: "They feed on the sin of my people." This brings us back to our point of departure.

What did Hosea mean when he spoke of the priests as feeding on the sins of the people? It quickly becomes clear when we realize that he is alluding here to the *sacrifices brought for sin*. The priests had to eat the flesh of animals offered as sacrifices. Hosea did not accuse the priests of eating the *sacrifices* which the people brought because of their sins–for there was nothing wrong with that. He accused them instead of *feeding on sin*.

Do you sense the breathtaking force of this accusation? Can you see what was going on in the hearts of these priests? The priests thought to themselves, "I hope the people sin a lot, for then we will have a lot of meat on the table." The more the people sinned, the more meat there was for them to eat. They could live off all that meat; it was a welcome source of income. They were delighted to see the people come with their offerings for sin, for it meant money in their pocket, so to speak. Therefore, Hosea went on to say that these priests were greedy for the iniquity of the people (4:8).

Now, the flesh from the sacrifices for sin was not the only source of income for these priests. Furthermore, we can rest assured that a true priest would much rather have a little less food on his table than have to hope for offerings brought because of sins committed. Depending on such offerings was an awful way to make a living. A man with the heart of a real priest would rather starve to death.

Our great high priest Jesus Christ died because of the sins of His people, but for these priests, the sins of the people were a source of enjoyment. The priests of the old covenant sought to line their pockets with something that meant the death of the Priest of the new covenant. In other words, they wanted to live off the sin for which Christ was willing to die. Through the sacrifices and other ceremonies, these priests were supposed to bring about a prefiguration and foreshadowing of Christ's work. But what they actually did was that hellish caricature: "They feed on the sin of my people."

In our time, there are many who live off the sins of the people, many for whom unrighteousness is a welcome source of income. Think of prostitutes who walk the streets openly. Everyone sees them and knows that they live off sin. There are those who manufacture equipment for sexual perversion and movie directors who pretend to be interested in art but really produce pornography. We don't always look down our noses at such people when we see them on the street, but they, too, live off sin.

The sad fact is that the world operates not with a double standard but with a whole series of standards. Therefore, it may happen that two men make a living off the sins of the people, one being universally despised while the other is held in high esteem. In other words, it is possible to feed on the sins of the people in a more refined and generally accepted way.

It's really a question of how you go about it. You can do it brutally or stealthily, in a shameless way or in a seemingly virtuous way, in an open way or in a secret way. But however you do it, the result is the same: you feed on the sins of the people and line your pockets with that which leads others to destruction.

The worst thing of all is that this evil is even to be found in Christian and Calvinistic circles. In this regard, we don't need to look down on prostitutes and tax-collectors. Are you wondering what I'm talking about? Have our Reformed people actually sunk so low? Do some of us actually live off "unclean" schemes? Is it true that there are Christians who derive their income from the sins of the people?

Now, I don't want to make the accusation that there are Christians who actually live off the sins of the people, but it is another question whether some of us are in fact engrossed by them. Don't you remember how the priests of Israel *delighted* in the sins of the people? The same kind of spiritual delight in the sins of others is present on many a Sunday evening when Christians get together to drink coffee and talk. As they drink their coffee, they simply "eat up" the sins of their own "brothers and sisters." They do not eat quietly, as mice invariably do, but lick their lips and chew noisily. They gobble up the whole thing, like a man at a fish market who puts a whole herring in his mouth. They delight in the stories about others. They feast on them and devour them. The sins of the people become a banquet for them.

There's always someone who has brought along some juicy morsel for these times of "sharing." His new delicacy is introduced by the question: "Have you heard about so and so?" Next, sweet-smelling Christian sauce has to be poured over the juicy morsel as people remark what a shame it is that the name of the Lord and the reputation of the church are once more dragged through the mud. Then the assembled guests eat their treat, slowly savoring every mouthful. That's how our priests feed on the sins of the people. Every sinful episode is seized on as a welcome opportunity for people to draw praise by contrast.

Let's not forget that all of us are priests in virtue of the universal priesthood of believers. Let's also remember that we may not do as we please with that office, and that we may not turn it into its opposite.

The heart of any true priest will *bleed* for the sins of God's people. The hearts of Jesus' disciples were full of sorrow when they heard that one of the twelve had made plans to betray Jesus. Christ poured out His soul in death because of the sins of His people. Are we then to derive enjoyment from those sins and use them to enliven our conversations over dinner? That's not what a priest is called to do!

Some think they have discharged the priestly office for all believers fully when they contribute a little money to help take care of the needy brothers and sisters. That's a fatal mistake. Priestly service goes much further. According to the Heidelberg Catechism, we must offer ourselves as "living sacrifices," and that includes the prayers we offer with our lips.

Someone who has properly understood the office of priest will avoid speaking ill of sinners in public conversations and will instead offer praise to God in private, intimate conversations with Him. He will *pray* for sinners. He will not gladly open his ears to hear all about the sins of the people. He won't be eager to discuss those sins with others. The one with whom he should discuss such matters is the Lord.

The sins of the people make him afraid. Therefore, he pours out his soul before God's throne and calls out to the Lord in his concern. Like Amos, he begs the Lord to forgive the people.

Never does he forget to look at *his own life* after he considers the sins of the people. He realizes that he, too, is a miserable sinner. He prays: "See if there be any wicked way in *me* and lead me in the way everlasting."

When this happens, God will no longer complain about us in heaven. He will not have to say to the priests of the twentieth century: "They feed on the sins of my people; they are greedy for their iniquity."

# 15

## Piety with a Flavor

*They sacrifice on the tops of the mountains,*
*and make offerings upon the hills,*
*under oak, poplar, and terebinth,*
*because their shade is good (4:13).*

THE PEOPLE OF HOSEA'S TIME were certainly religious! There was hardly a hill in the land without an altar on it, and hardly a clump of oak, poplar, or terebinth trees that was not used as a holy place. Not once a week but *daily* did the blood of sacrificial animals flow, as solemn hymns of sacrifice were sung. This must create a favorable impression, I would expect.

Any nation that destroys its altars and tears down its churches to turn them into bank buildings or movie theaters and builds entire cities without temples is anti-religious and secularized in the deepest sense. Such a nation is a commercialized nation. But Israel was not such a nation. The number of places where sacrifices were offered, and worship services were held grew day by day. The smell of religion and incense was everywhere. Truly those Israelites were faithful, vigilant sons of Abraham.

The course of Abraham's life was marked by altars. His exact path could be traced later because he erected altars everywhere. That was Abraham's piety; erecting altars was his life. The descendants of Abraham were doing the same: "They sacrifice on the tops of the mountains, and make offerings upon the hills."

Hosea, you man of God, what do you have against that? Shouldn't these people be praised? Aren't they following in the footsteps of the patriarchs? Aren't they in effect repeating what their fathers once said to Joseph: "We are honest men"? This honesty and piety had certain flavors–so much so, in fact, that the prophet, who liked nothing better than altars, shook his head. He did not applaud the building of those altars but criticized it instead.

We must be careful not to reproach these Israelites unjustly. No one should insinuate that the altars of which we read here were dedicated to idols. Hosea did not say that these holy places were devoted to *Baal*. The spirit of this man of God was not aroused at this point because the land had turned to idolatry, because the country was full of altars with inscriptions that said: "To the unknown God." On the contrary, the name of Yahweh, Israel's God, was mentioned repeatedly in these services. His praise was on the lips of these "servants of the Most High God." Idolatry wasn't the problem, then. Any priest and anyone who prayed under the holy oaks would have been indignant at any accusation of idolatry, protesting that the Israelites were pious people.

Neither should the "flavor" mentioned in the title of this chapter be sought in something unlawful in the religious ceremonies conducted on every hill and under every green tree. Of course, these practices were indeed unlawful. That's beyond dispute. The open-air services were out of bounds, for the Lord had designated Jerusalem as the central holy place where He wished to meet His people. What Abraham had done earlier and what Joshua had done when he erected an altar under the oak tree (Josh. 24:26) was not an adequate justification for these religious practices that the Israelites had devised for themselves.

Yet, because Jerusalem had become isolated through the splitting of the Kingdom, there was a partial excuse–but not a full justification–for this offering of sacrifices on the high places. After all, Elijah had built an altar on the heights of Mount Carmel, and God responded with fire to show that He was there. We should not assume that the Lord will always absent himself from unlawful worship services, nor can we always deny the name *church* to unlawful institutions claiming to be churches. "Lawfulness" is not a defining characteristic of the church.

Hosea himself clarifies his objections to what was going on in his time. What bitter aftertaste did he detect in the piety of the Israelites? The simple fact that they sacrificed on hills and in bushes could be overlooked, *if need be*, but what angered him was their *reason* for sacrificing there.

Why were these religious customs established? Was it to serve *God* and bow down in adoration before the Maker of heaven and earth? Was it gratitude to the Most High that led the Israelites to lay down their gifts on the altar of love? Was it perhaps a healthy awareness of their sin that led them to offer these sacrifices?

No, they had quite a different reason, sad to say. The cutting reproach of the prophet is that the Israelites offer their sacrifices under trees "because their shade is good." That's Hosea's characterization of their piety. It's nothing but a *pious egoism*. What concerns them is not God but themselves, that is, the shade of a tree, their own welfare. Israel's piety was nothing but a *worldly piety*. That's the bitter aftertaste.

What was going on in Israel? Israel lived in the midst of heathen nations, and heathen religions never stopped exercising their influence on the religion of Israel. Those heathen religions were pure *service of nature*. They represented religion without God. The heathens prayed not to God but to what He had made; they deified nature and the powers of nature. These heathens therefore preferred the tops of mountains and hills, for they believed they were closer to the heart of divinity there, the divinity they sought in the sun or the moon.

The bushes also became beloved sanctuaries, for the trees with their "pleasant shade" were a striking symbol of the beneficent character of divine nature. That was where the sacrifices were offered. That was where the gods lived. The more sacrifices were offered under "God's trees," the more shade and protection the trees would afford. The heathen says in his heart, "I give you the gift, my God, not *because* it's rightfully yours but *so that* you'll give me a great deal in return." The heathen is interested not so much in his god as in his own welfare and the shade afforded by the tree.

Israel's "worship" had been permitted by such a spirit. The Israelites were less concerned about God than about the "shade." The benefits to be derived from worship. Although Yahweh's name was mentioned repeatedly, they could easily do without Him, as long as He gave them shade. Therefore, they sacrificed in the bush, where they could enjoy the shade afforded by the trees. That was their religion without God!

To what extent this religion had become worldly and godless is made clear by the prophet by way of a few strong statements. "Wine and new wine take away the understanding," he charges (4:11). In short, their lives are dominated by the pleasures of the flesh. Religious observances have not been abandoned, but before, during, and after the services all their thoughts and words are focused on that which charms the eye and titillates the senses.

Even worse, the prophet complains: "My people inquire of a thing of wood, and their staff gives them oracles" (4:12). Here we have a reference to the oracles of the heathens. A piece of wood or a stick standing upright would be allowed to fall. Some decision about the future would then be made on the basis of the direction in which the stick pointed. This direction was taken to be a clear indication of what should be done. The children of Abraham followed the patriarch in such offering sacrifices, then, but they did not wish to live with God the way Abraham did.

Abraham was a man of prayer. His only desire was to go to the land which *God* would show him. But these Israelites got their instructions from a piece of wood. They did not fold their hands in prayer but used them to take hold of the great wheel of adventure. Fate and Fortune were their god and goddess to whom they entrusted their destiny and welfare. What is this but religion without God?

Hosea adds that the husbands and fathers should not be surprised if their brides and daughters later engaged in open adultery if they follow the Canaanite custom of devoting themselves to some goddess or other and even become prostitutes for the sake of that goddess. This is simply the inevitable consequence. The young are not blind: they are perfectly capable of detecting the emptiness and rottenness of the religion of the "older generation." All that remains for them to do is to get rid of the dead forms and empty language. In doing so, the young are not worse than their mothers and fathers but only more honest.

Those disappointed fathers and deceived husbands, whose daughters and brides take part in orgies of the heathens, should not expect the Lord to intervene on their side by punishing the guilty woman, for their fathers and husbands themselves brought on the disappointing behavior. "I will not punish your daughters when they play the harlot, nor your brides when they commit adultery" (4:14).

Hosea sums up the whole tragedy by saying: "A people without understanding shall come to ruin" (4:14). This text is not something for intellectuals to seize on, as though reason and rational knowledge were proclaimed central to a nation's welfare and success. Such a view smacks of Humanism. The knowledge that is immeasurable in meaning is the knowledge of God's word. A nation with "reason" as its only asset can easily go into decline and may well run around in intellectualism.

The word *understanding* in this text really refers to faith. It is the enlightened eye of reason that possesses insight into what fosters peace and human welfare. A nation that lives by a religion without God and does not live by faith will ultimately fail. The rising younger generation will attach no significance whatsoever to such a religion and will break with it openly!

The picture painted by Hosea again brings us uncomfortably close to our time. In more than one respect, our time shows us a religion in which the worshippers are clearly more interested in God's shadow than His glory.

Nowhere is this clearer than in the striking difference between New Year's Eve services and New Year's morning services. On New Year's Eve, all the worshippers are eager to seek refuge under the "shadow" of God's wings, but the smaller turnout on New Year's morning already shows that the worshippers have again decided that they can fly under their own strength. By then people are interested more in news from the stock exchange and the centers of finance. They focus on the desires of their own hearts and ignore the Lord and all His ways. They turn to a piece of wood for advice!

When we speak of the past on New Year's Eve, we see the hills and mountains shaking, but by New Year's morning those same hills and mountains are again secure enough to build on. How much we are interested in wine and oil and how little time we spend thinking of God is also apparent from our conversations before and after the sermon. These are just a few signs—I could list many more—of an externalized religion.

This kind of religion, of course, does not impart strength and devotion to the family. Family life then loses its backbone and spirit. There are many children in Christian homes who never learn from the lives of their parents that the service of the Lord is a source of strength and joy. They see their father pray before meals, but there is nothing to indicate to them that prayer is the secret of his success and the source of his strength. When things are going badly, it's not much fun to have him around, but once his fortunes take a turn for the better, he becomes pleasant company again.

In such families, the power of prayer is not the yeast that leavens all of life, and the joy which faith brings is not communicated from the one to the other like an electric spark. The family engages in both commercial and religious business, but the latter is something separate; It is set aside for Sundays and special occasions when we seek the "shadow" of God's wings.

Do you really believe that the young see and feel nothing of this? Do you suppose that children don't laugh inwardly at such an empty spectacle? When the rising generation of sons and daughters takes no pleasure in the church and its activities, when you have a hard time keeping them away from sinful pursuits, don't be so quick to join the many fathers and mothers who complain about "young people today." Look at yourself first. Have you shown your children that the service of the Lord is much to be desired? Have your children had the opportunity to see and feel that faith changes us, sure that it makes us joyful and confident people?

We hear a lot of complaints about the decline of organized youth work in our time. Many causes have been found and many explanations given. If you are interested in one of the most important causes, have a word with the prophet Hosea!

# 16

## What We Deserve

*Like a stubborn heifer,*
*Israel is stubborn;*
*can the Lord now feed them*
*like a lamb in a broad pasture? (4:16).*

OUR TEXT IS ABOUT SIN AND PUNISHMENT. The sin is indicated clearly enough in the first part: "Like a stubborn heifer, Israel is stubborn."

The people of Israel are here accused of stubbornness. Like an unwilling cow that is no longer content to be pulled along on a rope but tries to free itself from its yoke, Israel refuses to be subject any longer to the Lord's guidance. The bonds are too oppressive for Israel, and the yoke of obedience is too heavy. Those Israelites dig in and refuse to budge. God's presence stifles them, and hence they seek their freedom. This is stubbornness at work.

We all know what a serious sin stubbornness is. Rebelliousness, said Samuel, "is as the sin of divination, and stubbornness is as iniquity and idolatry" (I Sam. 15:23). The sin was what led to Saul's downfall and death, and he was not the first. Neither was he the last, as we now see.

The second part of the text tells us what the punishment for this sin is. Hosea asks: "Can the Lord now feed them like a lamb in a broad pasture?"

That this means punishment, that it represents a threat, is *not* so clear at first! We might be inclined to say that it sounds more like a promise. There seems to be something loving and tender in the Lord's talk of feeding Israel like a lamb in the broad pasture. It makes us think in New Testament terms of the Good Shepherd.

At the very least, it seems to suggest a kind-hearted indulgence, like that of a mother toward her son. Such a mother might say, "He's still so young. Having a son means giving a lot and putting up with a lot. His erratic behavior will come to an end eventually." That seems to be the attitude which Israel's Father–and Mother–takes toward the rebellious child. The child kicks up his heels like an energetic young colt, but let's not worry about that. He needs room to grow. Well, let's give him some room. Therefore, the Lord will feed him like a lamb in a pasture.

That's what the Lord *seems* to be saying. Yet it's not really what he says. What appears to be indulgence is really judgment. The "room" which Israel is given will mean his destruction. Israel will get what he deserves.

There's nothing more horrible than when the Lord lets the sinner have his way. A mother who lets her child have his own way and leaves him alone may believe that such lenience is good for the child. A gentle approach is much more effective than resorting to force, she reasons. But what she's doing is letting go of her child. That's her weakness.

When God lets his son Israel have his own way, this great pedagogue doesn't suppose that this will somehow be good for him. He does it instead to judge and punish him. He is fully aware that He is letting go of Israel. This very "lenience" is really a manifestation of God's *power*.

It is a horrible thing for man to get his own way. Man doesn't feel or see that—just as the boy may feel that his mother loves him only if she lets him do as he pleases. God the Lord shows us His wrath when He says to men, "I'll let you have just what you're asking for."

God's anger is also manifest when he assures Israel that he will feed him like a lamb in a pasture. Why? We'll find out soon enough. But first, let's look at Israel's sin.

We have already seen that Israel's sin is *stubbornness*. The Israelites themselves didn't call it stubbornness. On the contrary, they maintained that they were just looking for a little more freedom and elbow room. They wanted breathing space. It was a burden to them to have to restrict themselves to the path laid out so clearly in God's law. Therefore, they wanted to loosen the tight bonds somewhat; they wanted to bring God's demands into line with their own desires.

What they wanted was a compromise between the church and the world. They saw no reason why God should be so precise and rigid about everything. That was old-fashioned narrow-mindedness!

We have all sorts of ways of escaping the sound of God's voice so that we'll be able to follow the dictates of our own hearts. We even quote beautiful proverbs to each other to justify our sinful desires. We say, "As long as you enjoy peace of mind and a clear conscience, it's all right." We assure each other, "The whole world is ours in Christ." Bit by bit, we construct a perverted doctrine of "Christian freedom," forgetting in the process that being free does not mean acting on all your impulses.

The highest freedom is only attainable within definite limits. Only when we subject ourselves to *God's commands* are we free and truly happy. The "freedom" that shakes off any yoke or restraint isn't even a caricature of true freedom: it's slavery. It's the freedom of a ship without a pilot, a ship that bobs along the waves and sooner or later is dashed to pieces on the rocks. Let Israel be an example to us!

Israel is like a stubborn cow; he wants freedom. "Well then," says the Lord, "I'll give him his freedom. I'll feed him like a lamb in a broad pasture."

There's a powerful judgment contained in these words, for they mean that Israel will be left entirely on his own. What we must remember is that the lamb simply doesn't belong in the middle of an open field. A lamb belongs with the flock, under the watchful eye of the shepherd. As soon as a sheep ventures into the open and wanders away from the flock, it faces danger and death. It gets tangled up in the bushes or falls into a pit or is attacked and eaten by a wolf or a lion. In such a case, the open spaces mean danger and death.

For fish, water is not a prison but something that makes life possible. To take a fish out of water is to condemn it to death. Likewise, the sheepfold and the flock do not represent prison to the sheep; rather, they are a guarantee of continued health and safety. The open place means death.

In the same way, the bonds of the Lord's ordinances are not the death of man but the basis of life. As a rule, people are more stupid than fish. They want to escape from the bonds of God's commands–and when they escape, they die. What appeared to be a prison was really what sustained them. In their foolishness, they were not aware of this.

The open spaces look inviting to us. The young are not the only ones who yearn for them and would like to escape the Lord's tight reins for a while. For many of us, the air in the church is too stuffy. The net of the Lord's decrees is too tight and confining. We would like to be able to slip out once in a while.

The gateway and path leading to life are narrow. That, too, is experienced by many as something oppressive. Hence, they look longingly at the beautiful wide road leading elsewhere. There's lots of room on that road. They know perfectly well–although they don't quite believe it–that the wide road leads to destruction. That doesn't *sound* quite right to them. *Narrow* roads, after all, are the dangerous ones as a rule, but surely there's little chance of an accident on a broad highway.

It does indeed sound a little strange, but in the Kingdom of God, things don't go the same way as elsewhere. This is a truth that you don't just learn from experience. You simply have to believe it.

Israel didn't believe it at all. Like a stubborn cow, he shook the yoke from his neck and believed that he was totally free, that he was his own lord and master. But in that "freedom," he lost his life, just as a sheep left alone in an open field perishes.

The Lord gave Israel lots of room, and so Israel strayed beyond the boundaries of his own country–right into exile! Israel got the room and the freedom he wanted so badly, but not quite in the way he expected. The room became exile, and the freedom turned out to be slavery. That's how Israel got what he deserved.

There are two things in this story that stir us especially. The first is the realization that God never *forces* anyone to accept His guidance. God, who is all-powerful, could easily have tamed His rebellious creature. By using force, He could have brought the resistance to an end. He could have said to His people, "I won't let you escape. You'll stay right where you are. Whether you like it or not, you're staying here."

But that's not how God deals with man! He wants to be Lord over a people that serves Him willingly. God wants His people to serve Him freely–or not at all. The Lord is not a dictator who harshly imposes His will and forces His subjects to praise Him even when they don't mean what they say, and their hearts are full of bitterness and resentment. He is rather a King asking for the genuine and free love of His people. Anyone who cannot or will not give such love must leave. He is not to stay for this reason but must leave. That's all there is to it.

The service of the Lord is not something we are forced into. Anyone who finds the presence of God too oppressive is free to leave. Anyone who wants more room will get more room. Anyone who wants freedom will get freedom!

It's not that the Lord doesn't care or that it's all the same to Him what we decide. Not at all! He weeps when someone leaves Him, for He knows that false freedom leads to death.

Our Savior does not want half of your heart or mine, and He will not accept divided or partial love. He insists on all or nothing. Anyone who wants to remain with Him must remain freely. Remaining must be his highest desire.

Service in the Kingdom of God is not at all like working on the assembly line, where all the work is mechanical. The sea with its waves *must* glorify the Creator. It cannot help but do so. But man can choose; he is not forced to glorify God. He has the power to refuse. This is a frightening honor. It is an awful–and yet glorious–privilege of God's people.

Servants can be commanded to stay, and they will do so. To His children, God says, "you must choose whether to stay or leave. If you want 'freedom,' I'll give you freedom."

The second stirring element in the story is that the voice of love can still be heard in the horrible threat. Hosea does not say that the Lord will *push* them away like sheep into the open field; he says that the Lord will *feed* them like a lamb in the open field. In this way, we again recognize Israel's Shepherd.

The Israelites turned away from the Lord a long time ago in their false desire for freedom, but the Lord is not indifferent to His covenant people. He keeps a careful eye on those who have gone astray and does not forget them in their misery. With a heart full of love, He watches those who are moving in the direction of death as they follow a path of their own choosing.

He is prepared to carry the poor, lost, bruised sheep back to the flock triumphantly on His shoulders. He is listening carefully for the sheep to confess that it has gone astray and wandered away from the Shepherd. He is waiting for the sheep to cry out to the Shepherd, confessing its guilt and asking to be taken home.

# 17

# Noblesse Oblige

*Hearken, O house of the king! (5:1).*

PROPHETS ALWAYS SEEM OUT of place at the king's court. They're not good at flattery, for they love the truth. They know that the law applies to high and low alike, and that there is no place for any "double standard." Kings as well as their subjects must obey the ordinances of the King of kings.

Therefore, prophets, who are God's messengers charged with the task of defending His honor, cannot remain silent when there is something in the king's household that calls for reproof. Prophets do not wear fashionable clothes, and they do not have velvet tongues. They do not get tough with the "little man," only to slip away shyly and timidly when it's time to say something about the higher circles of society. Without respect of persons, they testify to *everyone* about God's law and will.

Elijah called king Ahab to order, and John the Baptist, who came armed with the power of Elijah, boldly admonished king Herod about his adultery. Paul did not shrink for a moment from speaking to the world's powerful figures about righteousness and judgment.

The prophet Hosea was cut from the same cloth. He did not call only on the "House of Israel" to listen to the word of God, he also told the priests to pay attention. Even more important, he focused the spotlight on the palace of the king. "Hearken, O House of the king!"

This required prophetic courage. The church of the Lord, which counts few prophets among its members, has not always manifested this courage. The history of the church gives us enough instances where courage was lacking.

When we are addressing ourselves to people of little earthly importance, we dare to call attention to their sins in an unequal way. But this boldness quickly disappears when we confront powerful people and intellectuals. The sharp words we address to the little man are then coated with honey–if, indeed, we dare to speak at all. Whenever the royal house in the Netherlands is criticized for somehow violating the Sabbath, there is a storm of protest against the criticism. Therefore, those who work in the areas of the church and evangelism have good reason to study anew the prophetic spirit that dares to cry out, "Hearken, O House of the king!"

The words which Hosea addresses to the royal house are far from mild. The princes and other members of the royal household had been given the highest important task of administering justice.[7*] Thus, we could rightly expect them to take the side of the oppressed and release people from the snares in which others had trapped them. Yet they did just the opposite!

Those who are oppressed and trapped were bitterly deceived when they looked to judges for help. Instead of untying the knots and snares in which these people had been caught, the royal judges had more pitfalls and traps ready, with the result that anyone who dared to appeal to a higher authority got even more entangled in legal problems than before.

Therefore, Hosea condemns the house of the king by saying: "You have been a snare at Mizpah, and a net spread upon Tabor." Tabor was probably a favorite hunting spot for people who hunted birds. That's what the prophet compares Israel's courts to. In other words, anyone who took his case to

---

7. In 5:1, we read: "for the judgment pertains to you." The Jerusalem Bible gets at the idea by saying: "You who are responsible for justice."

court flew right into a trap. By "anyone," I mean anyone who did not come armed with a lot of money, that is, anyone who did not have the means to bribe the judge and thereby assure himself of a favorable verdict.

It was the little man, then, who was trapped like a bird in a snare. Those who came to court with money in their pockets could count on getting their way, but to all the rest, the judges shook their wise heads. Even if some poor person who had come to court was completely in the right, the judges and lawyers knew how to twist things in such a way that the accusers wound up being accused and those who sought justice were trapped by some artificial snare. All who were oppressed and downtrodden in Israel were trapped by the court like so many harmless birds and put behind bars.

That was going on in Israel. In each courtroom, there should have been signs that read "Beware of pickpockets" and "watch out for snares and traps." Justice had been turned inside out. Bandits were walking around in judges' robes. Bloodthirsty beasts paraded in evening clothes. Halls of justice became slaughterhouses, and judges became hunters.

All of this was done by judges of royal blood, whose *nobility* should have led them to conduct themselves in a more honorable way. In Israel, the theocratic kings were supposed to reflect the image of the coming Messiah and king, especially in the way they administered justice.

The Israelites loved to sing of this Messiah and king. Perhaps the hymns from the nearby temple could even be heard in the courtroom. The Israelites often sang that God rules his people in a righteous, wise, and gentle way. He turns to those who live in misery and hears their complaint. Those Israelites would go on to sing that God rescues those who are unhappy because of their suffering, and that he frees the needy and crushes their oppressors.

We are privileged to live in a land where justice is not for sale, where there is only one law applying to all classes. Rich and poor are treated alike in our courts, which bear no resemblance to that awful place Tabor, where greedy hunters went about their gruesome work of trapping birds. Therefore, we might be inclined to shrug our shoulders at these nefarious practices and return to the order of the day.

But the word of the Lord will not let us off quite that easily! Its meaning is not restricted to the light it sheds on historical conditions and circumstances. It has implications for our life in the present. Whenever we read scripture, we must ask ourselves, "What does it mean for me today?"

When we listen carefully to the Bible, we realize that this passage about degenerate judges who trapped the poor like royal hunters snaring birds is overflowing with meaning for us. This passage, too, is intended to admonish and instruct and reprove us–if we will only listen.

When Hosea talks about royal princes who are supposed to uphold what is right and just, he also means *us*, for all believers, as children of God, are members of a royal household. Housewives and servants, employers and butlers, cleaning women and chauffeurs, teachers, and construction workers, regardless of their social standing or personal characteristics, are all kings and queens, princes, and princesses. God does not just place us *among* the princes and important people of this world; He actually makes us kings.

Thus, we are all members of the nobility. And this, in turn, means that much is expected of us. "Noblesse oblige," as the French put it. In other words, we must live up to our position. Of course, we expect much more of a king than of an "ordinary person." Furthermore, kings and queens and princes are public figures. Everyone takes careful note of what they do and fail to do. It's not easy to live in a palace, we tell each other, for such a life has definite disadvantages. Kings and queens can hardly take a step that is not reported in the newspapers. In their own country and abroad, they are followed by an army of newsmen and photographers.

Let's remember that the same applies to us. As Christians, we, too, live in a palace or a glass house. The world watches what we do very carefully and takes more than a passing interest in our actions. If we did something wrong today, there were probably people who observed it and quickly told others about it. We may get tired of this or find it painful and troublesome, but it simply goes with being members of a king's family.

Furthermore, the world is justified in expecting a great deal of us. It's only right and proper to expect the children of God to live and act differently from other people, for they are the only ones who can truly do *good works*. This is the exclusive privilege of the church.

If a deed is to be "good" in *God's* eyes, it must satisfy three conditions: (1) it must flow from a true faith; (2) it must be done in accordance with God's law; and (3) it must be done to God's glory. Many of our alleged good works just don't measure up to this standard, even though we are satisfied with them ourselves. Careful examination makes them melt away like snow before a hot sun.

Yet, doing good works is a *total impossibility* for someone who is not born again. However much the noble attitude of such people may be praised, their deeds do not flow from faith in God and are not intended to glorify God; therefore, Augustine liked to speak of the "glittering sins" of the heathens.

God refuses to accept such works. Good works are only possible as the fruits of a new life that began with a rebirth. Only God's children are capable of such works. Therefore, no Christian should say, "Let each one look only to his own life." The Lord Jesus himself said that we should pay attention to how others live and act.

This means that their conduct–and ours as well–must be able to stand exposure to the light. "Let your light so shine before men, that they may *see* your good works and give glory to your Father who is in heaven" (Matt. 5:16).

Do we live up to this high calling? The world expects much more of believers than of "ordinary people"–and rightly so. Unconsciously it honors the power of the gospel and the effect of the new life within us.

Do we disappoint the world in this expectation? Do we win our neighbors for Christ through our holy way of life? To ask these questions is to answer them. Not all the deeds of the princes and princesses of the church are worth reporting in the newspapers, and not all their words should be published. Let's admit that it's fortunate that the newspapers don't have room for all of it. And let's never forget that we are being watched closely, for what we do often brings shame on the royal house of which we are members.

"Hearken, O house of the king!" Hearken, you who are kings and queens by the grace of God! The fact that you are members of the royal house imposes certain obligations on you. *Noblesse oblige!* The world expects you to act more nobly and royally than other people do, and God expects the same thing.

The world expects you not to act like those princes who let guileless fools stumble into the traps and harmless birds fly into their nets. Are such sins entirely a matter of the past? Was Hosea just talking about a degenerate condition of the House of Israel in the distant past?

# 18

# God's Knowledge and Our Knowledge

*I know Ephraim... (5:3)*
*...they know not the Lord (5:4)*

ONE OF THE THINGS THAT REPEATEDLY surprises us about God's word is that it tells us such ordinary things. Often it seems superfluous to repeat those *ordinary* truths or remind each other of them.

In this respect, the *preaching* of the word is often very different from the word itself, for many preachers and Bible expositors outdo themselves in hauling the most extraordinary ideas out of the scriptures and dressing up ordinary truths in the most startling, flashy garments. There's no reason for this sort of thing. Some scriptural "truths" have already become so well known that they are in danger of being lost entirely. They may well turn into meaningless formulas and clichés. Slowly but surely, we're getting to the point where church members interested mainly in sensational preaching know nothing whatsoever of the basic biblical truths, which they regard as "old hat."

Take such a statement as our text, where God says that he knows Ephraim. Isn't it unnecessary to make such a statement to a people schooled in doctrine and theology, people well versed in dogmatics and well aware that God is omniscient, that he knows everything? It may be that God has some attributes beyond our comprehension, but it's nothing new or strange for us to hear that God knows everything, that he knows Ephraim, that Israel has no secret of which God is unaware. A man may be sly and cunning and may hide the various sides of his life and personality from others, but even a child can tell you that God knows us through and through. There's nothing that fills the soul of a child more than the awareness that God knows everything, and there is nothing more likely to give rise to cautious respect than the thought of that all-seeing eye.

We've all grown up with God's omniscience. And once we're adults, we learn to speak about it in a more sophisticated way. Those rare individuals who go on to become theology professors may write a chapter on God's omniscience in a doctrinal handbook. A few scholars may even write a dissertation on the subject. Thus, all of us, whether we're amateur theologians or professional theologians, are so well versed in God's attributes that we know perfectly well that God knows everything, that he knows people, that he knows Ephraim. No one can call this truth into question. It has become so widely accepted and seems so ordinary that it no longer has any effect on our consciences.

"I know Ephraim!" Now, Ephraim (another name for Israel) was also well aware of this before Hosea came along to inform him of it in God's name. What did you think? Did you suppose that Israel's theologians were not aware of God's omniscience? What else is new? They could give you a whole series of proof texts to support that doctrine.

Come now, Hosea, don't give us a stale sermon with nothing new in it. Don't preach to us about things we've heard so often before. Did you think we haven't read the psalms of David, where God's omniscience is mentioned repeatedly? As children, we already learned to recite the psalms. We learned:

> The Lord looks out from heaven,
> he sees the whole race of men;
> he surveys from his dwelling place
> all the inhabitants of the earth.
> it is he who fashions the hearts of men alike.
> who discerns all that they do (Ps. 33:13–15 NEB)

There you have it: He fashions the hearts of men and discerns everything. From another Psalm of David, we learn:

> Yahweh, you examine me and know me,
> you know if I am standing or sitting,
> you read my thoughts from far away,
> whether I walk or lie down, you are watching,
> you know every detail of my conduct.
> the word is not even on my tongue,
> Yahweh, before you know all about it (Ps. 139:1–4 JB)

Thus, Hosea should not assume that he was telling Israel something new. Those Israelites schooled in doctrine knew all about God's omniscience!

But the omniscient God, who knows these theological Israelites better than they realize, declares simply: "They know not the Lord!" When it comes to theological knowledge of God, they deserve an A, but they get an F for their practical knowledge of Him.

They're so totally lacking in practical knowledge that they weren't even aware that the Lord knows all about them. Before the altar, they sang, "Lord, You have searched me and known me," but at the same time, they thought they could use the altar and the smell of incense to hide things from God. They thought they were being cunning. They behaved just like children. Therefore, God had to treat them like ignorant children and feed them milk. He had to keep on repeating a seemingly elementary truth well known to everyone until he was sick of saying it: "I know Ephraim, and Israel is not hid from me."

Why did God say that? Why this tiresome repetition of the most ordinary truth? God had to point this out because Israel did not live by its own doctrines. Everyone knew it so well in theory but seemed to forget about it in practice. This truth was so well known that it had become unknown. It no longer stirred anyone's conscience.

The Lord had just given the Israelites an impressive demonstration of His omniscience and His knowledge of human affairs. Israel's rulers were told in no uncertain terms what God thought of their conduct. God was not fooled by the hidden snare they had set up in the stately halls of justice to trap the unwary. "I know Ephraim!" If that's the sort of thing that went on in the highest circles, then we hardly need to wonder how far the moral decay had gone in the lower circles.

No doubt the Israelites thought they would continue to go unpunished for their sneaky misdeeds; no doubt they assumed that the Lord hadn't noticed anything amiss. They were so used to deceiving each other that they thought nothing of trying to deceive the Lord as well. They thought that they could nicely mask cunning and deceit with an extra prayer. It was inconceivable to them that their pious fraud would be detected. Therefore, the Lord warned them in advance to give up these illusions.

It's impossible to fool the One who knows everything. Hence, the hope of escaping punishment was an idle dream. "I know Ephraim, and Israel is not hid from me."

Of course, he knows Ephraim! The Lord had called him out of Egypt when he was still a little boy and had kept a close eye on him ever since. The Lord had seen him cry out to God in his hour of need and turn away from God when things went well. He had helped Ephraim along and put up with his wiles for a long time.

But there is an end to God's patience. Precisely because I know you so well, Ephraim, because I know how hard your heart is, My judgment is completely just. In God's name, the prophet Amos had cried out to Israel:

> For you alone I have cared
> among all the nations of the world;
> therefore I will punish you

for all your iniquities.
Do two men travel together
unless they have agreed? (Amos 3:2–3 NEB).

It is certainly no waste of time to remind today's Ephraim that the Lord knows him through and through. Today's Ephraim is bursting at the seams with theological knowledge. With great relish, all sorts of theological topics are dealt with and disposed of. Yet, all the motives and intentions of this Ephraim are known to the Lord. It's easy enough for us to convince each other of something, but we'll never fool God. He sits on His throne in heaven and laughs at us.

This also applies to the comical scene played out in churches and other seemingly serious locales. One person may say that he fights on the side of truth. A second declares that Jerusalem's peace and security is his only concern. A third maintains that the real issue is God's honor. All three may be fully convinced of their own sincerity, but the Lord knows Ephraim. He observes what's happening behind the stage on which this comedy is presented. His eye penetrates to the depths of the heart. All things are laid bare before the eyes of the one who watches us. He sees through all our pious words immediately.

Scholars and uneducated people, preachers and elders, writers and muckrakers, young men, and women, remember that the Lord knows Ephraim! The Lord knows you and me. If we carefully considered the consequences of this truth for only one day of the year, what a silence there would be! We would then learn to be much more careful about what we say and write.

What an overwhelming truth! Think about it. What do you really know about your neighbors? You know what they look like, but what are they like inside? Do you know what goes on in their minds and hearts? Of course not.

But we don't devote much effort to finding out either. We live in a busy and superficial era in which people no longer have time to tell each other about their ultimate concerns and hopes. Thousands upon thousands of people wander lonely and alone not just through the busy world but also through the streets of our ecclesiastical Jerusalem. Many parents know virtually nothing about their children, and many children show no interest in their parents. Many a husband is a mystery to his wife, and vice versa.

When you get right down to it, what do we really know about *ourselves?* The psalmists were accustomed to speaking with their *souls:* "Why are you downcast, O my soul?" (Ps. 42:5). But this sort of thing went out of style long ago. Modern man and the modern churchgoer are becoming more and more afraid to be alone with themselves.

We don't know our neighbors. We don't know the members of our own family. We don't even know ourselves. But the all-knowing God knows me and everyone else as well. He knows everything about me, including the base and shameful motives on which I often act. He knows just what I've said and what I've considered in the inner recesses of my mind.

Yet this truth is also a *comfort*. What a joy it is to realize that the Lord knows not only my name and address but also all my problems. The fact that He knows does not mean that there will be an immediate change in my situation but knowing that He knows already makes me feel better. In a way, it's an answer to prayer. Because He knows, we can let Him shoulder all our burdens.

But this truth is also very *unsettling*. Now my godliness will have to survive the test of God's flaming eyes upon it. We can lie through our pious words. We can even lie by conforming to "Christian" customs. It's easy enough to deceive people that way. But the Lord looks into the heart. He sees through every disguise. "I know Ephraim!"

The Lord knows us. He knows each and every one of us. He knows all about our personal life, our family life, and our church life. Therefore, there is no point in pretending to be better than we really are. There's no point in trying to keep up "appearances." We're wasting our time when we try to use our standing as church members to fool God. There's simply no way to fool the Lord–not even through the most immaculate church credentials, not even by zealously defending our principles and all the decrees of the Synod. "I know Ephraim."

Do we know the Lord? Of course, we know a great deal about Him. We even seem to be making remarkable progress in our knowledge of God. We're outdistancing earlier generations in this respect. But is this knowledge paired with true piety? Do we know the Lord in a deeper and more *personal* way, or do we only know *about* Him? Is it apparent from how we live that the Lord knows us through and through?

Is it possible that our theologically learned generation, which takes up the most complex theological issues and holds meetings and conferences to discuss them, which devours church papers and theological journals by the dozen, is like Israel? Will God say of us that we don't know the Lord?

If we know all about the Lord but don't know the Lord Himself, we're in serious trouble indeed! Remember, there is an omniscient God who knows all the theologians, while there are theologians who do not know the Lord. That's a painful, difficult puzzle, and we can only solve it if we keep our gaze fixed on the cross.

# 19

# The Stumbling Block

*The iniquity of Ephraim knocks him down*
*and down comes Judah with him.*
*Though they go in search of Yahweh with*
*their sheep and oxen,*
*they do not find him;*
*for he has withdrawn from them (5:5–6 JB).*

IT IS SOMETIMES SAID that we are tormented most of all by our *own* guilt. Yet it's my impression that our own guilt is what usually bothers us least. We are deeply concerned about the faults and shortcomings of sister A and brother B. Whether their sins actually bother us so much that we drop to our knees in prayer on their behalf, of course, is a question that we would rather not look into too closely. But be that as it may,

I don't see too much evidence of people being tormented by their own guilt.

We ourselves are never the ones to blame. We point the finger at the serpent that deceived us, or at the woman God gave us to be our partner in life. The cutting and ironic question asked by Jesus still applies to us today: "Why do you observe the splinter in your brother's eye and never notice the plank in your own?" (Matt. 7:3 JB).

Jesus was right, for that's exactly how we act when this or that goes wrong in life. You can be sure that we will point the finger at someone else and maintain that *he* is the cause of the problem. It doesn't seem to occur to us that in most instances, we ourselves are the greatest cause. Hosea now declares:

> Israel's arrogance cries out against him;
> Ephraim's guilt is his undoing,
> and Judah no less is undone (5:5 NEB).

That's nothing new. That's the monotonous chorus which all the men of God of that time sang. "Things are bound to go wrong," they warned. "Israel will soon be in a jam." If *Israel* could escape unharmed this time, then no one would ever have reason to fear. In direct and indirect ways, Ephraim was told that he would perish.

It has already been established that Israel would go under. The prophet now goes one step further and lets Israel know what the cause of his death will be: Israel's own arrogance and guilt will be his undoing.

The obstacle that will cause Israel to stumble and will bring about his downfall is his own sin. Of course, Israel could never admit that. When Israel finally did collapse, its downfall would be attributed to the overwhelming power of the enemy, which Israel, of course, was not strong enough to resist. Or it would be the fault of the Lord Himself, who abandoned the land and no longer seemed interested in the fate of His chosen people. Their ways were hidden from the Lord, and their righteousness was ignored by God. They just couldn't understand why *they* should be given such treatment.

Could it be because of their own sin? Surely you don't mean that! Was there ever a nation on earth as religious as Israel? Was there ever a nation that brought sacrifices so faithfully in such numbers as Israel? No, their own guilt was *not* what bothered the people the most.

There were, however, a small number who were deeply troubled by their own guilt. They were the "remnant," the ones whom God had chosen. These people were tormented by their own guilt and by the guilt of the country and nation. Yet most of the Israelites said, "I just don't understand it! We, the people of the Lord, receive blow after blow!"

In this respect, things haven't improved much since then. Few and far between are the people who admit openly that they stumbled because of their own sin. The rest of us have become experts at tracking down the "causes" that "explain" the decline in the church, in society, and in our personal lives. After all, who wants to point the finger at himself?

There's always some seducer lurking in the background. Surely, we can pin the blame on satan! We simply attribute the sins of our own "flesh" to the evil influence of the devil, and thereby we give our consciences some rest. We see "obstacles" to virtue in all possible corners and places, but seldom do we recognize them in our own hearts–despite the fact that the Bible tells us unequivocally that man is his own greatest enemy.

When it comes down to obstacles in your path or stumbling blocks that cause us to fall, the Lord Jesus directs our attention not outward but *inward*. Your *own* hand or foot or eye may endanger you. Be careful that your own eye does not cause you to stumble, for that's how Eve and Achan got into trouble. Don't be so quick to point the finger at others. Take a good look at yourself first. If your eye causes you to stumble, pluck it out! If your hand causes you to stumble, cut it off! That's painful surgery!

What was the sin that caused Israel to stumble? How did Ephraim dig his own grave? It's not what you might have guessed. Normally, when we think of a sin that causes someone's downfall, we think of something very offensive and serious. The drunkard drives himself and his household to the brink of collapse. The adulterer brings shame upon his family and dishonors his posterity. There are many such sins that lead to ruin and even death. "God will punish those who surrender to their own desires and turn their backs on him in pride," we say to each other complacently as we observe the "world's" doings stealthily.

Of course, those are abominable sins! But there's another sin that causes even more people to fall. That sin was also Israel's great stumbling block. The sin I'm referring to is self-righteousness. Ephraim stumbled over his own piety and over the altars he built.

Let's not forget this possibility, for it's not a rare occurrence. Sins by themselves, no matter how great or numerous, will never block the path to heaven. Nowhere do the scriptures teach that someone's sins may be too numerous to be forgiven. That was Cain's way of thinking.

The purpose for which the Lord Jesus came into the world, after all, was to save sinners. He did not come for those who are righteous! Self-righteousness is a great stumbling block. There's much more hope for prostitutes and tax collectors than for polite Pharisees. Those Pharisees have never noticed that God justifies the godless and not the pious churchgoers. They have never understood that their "righteousness" is a filthy garment to be cast aside. It's one thing to confess this with your mouth, but it's quite another to practice it in your life.

In theory, there's no room for boasting, but in reality, there is a lot of boasting going on. *His* name must be praised eternally, but surely there is no harm in burning a bit of incense in honor of my name and *my* doctrinal soundness and *my* willingness to sacrifice! Thus, our faithfulness can become a stumbling block.

Who is to say how many may have stumbled over the countless prayers they have uttered and the numerous sermons they have heard? Who is to say how many people have died from overeating at the communion table or may have drowned in baptismal water?

I must do everything *out of* true faith, *according to* the law of God, and *unto* His honor. In other words, my actions must flow from the purest source, measure up to the purest requirements, and aim at the purest goal. If we measure our preaching and church attendance and personal life by these criteria, is there anyone who would not have to ask God to forgive him for his virtues and not be offended at his good works? Only someone who had come that far will escape stumbling over his own self-righteousness and will not have to be told that his own arrogance and guilt are his undoing.

> Lord, *teach* us to see our righteousness and unrighteousness!

That Israel's chief sin was a false religious fervor is obvious from Hosea's description of what will happen when the catastrophe actually comes. The prophet goes into great detail. He knows about it because of God's revelation to him, but at the same time, he knows his countrymen so well that he can see in advance just what they'll do. They'll start *seeking the Lord*. Of course, they will!

That people turn to the Lord for help and comfort in their hour of need is nothing new. That's life. When *we* are in a desperate situation, we're quick to turn to God, but as long as we have no problems, we can get along without him. The prodigal son got along fine in a faraway land until his hunger made him jealous of the pigs and their food. The disciples held out bravely against the wind and the waves until they saw the hurricane approaching. Then they cried out: "Teacher, do you not care if we perish?" It was their need that made them turn to Jesus.

One unbelieving wit writhing in pain on his sickbed cried out that he would go to church faithfully if only he would be allowed to move around again on crutches. But if he could walk without crutches, he added with devilish sarcasm, he would never set foot in a church. This mocker of the Christian faith is a preacher calling us to repentance. We use God to rescue us from shipwrecks and to provide a home for refugees and the homeless. But for the rest, we stay away from Him.

Thus, it's obvious: they'll start seeking the Lord. It's as certain as 2 plus 2 equals 4. It's a matter of simple calculation for Hosea.

*How* they will come is no problem for him either. Hosea tells us that they go in search of the Lord with their *sheep* and *oxen*. Of course, that's what they'll bring! That's what they always bring to appease the Lord. They offer him sheep and oxen–and that in the hour of extreme peril!

> From the psalms of David, they had learned:

> For thou hast no delight in sacrifice;
> were I to give a burnt offering, thou wouldest not be pleased.
> The sacrifice acceptable to God is a broken spirit;
> a broken and contrite heart, O God, thou wilt not despise
> (Ps. 51:16–17).

Yet these Israelites rely on the usual gifts–sheep and oxen. The Lord had said:

> All the beasts of the forest are mine
> and the cattle on a thousand hills.
> If I were hungry, I would not tell you,
> for the world and all that is in it are mine.
> Shall I eat the flesh of your bulls
> or drink the blood of he-goats?
> Offer to God the sacrifice of thanksgiving
> and pay your vows to the Most High.

If you call upon me in time of trouble,
I will come to your rescue, and you shall honor me
(Ps. 50:10, 12–15).

Yet these Israelites offer the Lord sheep and oxen.

In their hour of danger, they do not cry out anxiously, "O God, be gracious to me, a sinner!" They show no sign of remorse. They do not praise God in quiet reverence. All they do is present him with sheep and oxen.

We hear the noise of the animals and the bustle of the temple. We hear the rustle of priestly robes and smell the scent of burning incense. But behind all this bustle and noise, the Lord withdraws and hides in the thick curtains of smoke created by the burning sacrifices. "They will not find Me," says the Lord. He has withdrawn from them.

To our ears, which are so accustomed to the language of the Bible, this sounds a little strange. "They will seek the Lord, but they will *not* find Him." Doesn't the whole Bible say just the opposite? Seek, and you will find! Knock, and the door will be opened for you! The house of Jacob does not call out to God in vain. We are promised that all who call on the name of the Lord will receive a blessing. Aren't those promises true and genuine?

Of course, they are! They are glorious and blessed truths. But we must make *one* qualification. There is the possibility that this promise may be turned into its opposite, which would mean that people seek the Lord but are unable to find Him. When would this happen? When people come to Him with sheep and oxen, bearing gifts and pointing proudly to their own virtues. That's the one great stumbling block.

# 20

# Convincing Proof

*For they have been unfaithful to him,
and their sons are bastards (5:7 NEB)*

THE TEXT THAT NOW occupies our attention makes us think immediately of some sort of court case. When a dispute is brought to court, there must be (1) an *accusation*, (2) legal and convincing *proof* of the guilt of the accused, and (3) a *penalty* or *punishment* for the offense in question. All are present here.

The accusation is that the Israelites have been *unfaithful*. We must read this as meaning that they have been unfaithful to the Lord, for this brings out much more clearly what is involved in the accusation. Ephraim is brought before the judge on a charge of *adultery*.

In Hosea's way of thinking–as we saw earlier–the relationship between God and His people is like that between a man and his wife. In other words, it's a marriage relationship. The prophet even had to bring this to symbolic expression in public through his marriage to the unfaithful Gomer. Just as his wife abandoned him and threw herself into the arms of other men, Israel's sin, and neglect of the service of the Lord reeked of unfaithfulness and adultery.

This reproach of unfaithfulness is the sharpest accusation that could be brought against Israel. Even in the best of marriages, something goes wrong now and then; there is always something that comes between husband and wife. But as soon as unfaithfulness enters the picture, the very foundation of the marriage is dealt a devastating blow. Any other dispute between husband and wife can be settled, but unfaithfulness destroys the most beautiful and tender elements in the marriage bond. The most painful thing marriage partners can accuse each other of is being *unfaithful*. Now then, it's just what the bride of the Lord was told. She was accused of infidelity!

The frightening thing is that every sin committed by God's people is immediately put into that awful framework. In ordinary marriage, there can be a dispute without unfaithfulness entering the picture, but the relationship between God and His people is no ordinary marriage. The Lord is an ardent and jealous lover. For Him, every sin, even the smallest departure from the straight and narrow path, is a case of adultery. This is because His eyes look so deeply into our souls. And He wants His people to possess the same penetrating gaze. He wants His people to see that they are unfaithful each time they succumb to some sinful temptation. Thus, the accusation is adultery.

The punishment for this transgression is death. Hence it should not surprise us that the defendant guilty of adultery is given a stiff sentence. Actually, the accusation is placed between two sentences in the text. One comes before, and one after.

What is the sentence that follows the charge of unfaithfulness? In the King James Version, we read: "Now shall a month devour them with their portions." It's not clear what this might mean. More recent versions, relying on the Septuagint, the Greek translation of the Old Testament made in ancient times, suggest something different: "Now an invader shall devour their fields" (5:7 NEB). This is much clearer language. What the prophet foresaw, then, is that some sort of horrible affliction would attack both the people and their fields, resulting in the destruction of both the people and their prosperity.

Thus, it's a stiff sentence indeed. Even more severe is the punishment that *precedes* the accusation: "The Lord has withdrawn from them."

Of course, not everyone would agree that the latter punishment is more severe. If they were forced to choose between an invader devouring their fields and the Lord withdrawing from them, many people wouldn't hesitate to choose the latter. "We can get along without God," they reason, "but we can't get along without money and possessions." When God withholds His *blessings* from us, many people cry out in pain, but are they disturbed when God hides His *face*?

We often sing in church that our soul thirsts for God as a hart thirsts for water, but on the whole, we seem to have more thirst for something to drink than for God. If we are in good health and enjoy an adequate income, we feel we can get along quite well without the Lord for a while.

Israel is an excellent example of this attitude. The Lord had already withdrawn from His people a long time ago, but as long as the Israelites enjoyed prosperity, they didn't even notice. They found out about it when they sought the Lord with sheep and oxen in their hour of need and failed to find Him.

These people, who loved to talk about Moses and never got tired of declaring that God is great, and Moses is His prophet, had drifted a long way from the outlook of Moses. The Lord told Moses to lead His people to a land overflowing with milk and honey, which He would give them. He said He would send an angel along with them but would not accompany them Himself. What did Moses do then? He didn't want to go!

There are many people who would have replied, "I'd be delighted to go! What could be more beautiful than a land overflowing with milk and honey? We even get an angel to show us the way!" but not Moses. Moses said he only wanted to go if the Lord would be present with them (Ex. 33). That was the right attitude. It's much better to be in a desolate wilderness with the Lord than in a land of promise without Him. "I would rather be a doorkeeper in the House of my God than dwell in the tents of wickedness" (Ps. 84:10).

That's why I said that the Lord's withdrawing Himself from Israel was a much more severe sentence than the invaders devouring the fields. In the former case, the sentence means death. There's no getting around it. God is life, and anyone without God is *already* dead. Thus, anything would be better than being without God–even if an invader destroys all our crops. As long as the Lord has not withdrawn Himself, there's still hope for us!

I will say no more about this judgment or about the accusation brought against Israel. I will turn my attention instead to the legal and convincing *proof* that the accusation of infidelity was not a trumped-up charge. Hosea gives us proof because love does not act thoughtlessly–especially God's love.

Actually, it was completely unnecessary to offer evidence in support of this charge of unfaithfulness. We must remember, first of all, that Hosea made this accusation in the name of the Lord Himself. It is simply inconceivable that this mouth, which is incapable of lying, would make a rash and unfounded accusation.

The reason why Hosea nevertheless provided evidence of Israel's unfaithfulness is that the people had become so insensitive. If they had not already silenced their consciences, they would have sensed the truth of the accusation immediately and admitted that Hosea was right. But instead of agreeing with him, they contradicted him.

Unfaithfulness! Of all the charges to make! Hosea couldn't resist throwing that in too! We may have some faults and shortcomings, but on that score, we're as innocent as a newborn babe. Is there a nation anywhere on earth so faithful to its God and to the religion of its fathers as Israel? Is there a nation anywhere as pious as we are? Are there as many altars anywhere else? Do other nations celebrate as many religious festivals, and do they bring as many sacrifices? Of course not! Hosea's accusation is really a joke. He couldn't think of anything else to say!

Hosea listened to all of this calmly. Despite these vigorous denials, he could back up his accusation fully. The Israelites pointed to the *animals* they sacrificed, but the prophet pointed to their *children* and based his complaint on the fact that they had fathered *bastards*. The existence of these children was proof of Hosea's point that Israel is unfaithful.

An illegitimate child is proof of its mother's sinfulness. Such a child is not brought by the stork. A bastard is a living and continual indictment of its mother; it is irrefutable proof of its mother's unfaithfulness. What further evidence do we need?

Of course, what Hosea says here is not to be taken literally. He does not mean to comment on the condition of marriage in Israel. It's likely that husbands and wives were no more faithful to each other in other countries than in Israel. That's not the point at all! The prophet has something else in mind.

What he means is that there is now a generation in Israel that doesn't know what godliness is. This generation has been a long time in the making. These people are the bastards of whom Hosea speaks; they are spiritual bastards. God simply does not recognize them as His own children, for they don't resemble Him in the slightest.

Tell me, Israelite fathers, and mothers, where did those children come from? The stork didn't bring them. If you as fathers had served the Lord faithfully, if you had set a strong example of godliness for your children, they wouldn't have turned out that way. God's covenant with Abraham contains a promise for your children. God is merciful to the many thousands who love Him and abide by His commandments.

Thus, the Israelites could hardly pretend that they saw no evil. They could hardly act surprised at how these bastard children turned out, for they were not much better themselves. They had no right to complain about the younger generation. Instead, they should have complained about themselves, for they were the ones who fathered those strange children. That younger generation of bastards was a walking indictment; it was convincing proof of the unfaithfulness of the mothers and fathers.

I don't propose to discuss the question of whether today's younger generation is any better or any worse than the generations before it. But *if* there's some truth to the complaint that the number of bastards who make no pretense of serving the Lord is rising, if it's true that many who were baptized no longer show up in church, it should hardly come as a painful surprise to us, nor should it lead us to praise previous generations to the skies. Even less should we shake our heads in amazement as we complain about those "strange" young people. We ourselves fathered them, and as a rule, the apple doesn't fall too far from the tree.

Of course, there are exceptions. You can find weeds growing in the most carefully tended garden. There are God-fearing families for whom it is a painful *riddle* that there should be one of these "strangers" in their midst. In such situations, we must remember that the choice ultimately is not ours but God's.

Much more common, unfortunately, is the situation where we have no reason to act pained or surprised, where there is nothing "strange" about the "stranger," where there is no mystery about where he came from. There are plenty of fathers and mothers who became "unfaithful" a long time ago. Perhaps they are not outwardly unfaithful. Outwardly they may well be surprisingly strict and regular in their religious observance. But the important thing is what lives in their hearts. We see religious activity in their lives, but no genuine *godliness*. They go to church, but *spiritually* they are dead. They read the Bible every day, but Christ does not live in them.

It should not surprise us that godliness does not grow and increase in such homes. On the contrary, we would have reason to act surprised if there were no bastards there, no children alienated from true godliness. Thus, the complaint about bastards turns into an accusation of "unfaithfulness" directed at fathers and mothers, pastors and teachers, elders, and leaders.

Are *we* perhaps unfaithful as well? Do *we* live in close communion with the Lord, and is this clear to our children? Or is our spirituality merely a matter of custom?

Let's think about it carefully. The prophet Hosea is not accusing the children. He's accusing their parents, for they're the ones who brought those bastards into the world.

In addition to our natural children, we also have spiritual children. I mean the books and magazines we produce, the letters we write, the words we speak, the conversations we carry on. Can those who examine our spiritual children see clearly that they were born of fathers and mothers living by grace and not living in sin? Or is it immediately obvious that they are worldly "bastards"?

The tree is known by the fruit it bears. And our children–both natural and spiritual–will serve as legal and convincing proof of whether we are really as faithful as we want to think we are.

# 21

# Attack from the Rear

*Blow the horn in Gibeah,*
*the trumpet in Ramah.*
*Sound the alarm at Beth-aven;*
*tremble, O Benjamin! (5:8).*

THE SHOUTING IN PREPARATION for the battle doesn't surprise us at all–not after what Hosea had just said. As you recall, he predicted that some horrible invader would come to devour both the people and the fields in Israel–as punishment for the sins of unfaithfulness. The people will be attacked by some plague, some disgusting *disease*. The fields will yield no more crops: there will be *famine*. And we can also expect the third member of the unholy trinity–*warfare*.

Perhaps it was war that caused all the misery in the first place. War, disease, and famine always march together.

They are the three grim monsters that the prophet now sees approaching Israel.

Hosea's prophecy of the approaching danger of war is couched in vivid language that everyone can understand. When the trumpet is blown by the watchmen on the city walls, this usually means that some sort of misfortune is looming on the horizon. The sound of the trumpet was the command to mobilize. The enemy army could already be seen in the distance, and the defending army had to prepare to resist the attack.

The sound of the trumpet was also a warning to the people living in the surrounding countryside, who would then have to find safety behind the thick city walls as quickly as possible. It was all but impossible to put up any real resistance to approaching enemy columns in the villages and small towns.

The man of God now saw this danger of war in his mind's eye. There was not a watchman in a single city who saw trouble coming. Hosea, Israel's true watchman, saw it clearly. Because of what he saw in his prophetic mind's eye, he started issuing orders like a general. As if he were the commander in chief, he called for a general mobilization. He passed the word to all the forts in Benjamin and Ephraim:

> Blow the horn in Gibeah,
> the trumpet in Ramah.

> Sound the alarm at Beth-aven;
> tremble, O Benjamin!

But no one paid any attention to Hosea's commands. The Israelites all went on sleeping as though there was no danger to worry about. Here and there may have been people curious enough to stick their heads out the door, but once they saw who was raising the alarm, they went back to bed. It was only Hosea. That oddball always has something strange to say. There should be a law against scaring people that way! If only everyone would mind his own business and prophets would stay out of military matters!

It should not surprise us either that Judah, the kingdom of the two tribes, is included in Hosea's warning about the approach of war. The prophet had concerned himself for the most part with the Kingdom of the ten tribes, which he spoke of simply as Ephraim. That was his task. But he had already warned *Judah* once in passing. He had begged Judah not to join with Ephraim in sin.

There was indeed a real danger of this, for Bethel, the center of Ephraim's idolatrous worship, was right by Israel's border with Judah. Therefore, it was very tempting for the inhabitants of Judah to take a look once in a while at what was going on there. Bearing this in mind, the prophet declared: "Do not come to Gilgal, Judah, do not go up to Beth-aven" (4:15 NEB). By Beth-aven he meant Bethel.

Apparently, the warning had no effect. The prophet of the Kingdom and House of David just let the man from Ephraim talk. Therefore—and this is my point—it should not surprise us that Hosea also pronounced judgment on Judah. Ephraim and Judah had both joined in the fun at Bethel. Arm in arm they danced around Beth-aven's golden calf. Now they will also fall together before the enemy's sword.

Thus, the prophet mentions not only Beth-aven (Bethel), which lay in the kingdom of the ten tribes, but also the cities of Gibeah and Ramah, which were in Judah. There the trumpet was to be blown and the banner of war raised. There's nothing strange or surprising about it.

But there is something else strange, something that must have surprised the people in the cities mentioned by Hosea. In his mind's eye, Hosea saw the enemy armies approaching from the *wrong direction*.

If there was ever danger threatening Israel, it came from the north. There was a great military road leading from Israel to the *north*. Later it curved toward the east, the land of Babylon and Assyria, the great and powerful nations that threatened the existence of the people of God.

All the prophets agreed that Israel had to be on guard against the great and mysterious danger from the north. That danger was always present. The northern front always needed brave and strong defenders. But no one ever thought about the defense of Israel's southern boundary, for there was no danger to be feared from that direction.

Along comes the prophet Hosea and warns Israel about the possibility of an attack from the rear. He advises Israel to see whether the enemy might be approaching from a direction where we don't expect to see him. He orders that the trumpet be blown first in *Gibeah*, and then in *Ramah*. Finally, the alarm must be sounded at *Beth-aven*. (Beth-aven, of course, is the prophet's nickname for Bethel. The name means *house of idolatry*, and that's just what Israel made of the alleged temple of the Lord at Bethel.)

Pay careful attention to the order: Gibeah, Ramah, Beth-aven. The movement is in the direction south to north. Hosea did not choose this order at random. The prophet means to say that the enemy armies will first appear at the gates of Gibeah, and then they'll march on to Ramah, which is some distance to the north. After the enemy has occupied Judah and Benjamin, he'll also take Bethel, which lies even further to the north, in Ephraim. After Judah falls, Hosea explains, "Ephraim shall be laid waste" (5:9 NEB).

If enemy bombers were spotted over Texas, then over Kansas and finally over Chicago, we would conclude that the attack was coming from the south. That's what Hosea was talking about. And we know how important it is to know where the attack is coming from.

It might not seem all that important to know exactly which enemy Hosea had in mind; the significant thing about this prophetic warning is that we are told to keep our eyes open and look in the *proper direction*. Hosea alerts us to the possibility of an attack from some *unguarded* quarter. Everyone was watching the developments to the north, but the prophet reminded the people not to forget the southern boundary. Benjamin was watching what was going on in front of him, but Hosea warned that the danger was *behind* him. If our defenses on one border are solid while some other border is wide open to attack, we may lose everything in the end anyway.

Now, I hope no one is so foolish as to say, "What do I care if many years ago some unnamed enemy launched an attack on Palestine from the south, at Gibeah, rather than from the north, at some such point as Dan?" We begin to see the implications of Hosea's prophetic words. Now we realize what they mean for our time.

It's a very important question for us whether we're prepared for an attack *from the rear*, or from an enemy *behind* us. We should ask ourselves whether the trumpet is being blown in the right place in the midst of all the tumult of our time. Do we hear the trumpet in Gibeah? That's the first point.

The second point we should consider is the sequence in the text: Gibeah, Ramah, Beth-aven. In his mind's eye, Hosea sees the enemy moving forward *gradually* but stealthily. City after city falls into the hands of the enemy; province after province is conquered.

Thus, it happened slowly–not all at once. Yet, before the people had figured out just how the enemy had done it, all of Ephraim was "laid waste." This, too, applies to our time.

The first point, namely, that the danger sometimes approaches from a different direction than any of us expected, applies to all eras, including our own. In our own time, there are many trumpets being blown, and no one can say that their sound is uncertain. "Blow the trumpet!"

That's exactly what we're doing, man of God. No one can say in good conscience that we have deliberately disobeyed the prophetic command to raise the alarm. There are even people who claim we are in greater danger of raising too much of an alarm; they argue that we are making a much greater fuss over the danger than we need to.

Be that as it may, it's better to raise the alarm too soon than too late. That way no one will be able to say that he wasn't warned at all. All of this is praiseworthy and valuable. Obviously, we are not asleep on the job. The watchmen on Zion's walls are ready. They see the dangers clearly, and even where they do not see them, they smell them, so to speak. Trumpets, watchmen, warning systems, and battle flags are all familiar items in our circles.

Blow the horn! Sound the trumpet! Raise the alarm! What is it that you want to tell us, Hosea? What threatens the church now? Haven't all the threats and dangers already been fully exposed? We've heard the trumpets warning. Surely the danger won't catch us unprepared, for the trumpet has warned us already. Was the alarm in vain? Is there still a chance that we might fail to recognize the extreme danger posed by such phenomena as Barthianism and liberalism?

It's beyond dispute that we've been warned adequately about the mysterious dangers from the *north*. And that's a good thing! The question what Hosea could possibly have against us is not to be answered by arguing that the commotion about the danger to the north is a waste of time and energy.

No, Hosea's point is that we might forget all about *Gibeah*. We might be so preoccupied with the possibility of a frontal assault that the danger creeps up on us undetected from the rear. The enemy is behind you, Benjamin!

We must not position *all* the watchmen at the one point most likely to be attacked. Instead, we must scan the horizon in all directions for the approach of the enemy. There are dangers that threaten our *doctrine*, but there are also dangers that threaten our way *of life*. Hosea has already expressed his concern about what is wrong with Israel's way of life. There is a real danger that we may arm ourselves to the teeth against all possible heresies and false doctrines, while the flesh and the world penetrate our ranks from the "south" unchallenged and devastate our ecclesiastical landscape. Samson is not the only hero who defeated powerful enemies only to be overcome by a lesser enemy—a woman!

The most ominous thing is that this enemy does not advance in the *Blitzkrieg* style but pushes ahead *gradually*. The world does not plan to overcome the church in one quick battle. Instead, it tends to take over the church slowly but surely.

First, one town is taken, and then another: Gibeah, Ramah, Bethel. And in the territory conquered by the enemy, we do not see customs and moral standards changing immediately. It's a gradual process. If you stay away for about ten years, you'll see that everything is completely different when you return.

That's how things go when we "conform" to the world. First, we start thinking in a worldly way, and then we become worldly in our speech. Finally, we conform to the world in our behavior. We don't *start* by participating in worldly entertainment and fashions, nor are the churches abandoned immediately. Perhaps the churches will never be abandoned entirely. All the same, the churches' whole way of thinking, speaking, and acting becomes thoroughly worldly.

How far the world's troops have penetrated into the confines of the church and how much damage the "flesh" has already done may be hard to say. In any event, those troops have already invaded our borders. Yet we do not hear anyone telling us to blow the horn at Gibeah. The people of Gibeah are fast asleep.

The enemy is already past Gibeah! The cry, "Sound the trumpet at Ramah!" was heard too late. Ramah, too, has fallen, but there is no mourning and lamentation to be heard there.

Rachel thinks this is just as well, for the gentle world did not kill any of her children. They were allowed to go on living just as before. Thus, the enemy is already past Ramah.

Would it do any good to raise the alarm now in Beth-aven?

# 22

# Inheritance and the Rich Man

*The leaders of Judah are like men who display the
boundary mark (5:10 JB).*

WHEN HOSEA SPEAKS HERE of the "leaders of Judah," he means the nobility, the important people, the aristocrats (with titles and without). In other words, he means the powerful people who made their influence felt through their name and position, the ones who could get almost anything they wanted through their money. These gold magnates and financiers, these landowners and bank directors, and "leaders" are castigated here. Apparently, they didn't come by their riches honorably, for they are compared to people who displace boundary markers.

We're all acquainted with that trick. Moving boundary markings to increase your own landholdings at the expense of someone else was an offense committed by great and small alike. Large operators and small operators stole—but the large operators, the "rulers," stole the most!

The idea of getting something for nothing, something that is not rightfully ours, is in the blood of powerful leaders as well as ordinary people; it takes hold of entire nations as well as individuals. Blessed are those who hunger and thirst after righteousness—but most people hunger and thirst for more land, colonies, capital, and possessions. Every human being is an annexationist by nature. The leaders of Judah were also out for what they could get.

In Israel, the boundaries of each piece of land were marked by stones or landmarks. The land marked off was an inheritance from one's ancestors. Trying to take over someone else's inheritance was a very serious offense calling for severe punishment.

God did not want to see any poverty among His people. Therefore, no one was allowed to sell the land he had inherited unless he was in dire straits. It was even more strictly forbidden to take possession of another man's land in some illegal way. From Mount Ebal, the Israelites heard: "'Cursed be he who removes his neighbor's landmark.' And all the people shall say, 'Amen.'" (Deut. 27:17). The writer of Proverbs had this passage in mind when he declared: "Do not move the ancient boundary stone which your forefathers set up" (Prov. 22:28 NEB).

It should not surprise us that the rich and powerful in Hosea's day were filled with the desire to increase their riches, for it was an era when the Lord's commandments were trampled underfoot. Oppressing the poor and extorting money from the defenseless were the order of the day. Those who wanted more and more land went their way unchallenged. But that's not the main thing Hosea had in mind.

What he was really reproaching the people for was not that they moved boundary stones to steal more land and refused to curb their appetite for land, but that they had become *like* those who move boundary stones. Thus, Hosea was making a *comparison*. They were, in fact, guilty of moving boundary stones, but that's not Hosea's point. What he wanted to impress on them is that they were also guilty of moving boundary stones in a figurative sense.

What he meant was this: Just as someone who moved boundary stones had infringed on land owned by his neighbor, so these people in Judah–not just a few people here and there but the country's leading citizens, the leaders of the nation–infringed on *the Lord's rights*. They had become like those who move boundary stones.

How did they infringe on the Lord's rights? To understand this, we must remember that there are two ways of sinning against the inheritance of the fathers. We can move the boundary stones *outward* and thereby *enlarge* our own territory. But we can also sin by moving the landmarks *inward*, thereby making our territory *smaller*; in other words, we can squander what our fathers left us. The Heidelberg Catechism does not warn us only that selfishness and the legal expansion of our territory amounts to theft; it says the same thing about *squandering* God's gifts (Answer 110). The law which God gave to Israel forbade selling and disposing of inheritances needlessly. Anyone who did so thereby betrayed a lack of respect for his forefathers and was guilty of engaging in wastefulness that inevitably led to poverty and decline.

Naboth, for example, was well aware of this. It was not because of any stubbornness or poor breeding that he refused to sell his vineyard to Ahab. He felt bound in conscience to the ordinances of the Lord. It was because of his high calling to obey God rather than men that he said proudly, "The Lord forbid that I should give you the inheritance of my fathers."

This attachment to the inheritance of the fathers was foreign to the rich men and nobles of Judah. They simply couldn't understand Naboth's motives. Without thinking twice, they would willingly have given up their land, their people, their city, and their temples in the service of some alien god.

The Lord had chosen Israel as His inheritance. He had declared that Israel must be a holy nation, and that no one was to encroach on His territory. But this declaration didn't mean a thing to the leaders of Judah. They didn't concern themselves with the Lord's rights and claims but willingly traded them for a bowl of lentil broth, following Esau's example.

They got rich through such trade, but they left the Lord out in the cold. They moved their own boundary stones farther and farther outward, but they watched unmoved when God's territory shrank or was eaten away, when Yahweh's rights were violated on all sides. These great landowners measured their holdings by the acre, but it didn't bother them that the Lord's land was defiled on all sides by altars erected in the service of idols. The Almighty would just have to learn to be content with a little less land.

That's what happens when there are too many "leaders," when there are too many rich and powerful men among the Lord's people, when the "little man" becomes a "big man," when there are not enough people like Naboth around to hold onto their inheritance. Consider this for a moment: you might like the idea of playing the role of Naboth, but have you ever heard of Naboth getting anywhere in this world? People like Naboth are trampled underfoot; they are stoned. When it comes to loving one's neighbor, everyone is his own neighbor. The rich and powerful of Judah (and Israel) would not be stopped for long by legal principles about inheritance and the rights of the Lord!

Thus, the leaders of Judah live like princes and admit without batting an eye that the heathens are taking over the Lord's inheritance. Yet the little man who clings to his inheritance and dares to protest is ridiculed or put to death. Those leaders of Judah have truly become like men who move boundary markers.

Much to my regret, I must point out that there are many people in our time who watch calmly as the boundaries of the Lord's inheritance are violated by all sorts of forces and the territory of God's Kingdom shrinks visibly.

Actually, this is turning things inside out. The only Kingdom that can and must live by annexation is the Kingdom of God. Israel already knew that God would give her the inheritance of the heathens. This became even clearer in the New Testament, where the Lord Jesus lays claim to all men and commands His apostles to make disciples of them.

Therefore, the ones who should be in the business of moving boundary markers are the citizens of God's Kingdom. They must throw themselves into the struggle with a certain prayer on their lips and in their hearts: "Thy Kingdom come." This prayer means: "Preserve the church and make it *grow.*" It should be the passionate desire of God's people to see the territory of the "world" shrink steadily, as province after province is incorporated into the Kingdom of God. Christ's rule is the only lawful rule; satan's dominion is totally illegitimate.

The fact that the "world" is conquering pieces of the church's territory is not only regrettable but also hard to comprehend. Yet, this fact cannot be denied. Today's "leaders of Judah" are also like those who move boundary markers. They are great talkers, but they hardly concern themselves with the rights and property of the Lord.

Just look at what the *Word of the Lord* tells us. There was a time when people spoke of subjecting themselves to the discipline of the Word. They recognized that the Word of God makes authoritative demands on all of our life. The Word determines when we should speak and when we should remain silent. It instructs us about our conduct at home and in the church. It guides us in our relationships with God and our neighbor.

But today there are many people who want nothing to do with the discipline of the Word. The Word's sphere of influence extends much too far to suit them. They're content to let the walls of the church echo with the sounds of the preaching of the Word, but that's all they want to hear of the Word. Spending an hour in church each Sunday morning is long enough: half an hour would be much better.

The main thing, they argue, is that the Word must not meddle in my private affairs. It must leave me alone when I'm at the office. It must not make demands on my life at home, and it certainly has nothing to do with what goes on in my bedroom. (In the old days, people would ponder God's law day and night.) How my wife and I choose to arrange things between us in our marriage is entirely up to us, for we're "sovereign" within that sphere. We'll decide for ourselves what and whom we'll talk about when we go visiting. Do you get the picture?

This reduces the authority of the Word of the Lord to one hour on the first day of the week–when the preacher deals with spiritual matters. As for the boundary stones God has set up to indicate that His territory encompasses the four corners of the earth, they are moved and moved again until they enclose the four walls of the church where people come together on Sunday morning. The "leaders" of each family join in the worship service too, but after the service, they go their own sovereign way again. Those leaders of Judah are just like the people who move boundary markers.

Meanwhile, the extent of God's *property* and *possessions* shrinks. God's lawful property is the entire earth and everything on it, including all that moves and lives. We all know this in theory. We know that we are stewards who will have to render accounts someday of what we've done with what was entrusted to us.

Whenever the Lord needs something for *His* church, *His* Kingdom, *His* Christian schools, and colleges, it must be given to Him freely and willingly. There's nothing more to be said about it: the Master needs it.

But many of today's leaders of Judah regard themselves as absolute masters of what they own. They believe that no one else has any say in what they do with their property. It may be that the entire earth and everything on it belongs to the Lord, but surely this doesn't include my wallet and the contents of my safe!

Did I hear you ask for a contribution for the work of God's Kingdom? Those people who promote Christian causes are always begging for money! It's easy for them to talk, for they have nothing to lose. *We* are the ones who have to pay! The laborers in God's Kingdom live on *our* money.

Thus, the leaders of Judah sit down on top of their safes and strongboxes. There they decide on the boundaries of God's rights over wealth and property, running right past their homes. Those leaders of Judah are just like the people who move boundary markers.

I could easily give you many more examples of how the Lord's territory is shrinking, but I've already shown clearly enough that Hosea's words about the "leaders of Judah" are highly relevant to our time.

It's fortunate that there are leaders of Judah, rich men, and nobles who conduct themselves in a fitting way before God and man and work for the coming of God's Kingdom. But it's unfortunate that there are also "leaders" who follow the example of Hosea's contemporaries by not concerning themselves with God's Kingdom. We should be thankful that the church is not dependent on such leaders and never has been.

Throughout all ages, the church of the Lord has relied on little men—who were really great men! It has thrived on the spirit of people who know what inheritance means: "The Lord forbid that I should give you the inheritance of my fathers." Those are the words of a leader. That's the kind of leadership we need today. Leaders of this kind can be found among rich people as well as poor people and simple people. Yet a rich man needs a great deal of grace if he is to realize what the spirit of inheritance represents.

# 23

## General or Physician?

*When Ephraim saw his sickness,*
*and Judah his wound,*
*then Ephraim went to Assyria,*
*and sent to the great king.*
*But he is not able to cure you*
*or heal your wound (5:13).*

No, THE FALL OF THE KINGDOMS of Ephraim and Judah did not come about suddenly and unexpectedly; it was not a bolt of lightning from a clear blue sky. Things simply don't happen that way. Just as someone who turns to Christ in faith does not immediately become holy but is sanctified gradually through a process of daily conversion, so the sinner living on the slippery slope of sin slides to his doom slowly but surely.

Some people die suddenly because of heart failure or a heart attack, but most people get sick first and send for the doctor before death takes them away. If God has decided that a man's time has come, the most talented physician will not be able to heal him. "He is not able to cure you or heal your wound," Hosea declared. These words addressed to Israel apply to all of us.

That's also the way it went with Ephraim and Judah. On many occasions and in many ways, God had already said that the existence of these two kingdoms would come to an end. Now we see that this end will come through a gradual process of sickness and declining health. Ephraim saw his sickness, and Judah was well aware of his wound. They sought medical help from a certain Jareb (whom I'll discuss later), but it did them no good. There was no escape from their doom.

The prophet Hosea also gives some precise information about the *nature* of the sickness. In the verse before, he speaks of a "moth" and of "dry rot." These are two different metaphors intended to cast light on one and the same disease. The difference between these metaphors is that the moth brings about the decay of the *garments* man wears, while dry rot eats away *at man himself.* The moth is a tuberculosis destroying man's clothes, while dry rot is a tuberculosis destroying his bones.

This "moth," referred to by Hosea, has drawn the attention of commentators. They point out that moths are a greater problem in Palestine than in a more temperate climate like ours, which is why the moth is referred to regularly in the scriptures as a symbol of destructiveness. Some moths lay eggs in clothes and garments. The caterpillars hatched from those eggs then use the cloth for food and other needs.

The operation of those caterpillars can be very deceptive. From the outside, there's nothing to be seen when they first go to work. Yet the beautiful garment is being eaten up from within. Before long, there will be large holes in it, and it will be completely worthless.

There were few things that plagued housewives in Palestine as much as moths. But Ephraim wasn't afraid of moths. He only looked at outward appearances and thought of himself as a well-dressed young gentleman—until it became clear at a certain point that Ephraim had no clothes on but stood naked in the cold.

Hosea goes a step further by speaking not only of moths but also of dry rot. In other words, the decay will affect not only Israel's clothes and outward appearances but also his inward existence. The disease of the clothes will give way to a disease of the body. In fact, the latter is a result of the former.

Now it's quite true that most people are more afraid of moths than of the spiritual dry rot that gnaws at our inner life. People cry more over a garment that is being ruined than over a corrupted heart. The loss of goods and possessions, food and clothing is usually regarded as a greater reason for lamentation than the loss of heavenly treasures. That's why Jesus warned us to lay up treasures in heaven where they would not be consumed by moths or rust. He pointed out that it would do us no good to gain the whole world and then lose our own soul.

The latter warning had a direct bearing on Hosea's warning about dry rot, by which he means a kind of tuberculosis of the bones. Like the moth, this dry rot works from within as it attacks the bone system in our bodies. This dry rot leads ultimately to the formation of an abscess that will cause death unless it is completely removed by surgery.

Ephraim was suffering from this horrible disease, but, like many other tuberculosis patients, he saw nothing wrong with himself and didn't believe he was sick. Such people often believe they are in perfect health at the very moment when the bacteria of sin are going about their destructive work, gnawing at the root of their existence, and consuming it. Ephraim's communion with God was broken, but he didn't know it yet and thought he was still on the best terms with God.

The harmony and unity were destroyed by factionalism, especially when various pretenders to the crown fought to the death after the reign of Jeroboam II. Yet, no one paused to point out how all the internal unrest, quarreling, and factionalism gradually stripped the country of much of its defensive power. Finally, Ephraim *saw* his sickness and Judah became aware of his wound, but it was too late, for the inner process of the disease had already advanced so far that it broke out in an abscess on the body.

Furthermore, Ephraim was so foolish as to turn to a charlatan for help. In the King James version, we read that when Ephraim saw his sickness, he turned to "King Jareb," while modern translations say simply that he went to Assyria to seek the help of the "great king." The only one with enough power to arrest the horrible disease at the advanced stage was the Lord. But Ephraim didn't need the Lord. He was no longer used to seeking help from above.

God complained about this in holy jealousy and great amazement. His people, stricken with a fatal illness, did not turn to Him for help but went instead to a charlatan!

It is not clear just whom Hosea had in mind when he spoke of King Jareb. The history books about that era mentioned no such king. Yet, by combining a few facts, we can venture a guess that's probably not too far from the truth.

We know that Menahem, one of the usurpers who occupied the throne of Israel around that time, made some sort of treaty with Tiglath-Pileser, a well-known Assyrian king. Menahem made a large payment to this king, hoping, no doubt, that this would assure him of Assyrian help in times of trouble.

That Hosea does not call Tiglath-Pileser by his own name but refers to him as "Jareb" may be because *Jareb* means *fighter*.

*Jareb* was certainly an appropriate name, for this Assyrian monarch loved to fight. The whole world trembled when he took up arms. This helps us understand little Menahem's treaty with the great Jareb–from a psychological point of view, at least–for who wouldn't want to make friends with the rich and powerful titans of this earth in order to find safety under the shadow of their wings?

Hosea makes a joke of Menahem's treaty. There's divine irony in the fact that someone with a fatal disease turns to a fighter for medical help. Generals and commanders are not people to whom we normally look for healing. Sometimes they like to pretend that they can heal the world's ills by restoring order, but such claims, on the part of these pretended lovers of peace, are based on a misunderstanding. Those generals are mistaken, and so are the people who believe in them.

Israel's abscess was certainly in need of medical treatment and healing, but a *general's sword* would hardly be the suitable instrument to use. In medical handbooks, we read that a patient suffering from tuberculosis of the bones needs rest in especially fresh air. Thus, turning to someone named Jareb, someone who loves to fight, someone who will make him breathe in the poisonous fumes of the battlefield, is just what he shouldn't do.

Seeking rest on the battlefield, seeking healing from a warrior, seeking reformation from someone looking for a fight makes no sense to Hosea. Therefore, he ridicules this tuberculosis patient who needs rest above all but looks for a fight, who walks right by the great Physician and consults a general about his illness instead. There have been fools in every era of history–and there are still fools today!

It's most unfortunate that evil sometimes grows like a cancer in the life of an individual or in the life of the church. Sin then gnaws at the very root of our life, just as a moth ruins clothes and dry rot undermines our health and demolishes our bone system. The sin may bear any one of a number of names. *Every* sin is in the demolition business.

Sin does not do its work in a flash but proceeds slowly, step by step. First, we sin just to show that we *can* sin. Then we sin because we *want* to. Finally, we sin because we *must* sin. What was hidden at the outset then breaks out in an open abscess. According to a certain story, the man who did the famous painting of Christ's Last Supper with His disciples had a hard time finding a model for the face of Judas. He spent years looking, and finally, he found someone with the false face of a traitor. Then he suddenly realized that he had already used the same man as his model for the face of Jesus! When we sin, we become slaves to sin, as Paul points out.

The scriptures indicate that *envy* is the sin that comes closest to dry rot in its effects. Envy eats away at our insides. Thus, we could say that envy is like the bacteria that cause tuberculosis. Slowly but surely, it goes about its destructive work inside us where no eye can observe it. Anyone who allows envy a place in his life thoroughly destroys his "life with God." He also destroys the life of the church. The process advances slowly, but in each case, it is sure.

Whenever envy and jealousy and factionalism gain a foothold in the church of the Lord, the church suffers from the most fearful disease of all. The diagnosis of the scriptures is tuberculosis, that is, a dry rot eating away at the bones. The moth has already devoured the garment in which it wraps itself. From the *outside*, the church may still look beautiful. It still appears to be dressed in a stylish Reformed suit. It goes to great lengths to defend its principles, and it remains a church that loves its creeds and doctrine. The church appears to be flourishing, but appearances are deceptive. What do we care how things look from the outside if the inside is rotten?

The Heidelberg Catechism points out that the church that confesses the truth of man's misery and redemption will be renewed by the Holy Spirit to be like Christ (Lord's Day 32). Christ is a *complete* Redeemer. He was busy with His work before we were born, and He still works in us today, although we often prefer not to speak of that work of Christ *in* us. He makes the church not only a *confessing* church, not only a church that will be blessed in the life to come but a church that includes *other* people who have also been renewed in the likeness of Christ, people who remind us of Christ.

But what is left of all of this if envy makes us unable to assume Christ's likeness, if jealousy makes us speak bitter words to each other and write polemical articles, if quarreling destroys the unity of the church? Envy is the tuberculosis of the soul!

Do *we* suffer from that disease? Are the symptoms of that horrible disease present in *our* lives? Some people say, "Of course not! I see no evidence of that whatsoever. There's nothing wrong with me." That may be. But it's usually too late by the time Ephraim sees his sickness and Judah becomes aware of his wound. By then the disease has reached its final stage.

Surely you can *feel* the disease. You feel weary and lethargic. You become tired easily. Apathy sets in. You lose your appetite. You notice yourself becoming more irritable. I'm sure you know what I'm talking about!

The cure for the disease is to be sought in rest–and not in fighting. Don't look to the general for help. Go to a doctor instead. Turn to the great Physician. We are to send our messages and prayers to Him and ask Him a most important question. We are to ask Him whether He, in His omnipotence and grace, will heal us from the worst of all illnesses, the rotting of our bones.

# 24

# The Prodigal Son

*Come, let us return to the Lord;*
*for he has torn us and will heal us,*
*he has struck us and he will bind up our wounds;*
*after two days he will revive us,*
*on the third day he will restore us,*
*that in his presence we may live (6:1–2 NEB)*

THERE'S ALSO A PRODIGAL SON in the Old Testament. His name is Ephraim. Although he was still "at home" when Hosea wrote these words, in his mind's eye the prophet already saw him in a faraway land, in exile. He heard him saying to his fellow exiles, "Come, let us return to the Lord." That's just what the prodigal son in Jesus' parable said: "I will arise and go to my father."

Yet the prodigal son didn't say that as soon as he left home. On the contrary, he first had to try it on his own, with the swine. Only when he felt completely defeated and all the props were knocked out from under him did he come to his senses and remember his father's home.

At first, Ephraim turned to Jareb to heal his "abscess," as we saw in the preceding chapter. But Jareb was unable to heal him (5:13). Instead, the disease got much worse, and Ephraim had to go into exile. Then, in the hour of his greatest need, when his existence as a nation had been completely crushed, when Israel wandered aimlessly in unhappy exile, his thoughts turned to the Lord again. It's about time!

Hosea prophetically hears the splinters of the broken heart falling as the nation comes to its senses and finally wakes up. It's unfortunate that they seek the Lord "in their distress" (5:15). It almost looks as though God provides a refuge only for the homeless. But turning to God in such circumstances is better than not turning to him at all.

The Lord is most merciful! He does not turn His back on deprived and beggarly refugees but takes them in. He is merciful to those who turn to Him for comfort in their hour of need. The main thing is that He gets His child back, and that child has learned something and will not run away again.

Ephraim isn't planning to run away again. He promises solemnly that he will live in God's "presence," that is, that he will stay close to home and will not stray away from God's watchful eye again. That's the "gratitude" expressed in this act of turning away from idols and returning to the Lord. (I'll have more to say about this later.)

This gratitude is the third of three things we must know in order to live and die in the comforting knowledge that we belong to Christ. The first is the extent of our sin and misery, and the second is how we can be freed from them. Ephraim had to learn all three the hard way. Actually, there's no end to learning about these things.

First, there is his sin and misery. Ephraim says that he wishes to return to the One who has torn him. These words already contain the humbling confession that he has forsaken the Lord and therefore deserves his wounds fully. In these words, we hear echoes of the Heidelberg Catechism, which asks whether God perhaps created man evil and even asks whether God may be doing man an injustice by punishing him for his sins. (That question was often raised by Israel!) Finally, the Catechism asks a question that contains a confession like Ephraim's: "according to God's righteous judgment we deserve punishment both in this world and forever after: how then can we escape this punishment and return to God's favor?"

This is the confession of the prodigal son: "I have sinned." It is also the confession of the tax collector, "O God, be merciful to me, a sinner." And it is the confession of the repentant murderer on the cross: "We're getting what we deserve." Wandering around aimlessly as a miserable exile, Ephraim finally learns how great his sin is.

He has also learned about his deliverance. Ephraim's eyes were already open to God's righteousness, but now he becomes aware of God's mercy as well. With all of Israel, he confesses that the mercy of the Lord is unto all eternity. His jubilation about his deliverance is just as intense as his lamentation about his misery.

Not for a moment is he in doubt whether the Lord will take him back, and he doesn't just wish it might happen. He is firmly convinced of God's willingness to take him back: it is the Lord who has torn us, and He will heal us. God will be like a father and also like a mother. With the gentle hands of a mother, He will bind up our wounds, for He is the One who has torn us.

Unlike the prodigal son, Ephraim does not consider asking the Lord to take him back as one of the hired servants. He knows it would hurt the Father deeply if the son were to beg to be taken back into the house as a servant.

Furthermore, the request to be taken back as a servant is a form of pure Phariseeism. (The Pharisee wants to earn his salvation: by working industriously he hopes to repair the damage.) Fortunately, the prodigal son also realizes this later. He was planning to ask the father to take him back as a servant, but he didn't go through with it.

Thus, we have the blessed assurance of deliverance. This assurance is so strong that Ephraim expresses the hope that the deliverance will come in the shortest possible time. He says:

After two days he will revive us,
on the third day he will restore us.

We would say: "After a few days he will revive us." That's roughly what Ephraim meant. This testifies to his faith in God's miraculous power.

When a sick person is so far gone that he has to be made "alive" again and has to be brought back from death's door, so to speak, it already requires faith to believe that a restoration will take place. It requires even greater faith to expect the healing to take place in the shortest possible time. Usually, it goes just the opposite way: as we all know, disease comes very quickly but goes away slowly.

Isn't this expectation a bit too optimistic? Isn't Ephraim forgetting the seriousness of his sin when he assumes that as soon as he returns to the Lord, everything will instantly be in order again? No, not at all! Ephraim bases this hope on a promise!

God has already said: "I will return again to my place, until they acknowledge their guilt" (5:1). There is a world of grace in this "until." God was not planning to chastise His people forever or make them feel His wrath eternally. Through the mouth of Isaiah, He said:

> In overflowing wrath for a moment
> I hid my face from you,
> but with everlasting love I will have compassion on you
> (Is. 54: 8)

Ezekiel spoke of the return from exile in terms of rising from the dead (Ezek. 37). Thus, the song of Ephraim's faith is in complete accord with the promise.

Faith must go no further than the promise extends. It must not run ahead of the promise, but it should not lag behind either. Faith can never expect too much, but it may never expect too little. The scriptures are overflowing with different statements that all make the same point, namely, that God is exceedingly merciful. He forgives gladly. He forgives numerous sins. He hastens to help us.

The prodigal son is not put on probation–not even for two or three days. The father does not hesitate for a moment about taking the son back. He embraces him and kisses him. He gives him the finest robe and kills the fatted calf. All the orders are given immediately. Ephraim, your delay of two or three days is fairly long, after all!

Of course, sin and deliverance are followed by gratitude. We ask: "How shall I repay the Lord for all His benefits to me?" Reborn Israel gives us the proper answer: we will live "in His presence."

This is the language of true conversion, and thus of true gratitude. We see this in two respects in Ephraim's conversion. In the first place, living "in God's presence" is the result of "seeking God's face." Living in God's presence means living a life of contact with Him. Such a life isn't possible if we don't seek that contact first. We can't walk with God if we don't turn to Him.

Up to now, Ephraim had never done that. He had never sought God's face and thus he never tried–or dared–to look God in the eye. He had prayed, but there was not much more to his prayer than folded hands and closed eyes, which really isn't worthy of the name prayer. Prayer means seeking God's face; it means looking right at Him. That's enough for someone in prayer–more than enough. He must read the message in God's eyes.

But that didn't concern Ephraim at all. He didn't care about it in the least. He did not try to look God in the eye, nor did he reach out to God's outstretched hands. He was interested only in the gifts in God's hands. Those generous hands were more important to Ephraim than friendly eyes. He kept his gaze fixed firmly on what the Lord had to offer, but for the rest, he could get along quite nicely without the Lord. At least, that's what he thought.

The Lord once said to Moses that He would send an angel to be with Israel, an angel who would drive away the enemies of the Israelites and turn over the promised land to them. But He Himself would not go along. The Israelites of Hosea's day would have jumped at such a chance. They would have said, "Let's go!" What could be more beautiful? They would have an angel as their guide. There would be milk and honey all around them. Their enemies would be defeated.

There are also many people today who would take God up on such an offer. Who cares if God Himself is not present? But Moses said no. He would rather live in God's presence in a barren, howling wilderness than enjoy all the delights of the promised land without God.

Thomas à Kempis also thought along such lines. He declared that all of God's rich gifts would mean nothing to him if God Himself was not present. He was right! Anyone who enjoys those gifts apart from the Lord's presence is a pauper.

Fortunately, Ephraim now retreats from such an attitude. For him, the only thing necessary is no longer prosperity or happiness but God's presence. "We will live in his presence," he declares.

Those who have been freed by the Lord no longer sing about grain and wine and oil. They sing instead about God's name, which is so full of honor. That name is their delight. God's friendly presence brings joy and light into their lives.

In the second place, the authenticity of Ephraim's repentance and conversion is apparent from the fact that he wants to live in God's presence. Ephraim wants to "stay home"; he doesn't want to stray from his Father's sight anymore. No longer will he yearn for a faraway land, for he knows from experience what it's like to live far away from his Father. Nor will he ask for a kid to feast on with his friends, as the older brother did, thereby making it known that his life at home left something to be desired, that he felt more like a servant than a son in his father's home. Ephraim now understands what gratitude means: that we show in all we do that we are thankful for God's gracious gifts.

The life of repentance and conversion does not consist of seeking God's presence in church services and at fixed times set aside for prayer, only to turn back to one's own way and seek luxuries far away from God. The search for God's presence is not a mountain peak jutting out here and there from the flat plane of our daily existence. Our entire life is raised to the heights. It is presented to God; it is lived in His presence.

Seeking God's face means living in His presence. The latter is the result of the former. Living in God's presence does not mean rest. It means living under the watchful eye of the One who never sleeps. Thus, it means that God checks up on us. He sees us wherever we are—in the living room, in the bedroom, at work, or in church.

The believer wouldn't want it any other way. He's not like a lazy servant who takes it easy when his master's eye is upon him. He goes about his work like a child performing a labor of love. He never finds the work he does a burden. Therefore, it's a pleasure for him to live in God's presence.

The desire to live in God's presence is what distinguishes genuine faith from temporary faith. Someone who believes only temporarily wants to come to the Lord, but he doesn't stay with the Lord. That's too much of a bother for him; he didn't realize that following the Lord would also mean taking up his cross.

He's willing to walk one mile with his neighbor, but not two. It's simply impossible for him to pluck out the eye that offends him. In the long run, the demands of God's word are too much for him, for living in God's presence also means placing his feet on the glowing coals of the altar, to be burned alive in the service of the Lord.

This is the new life to which Ephraim will be awakened through God's amazing power and grace. This is true revival!

Ephraim says that God will revive him after two days and restore him on the third day. Some commentators warn against regarding these words as an allusion to the death and resurrection of Christ, but I must differ with them here. What we have in this passage is more than an allusion. In fact, this text is primarily about Christ, for Christ speaks here through the mouth of Hosea.

Christ was torn and struck down by God, but after three days He rose again. There is no doubt in my mind that the Savior also explained this text from Hosea to the two men on the road to Emmaus when he set their hearts on fire. The revival of Israel (the body) was only possible through the resurrection of Christ (the Head).

How does Christ's resurrection benefit us? Through His power, we are awakened to new life. Through our faith in Christ, we gain the power to live a life of gratitude. That life of gratitude means living in His presence. It is the beginning of eternal life. That doesn't mean that we no longer stumble. Our joy will be complete when we are able to see Him face to face. And what that will mean simply can't be expressed in impoverished human language.

# 25

# Of Sunshine and Rain

*Let us know, let us press on to know the Lord;*
*his going forth is sure as the dawn;*
*he will come to us as the showers (6:3).*

ALTHOUGH HOSEA DIDN'T KNOW the Lord's Prayer, he certainly understood what was behind it. Among the first words he put in the mouth of God's repentant children, full of sorrow for their sins, are: "Let us know, let us press on to know the Lord." (These words are a continuation of the text discussed in the preceding chapter.)

This amounts to the familiar petition "Hallowed be Thy name," which the Heidelberg Catechism explicates as follows: "Help us to really know you, to bless, to worship, and to praise you for all your works and for all that shines forth from them: your almighty power, wisdom, kindness, justice, mercy, and truth.... Help us to direct all our living—what we think, say, and do—so that your name will never be blasphemed because of us but always honored and praised" (Answer 122). This is now the passionate desire of God's repentant people. Their first concern is to press on to know the Lord.

But knowing the Lord means paying careful attention to all that he does, seeking his presence, and inquiring into his will and his law. We do all this so that God's name will be honored and praised instead of slandered.

This new *life* is already revealed in this desire, for the breath of the new life is *prayer*. Of course, I don't mean just any prayer. If the prodigal son had asked only for his daily bread when he returned home and stretched out his hands eagerly for God's gifts, we would have good reason to doubt the authenticity of his repentance and conversion. Fortunately, that's not what he did. The prodigal son did not worry, first of all, about food and clothes, but about his father's honor.

Here, the spirit of Christ, who spoke earlier through the mouths of the prophets, already responds to the unexpressed desire of these prodigal children: teach us how to pray! This Hosea—remember that his name has the same meaning as *Jesus*—is their teacher. He tells them: "Whenever you become afraid, stretch out your hands to God and say, 'Our Father, who art in heaven, hallowed be Thy name.'" In other words, they are to "press on to know the Lord."

As soon as the children of Israel appropriated these words of prayer in a wholehearted willingness to seek God's honor in their lives, they felt deeply that they were weak *in themselves*, that they could not stand even for a moment on their own two feet. Experience had taught them that. Therefore, they immediately added the hopeful expectation that the Lord himself would sustain the new life, just as the sun and the rain foster the development of a young plant in nature. As they lived the life of grace, they felt just as dependent on heaven as a young plant in its natural environment is dependent on the sunshine and rain. This is what is meant by the other words in our text:

> His going forth is sure as the dawn;
> He will come to us as the showers.

The reference to showers needs no explanation. As for the words about the dawn, it is Israel's hope and expectation that the Lord will hover over His people and shine on them just as the sun imparts light and warmth to the earth when it shines on the fields. Israel needs sunshine *and* rain. If anything is to come of the new life and the beautiful promises, Israel will have to rely on the fruitful operation of the Holy Spirit.

These metaphors–like those of other prophets–point clearly to the *outpouring of the Spirit*. Thus, we see that this passage is full of Easter and Pentecost thoughts. In the preceding chapter, we already discussed the Easter expectation and resurrection. In the next text that concerns us now, we see an anticipation of Pentecost.

Hosea himself would not have known what the words *Easter* and *Pentecost* mean. For him, the risen Lord of Easter Sunday is one with the Spirit of Pentecost. The one who awakens new life within us is the one who brings it to completion. The one who sows is also the one who reaps, who ripens the crop until the sheaves are ready.

The ultimate issue here is the *harvest*. The harvester comes for the fruit. That's why He devotes so much attention to Israel and to all of us. Let's find out what he had to go through on our account and then ask ourselves whether the fruits in our lives are a proper return on that investment.

"His going forth is sure as the dawn." This makes us think of the full salvation given us in Christ Jesus, who makes a new day "dawn" in our lives. We like to say that Christ makes us walk in the light of the truth. But in him and with him *all* things are given to us, so that God's mercy is as right to our amazed eyes as the dawning of a new day. That mercy shines down on our heads in never-faltering strength like the sun.

Because of Christ, God's goodness is not a short eruption but a constant, even emanation of sunshine. It continues even if a foolish man closes all his doors and draws all his curtains, complaining in the dark that he sees little of the sun and always has to walk among the shadows in dim light.

God is like the dawn of a bright new day, like the sun in all its splendor. Therefore, we are continually amazed at the chain of answered prayers.[8*] The Lord never gets tired of giving us everything. God is generous with his gifts, just as the sun is generous with its sunshine. That's the amazing thing.

Even so, we are still dissatisfied, and sometimes we complain that God doesn't give us enough. He makes his sunshine on the *evil* (which includes us, and not just the "wicked world"). He puts bread in the mouths of those who dishonor his name, and he gives extravagant gifts to those who are out to do evil.

We all want to bask in his light. We certainly don't find it unpleasant when the sun of God's goodness shines in our lives, and we're quite willing to sing about it on Sundays too. God's smiling face brings light and even joy into our lives, and we're happy to live in that light. We tell each other that one never gets tired of sunshine.

But the Lord asks more of us. He is not entirely satisfied when we sing about the new dawn and simply gather up His good gifts.

---

8. See 2:20 and Chapter 11 above, which deals with the harmony of prayers.

Now we remember that Israel looked in hope to the rising sun of God's favor because that sun would foster the growth of *new life*. We also remember that Paul said to the Romans: "Do you not know that God's kindness is meant to lead you to repentance?" (Rom. 2:4). God did not create the sun to move poets to ecstasy, nor did he create the light of the dawn to stir the soul of the singer. His main purpose was to give light and make us *fruitful*. God himself is like a sun whose rays wake the sleeper gently with a kiss and advises him to repent.

God has many different ways of leading man to repentance and thereby making him fruitful. Some of them are painful. One of the means God uses is the shining sun; He uses the sun to disarm us. What he demands of man, the creature created in his own image, is what he himself does day after day: he asks man to *overcome evil with good*. That's the fruit of repentance he seeks; that's the new life he waits for. He wants us to be *thankful* in all our prosperity.

This demand that we be thankful is far-reaching. It is certainly not enough to confess piously–or impiously–that the Lord has blessed us richly. This demand involves a total renewal of our lives as we bind ourselves to God's commands. The life of gratitude is lived under the banner of two words–*commandment* and *prayer*.

A thankful man is a repentant man; that is to say, he is a different person. With revulsion, he turns away from the usual excuse that we all remain "sinful human beings." Instead, he takes seriously the promise that he has become a "new creature." Through the power of God, he turns his life into a song and learns to sing God's commands. He turns his life into a prayer: "Hallowed be thy name."

If it is to mean anything to me that God's presence in my life is as sure as tomorrow's sunshine, then there must be *fruits* in my life. Otherwise, my joy is in vain and my psalms about God's gracious presence in my life will become a curse.

God will come to us as a *shower*, says born-again Israel. But the showers meant here are not the late rains or spring rains but those during the harvest season. It rains cats and dogs as the rivers swell rapidly to form turbulent torrents of water. God's sluices open and the water pours onto the earth with a mighty roar, filling all the chasms. We would hardly speak of those pelting rainstorms as refreshing. Yet, what farmer would want sunshine *all the time?* (Perpetual sunshine is the foolish wish of the pampered city dweller too used to the comforts of human culture.)

Doesn't the rain also mean blessing? Don't those dark clouds bear the promise of deliverance? Doesn't God enrich us when He sends rain that dampens the soil holding the roots? Doesn't the falling rain make the fields more fruitful? Doesn't it preserve the waving fields that would certainly wither without rain? Who is so foolish as not to be thankful for the storms that rage over the grainfields on dark days before the harvest season? Who is so foolish as not to rejoice at the dark clouds that burst over his head?

Just as we can complain about the stormy weather without remembering that the fields need the rain and that we must live off the produce of the fields, we pout when the sun of our life hides behind thick rain clouds as lightning flashes and the heavens are emptied. We don't stop to think that those unrequested showers may bring with them unexpected blessings, that all things, even raging storms (perhaps storms most of all), work together for good and make the great harvest possible.

The rain as well as the sunshine is intended by God to lead us to repentance. In other words, it is to make us fruitful.

One of these fruits, according to the Heidelberg Catechism, is that we become patient in adversity. This patience is not the passive attitude of the man who says to himself, "I can't do anything about it anyway." The unbeliever can and must be "patient" in this sense. But this kind of patience is not the fruit of a new life.

Christian patience is full of turbulent activity. The Christian doesn't *drag* his cross; he carries it–*joyfully*. He rejoices. He is always full of hope and courage. In faith, he embraces the paradox that all adversity will turn out to be prosperity, for the dark rain clouds contain a silver lining.

The conversion of the Christian, that which makes him different from other people, means that he sees things differently and therefore gives them different names. Whenever you ask him how things are going in his life, he answers, "Fine!" He knows that God will direct all things for his good. He knows the meaning of the paradoxical claim that man can thank God in everything, that man can always be happy. He learns to rejoice always in God's name, as God's goodness (the sun) warms him and sheds light all around him and God's strength (the rain) supports him in his suffering.

We must conclude that we have walked only a few steps down the path of *genuine* conversion. God's work in us has not yet led to great results. The sun and the rain God has sent have borne little fruit. But it would certainly be a sorry matter if there were no fruit at all, for any life that bears *no fruit* is ultimately consigned to the flames.

It's frightening how many lives there are that bear no fruit–many of them "Reformed." Those lives are full of thorns and thistles, but we find no fruit in them.

The great harvester is coming to pluck the fruit. What will he find?

# 26

# God's Predicament

*What shall I do with you, O Ephraim? (6:4)*

THERE WAS A TRAGIC misunderstanding between God and Ephraim. Ephraim thought that God needed him, while God declared that He didn't know what in the world to do with Ephraim.

The idea that God somehow needed His people was the reason for the custom of offering so many sacrifices. The Israelites believed that the sacrifices somehow sustained the Lord and put Him in a good mood. It must have pleased God that there was a nation in Palestine–alongside so many heathen nations–that thought of Him at their altars. "It's a good thing You have us, Lord!"

The prophet Hosea now comes along to brand this notion that God is dependent on sacrifices as a presumptuous conceit.

He dismisses it with the startling words: "I desire steadfast love and not sacrifice" (6:6). He informs the Israelites that they have misunderstood the matter completely, for the truth is that the Lord is in a very different predicament: He doesn't know what to do with His people. "What shall I do with you, O Ephraim?"

What this question echoes is not so much indignation as perplexity.[9] God just doesn't know what to try next. Nothing seems to work with Israel. He has all but given up hope of even making anything of Ephraim. Thus, it might be better to read the question in our text as follows: "What will I ever make of you, O Ephraim?"

It is always God's purpose to make something of man. God is the great sculptor, who fashions man in His image. He glories in turning the splinters and little pieces He works with into people whose features are like His own. But the material He works with is hard and resistant. He would have an easier time with granite or marble. God found it easier to write His law on tablets of stone than in the heart of Ephraim. When God asks what He can possibly make of Ephraim, we should really answer: "Nothing! He is a hopeless case!"

---

9. Some commentators regard these words as an expression of divine wrath. While this possibly can't be ruled out completely, the contacts make it appear more likely that God is perplexed.

Yet there had been many attempts to make something of Israel. Hosea reminds the Israelites of the arduous labors devoted to them through the ages:

Therefore I have hewn them by the prophets,
I have slain them by the words of my mouth (6:5).[10]

God had sent prophets to *hew* the people. The prophet's work is sculpture–nothing more and nothing less.

Nothing more! They were not to hack away at Israel recklessly and smash everything to bits. The prophets were not wreckers but builders; they were not wood choppers but artists. Turning a block of marble into an image of something requires more than a hammer and chisel; it requires a great deal of love and skill!

Nothing less! The words of the prophets had the effect of a hammer and chisel. They were not empty sounds or rambling speculations; they were not literary outpourings or lectures on doctrine.

The prophets knew that their task was not to present their views on various topics but to cut the Israelites down to

---

10. Some commentators regard this verse as an answer to the question in the preceding verse: "What shall I do with you, O Ephraim?" But the prophets had already tried this and failed. Now it was time to try something else.

size and whip them into shape. Therefore, they spared no one and nothing. They did not hesitate to hit so hard that splinters flew in all directions. They did this not because they loved destruction but because they had to make something of Israel. They were trying to make Israel conform to God's image.

Their words were so far removed from idle sounds that lives were lost from time to time as the judgments announced by the prophets were fulfilled: "I have slain them by the words of my mouth." But the vast majority of the people remained unmoved. The sharpest threats and the most moving promises had no effect on their unyielding hearts. Israel did not change in the slightest.

All the efforts to make something of Ephraim through the words of the prophets had failed. The prophets had no success whatsoever with Ephraim. "What shall I do with you, O Ephraim?" That was the predicament of God's exhausted love.

When the *Word of God* has no effect on us, we're in bad shape! We, too, have heard the words of the prophets, those uncompromising and painful words, and we would do well to pay attention to the purpose God has for those words. Here in Hosea, we find out what that purpose is: to cut us down to size and whip us into shape! The words of God's mouth are ready to kill what needs to be killed–our old nature. Then the new life will be able to blossom, and we will assume the new nature

God has destined for us. In other words, we will manifest His image.

It's important for us to ponder this unexpressed goal of preaching. Both the *preachers* of the Word and those who listen to them should think about it. The preacher should concern himself more with cutting and shaping the people of God than with presenting doctrines. He should not make it his main concern to present his views of the scriptures or the church or the covenant or baptism.

Proper doctrines, of course, are as essential as food. Mistaken ideas must be cut and shaped and chiseled and hammered. But man is more than his mind, for even if he affirms all the correct "doctrines," he may still remain unrepentant and unconverted.

Cutting and shaping, then, involves more than just presenting doctrines. It is not enough for the preacher to inculcate the correct ideas; he must work toward the renewal of the *whole person* in God's image. It's not enough for the believer to have some idea of what God is like: he must be the very *image* of God. Christ must *take shape* in his life.

This kind of cutting and shaping requires the soul of an artist. The preacher must devote much love and attention to the overall proportions. He must see that enough is cut away, but he must be careful not to cut away too much. There must be harmony in the image. The "word" is a genius when it comes to sculpture, and not a blacksmith hammering continually on the same anvil. The Word is interested in forming not human skeletons but the people of God with flesh and blood, with intellect and feelings, with head and heart and hands, with body and soul, properly equipped for any and every good work.

As far as the hearers of the Word are concerned, is there anyone who still goes to church to let himself be cut and shaped, to let himself be "killed" by the words proceeding from God's mouth? Rather than subject ourselves to cutting and shaping, we would prefer to bask under a shower of edifying sermons. We enjoy those sermons, but we go on living just as we did before.

We sing that we despise a tree that bears no fruit. Without blushing, we even sing that we have tried to curb our evil inclinations, but there aren't many who are serious about it. We also repeat some of the things that "the poet" said in the Psalms. Poets, of course, live in elevated spheres: there's quite a difference between the prose of daily life and the poetry of the Psalms.

Is there anything wrong with getting up in a bad mood on Sunday morning, being hostile to others, and then saying to God in His holy house of worship that you have done your best to curb your evil inclinations? After the church service, we tell each other how beautiful the Psalms are: they give us a picture of the hearts of God's holy ones.

Hosea mentions one of the features of God's image–no doubt the most important one–that God loves to find in His people, namely, love. He talks about it first in a *negative* context, saying that God has not succeeded in developing this trait in Ephraim and making it part of his nature:

Your love is like a morning cloud,
like the dew it goes early away (6:4).

Later he discusses love in a *positive* context, pointing out that love is a quality that the Lord would like to have found in Ephraim: "I desire *steadfast love* and not sacrifice" (6:6).

In the King James Version, the word mercy is used in place of *steadfast love*. Other students of the Bible maintain that Hosea was talking about piety here. In any event, what he meant was an attitude, something that proceeds from the heart. The word *steadfast love* comes very close to this.

I don't propose to go into the question of whether Hosea had our love for God or our love for our neighbor in mind. I take it that he meant both, for that is the fulfillment of the law: love God above all else and your neighbor as yourself.

Anyone who has this love in his heart manifests the most glorious aspect of God's image, for God *is* love. Therefore, when Paul extols faith, hope, and love, he declares that love is the greatest of all the three. It is faith that makes a man throw himself into God's arms, and hope is what makes him look always to God. But *love* is what makes him *look like* God. Thus, it is no wonder that the Lord, who wanted to make something of Ephraim, who ordered the prophets to cut and shape him, looked especially for this one feature of His image–love.

Unfortunately, He didn't find it. What He found instead were numerous sacrifices that the Israelites made. Everywhere the altars were in use, but what did the Lord find on those altars? Instead of a burning heart full of love, Israel offered Him animals. Such offerings are worthless.

Anyone who obeys the fourth commandment scrupulously and supports the work of the church and the ministry of the Word but withholds his soul, offering his money in a grumbling mood rather than joyfully, would be better off keeping the money. The Lord tells us that He doesn't want such offerings. That kind of money is no more to be desired than the 30 pieces of silver that Judas threw down on the floor of the temple.

Collecting that kind of money will not build a healthy church. All it's good for is buying a field of blood. This text is an important statement from the era of the *old dispensation*, teaching that the important thing when it comes to serving God is not the external ceremony but what lives in the *heart*.

This may be. Yet we are still so attached to those "external ceremonies." We're inclined to be satisfied with the outer side, using it to fool ourselves and others. If we could, we would even use it to fool God.

The civil authorities are completely satisfied with the outward show. As long as you pay your taxes, everything is in order. The government doesn't care whether you pay them with joy and with true patriotic feelings in your heart. But the divine authority picks up where the civil authority leaves off.

God isn't satisfied when you make your pledge and contribute to the church with a sigh and always stay on the straight and narrow. He looks into your heart to determine whether you're doing all of this out of *love*. He looks into the very depths of your soul. If He concludes that you are honoring Him with your lips while your heart is far from Him, His judgment will not be favorable. What will He say about those scrupulous Israelites (and Christians) who sit in the synagogue on the Sabbath day plotting murder in their hearts (it's far from impossible), observing all the holy days while they fail to abide by the law's strictest demand, that of love?

Hosea tells us that Ephraim's love was like a morning cloud that disappears as soon as the sun rises, just as the dew soon vanishes. Those clouds and that dew are not fruitful. They are like promises, rich promises, that are not kept. They are appearance without substance! They are fleeting and transitory and superficial.

When those sheep are shorn, there's a lot of commotion, but we get little wool. The features of God's image were not impressed upon them. At best, they were painted on; they only went skin deep. It's clear as daylight[11] that God's judgment will consume those people who didn't want to heed His word when it called them to repent.

Just in case any of us have the idea—one can never be sure—that the Lord is somehow in need of the churchgoers in our part of the world, that it's a good thing we're here to build and maintain His tabernacles, we should ponder what this passage means for us. We should turn things around and consider the possibility that God may be wondering what to do with us.

Because we have the figure of Jesus Christ clearly before us, God seeks loving qualities in our personality and character. Does He seek those qualities in vain?

"What shall I do with you, O Ephraim?"

---

11. In 6: 5, we read that God's judgment "goes forth as the light."

# 27

# Conforming to the World

*Like Adam, they have broken
the covenant (6:7 NIV)*

THE SIN OF WHICH ISRAEL is now accused is covenant breaking. The somewhat strange claim that the Israelites have broken the covenant "like Adam" has caused exegetes and translators a lot of pain. (I'll return to this point later.)

First, I would ask in what way Israel broke the covenant. When we speak of covenant breakers today, we think immediately of people (usually young people) who have turned their backs on God and cast aside their birthright. In addition to this open covenant breaking, there is another kind. It's much more common, but it attracts much less attention. That's the kind Hosea is talking about here.

Those who are lacking in *love* are covenant breakers–even if they bring abundant offerings. Let's not forget that possibility. They may spend a great deal of time at the altar and visit the temple frequently but still be unfaithful to the covenant. They may talk often about the covenant and develop intricate doctrines of the covenant but still act contrary to its most basic principles.

The law of the covenant is love. When love is turned into an idle game and disappears as quickly as a morning cloud, the prophet of the Lord must protest: "They have broken the covenant."

Here we're talking in negative terms; we're talking about the lack of love. But Hosea also demonstrates this in positive terms by pointing to a series of transgressions against both the tables of the law.

As far as our relation to our neighbor is concerned (the second table of the law), it was just as though the commandment forbidding murder didn't exist in those days, for murder and killing were the order of the day. Hence, Hosea speaks of Gilead as "a city of evildoers tracked with blood" (6:8). It may well be that he was alluding here to the fact that Pekahiah was murdered by Pekah with the help of 50 men of Gilead, as we read in II Kings 15:25.

Even the priests, whom Jeroboam I had recruited from the dregs of the population, joined together to form a band of robbers, and made the road between Bethel and Shechem unsafe (6:9). Apparently, they went as far as to kill some travelers, which is worse than what happened in Jesus' parable of the Good Samaritan, where the priest only left the poor man lying half dead by the side of the road.

Some commentators believe that the priests were not actually robbers themselves, but that they refused the right of asylum–Shechem was one of the six cities of refuge–to those who were fleeing for their lives. Whichever interpretation is correct, it is clear that the priests did not act as we would expect priests to act.

Add to this the sinful cultic practices (transgressions of the first table of the law), which Hosea speaks of here as "harlotry," as a "horrible thing" (6:10), just as he does elsewhere. The command to love God was not taken any more seriously than the command to love one's neighbor!

That's how things went in Hosea's day. We are inclined to shake our heads and say, "What a horrible time!" But are we in any position to look down on those Israelites?

What are the simple truths taught to us in this passage? We learn that envy, hatred, and quarreling are just as awful in God's eyes as killing. We also learn that many "believers" (priests of the Lord) are so lacking in priestly concern that they calmly deny asylum in the church to those who have been shipwrecked in life, and that they regard evangelization as some sort of strange hobby–or at best a secondary concern.

When we consider all this, we realize that we have no right to look down on those Israelites, for things are no better with us. Furthermore, if the notion of the "covenant" is popular while the covenant law of love is tampered with, we hear creaking and grating on all sides and the Lord can certainly say He has found something horrible in the House of Israel.

Yet this surprises the theologians of the covenant! Even if the covenant held no more secrets for me and I became fully immune to non-reformed views of the covenant but had not love, I would be a sounding gong and a clanging cymbal.

Our generation, which writes and quarrels about the covenant in a loveless way and is equally loveless and unpriestlike in denying asylum to those who have wandered away from the church, will be told that it has broken the covenant like Adam. Yet those very same people thought everything was in order with the covenant, down to the last detail. People can certainly make mistakes. Such mistakes are even less excusable when we have clear historical examples before our eyes.

They have broken the covenant like Adam, we are told. Let's take a closer look at this sudden reference to Adam, which seems somewhat strange in this context.

We might prefer another translation, which is equally justifiable from a purely linguistic standpoint. We need not take *Adam* as a name, for in Hebrew it is also used as a noun to mean man as such. In Genesis 1:27, we read that God created *Adam* in his own image, but this is usually translated as: "God created *man* in His own image." This translation is justified. Thus, our text from Hosea could also be translated as follows: "*Like a man*, they have broken the covenant."[12]

If the latter reading is correct, the reproach becomes even sharper. Hosea would then be saying that Israel acted in an all too human way with regard to the covenant. (We would say a purely worldly way.) Becoming unfaithful and violating agreements is the sort of thing we expect of the natural man–who does still set a fine example of faithfulness from time to time–but it's hardly what we would expect of the people of God, who are fully equipped for every good work.

That a heathen nation like Tyre forgets about the *covenant of brotherhood* as Amos charged (Amos 1:9), is a serious matter, for this represents a tearing of the bonds of *common grace*. What, then, are we to say about the nation that forgets all about *redemptive grace* and the *covenant with God?* Just as people no longer regard the marriage bond as sacred, Israel's marriage bond with God was no longer holy. Just as some nations rip up treaties as though they were mere scraps of paper, Israel broke its sacred agreement with the Lord.

---

12. In the King James Version, we read: but they like men have transgressed the covenant."

Thus, the nation of redemptive grace has sunk to the level of the nations of common grace. It has conformed to the world! It has transgressed the covenant just like anyone else. In fact, the natural man often lives a better life than these people of the covenant. Perhaps this talk of conforming to the world is even flattering. It's certainly the most somber complaint and the most serious accusation Hosea could make: the new man acts just like any other man.

In the land of Israel of our time, we often assure each other that we are and remain human beings. This is a godless way of speaking, for it serves to cover up a multitude of sins. Like most commonly used sayings, it contains an element of truth, but when it is stated in general terms, it is a lie.

The truth is that our "old nature" remains active within us until our death, and that even the holiest people achieve only a beginning of true obedience as long as they are still on earth. But it is a lie to say that the believer always remains a mere "human being" and never rises above the level of ordinary human existence. On the contrary, he becomes a *new man*, and the old nature passes away.

First, he was a sinner, and then the process of sanctification began. Only God knows him by his new name as someone who has been sanctified. In the scriptures, God speaks of him as such. He acts not like Adam but like the second Adam. Christ takes shape in him and lives within him.

The first Adam may still be present within us and seek to pull us in a sinful direction, but it is the second Adam who gives direction to our lives. The wicked desires of the flesh no longer rule over us, as the Heidelberg Catechism points out; they are nothing more than rebels that rise up in defiance now and then.

Thus, the believer does not remain a sinful human being. On the contrary, he becomes a *different* person, one who thinks, feels, acts, and speaks differently. In short, he conforms to Christ in all that he says, feels, and thinks. If he does not conform to Christ, he conforms to the world, breaking the covenant like a man!

It may be that there are some who still do not know what conforming to the world means. We usually look for such conformity in all sorts of external things, things we can see. Pin-up girls, sensual movies, and so forth are what most of us think of when we talk about conforming to the world. But the whole matter is much more serious than that.

Our conformity to the world goes much deeper than many people think–especially those who speak out most vociferously against the degeneration in our time. Remember that Christ judges the heart. Anyone who thinks like other people, has the attitudes of other people, and speaks like other people instead of thinking and speaking as a renewed, born-again Christian, has conformed to the world.

This conformity to the world is evident when our conversation does not rise above the level of the world's conversation—even if it remains completely polite and touches only on the weather, the neighbors, and politics. It is present when we evaluate events in society by the world standard (i.e., self-interest), even if we preserve our own honor scrupulously and strictly. It is present in our worries about what we will eat and drink, for those are exactly the concerns of the heathens. It is present in the worldly question of who will be the greatest among us, which is a question we like to ask.

This conformity to the world is manifest everywhere in the lives of our families and churches as well as in disputes and in meetings and in what goes on in the depths of our hearts. Wherever and whenever *nature* comes to the fore rather than the *spirit*, whenever we act as mere human beings and not as new creatures, the flag of conformity to the world flies higher on our flagpole than the flag of the covenant, with its attitudes and way of acting and speaking.

In what way they do and fail to do, they're still like mere human beings. That's the grave reproach Hosea directs at Israel and at us. It makes him angry and anxious at the same time. That's the tragedy of a covenant people.

At the same time, it's an incomprehensible riddle! We can't get over it that there are still people who can act like animals. But Hosea declares that there's something even worse, namely, that people with new natures act like people with old natures.

A psalmist once prayed to God as follows: "Let the nations know that they are but men!" (Ps. 9:20). We can well understand this sentiment, and we can join him in this prayer. Yes, Lord, let those heathens know that they are mere human beings who also have a soul. Don't we claim to be greatly concerned about the heathens?

But what if this prayer continues and becomes more personal? What if we pray to the Lord to let the Christians know that they are new creatures? Could we join in the prayer then? That's just the prayer we need to pray–because of our conformity to the world!

O Son of God, mold me until I conform to your image. O Second Adam, dwell in me so that I may be sanctified, so that I, as a party to the covenant, will no longer transgress the covenant like a mere human being. I want to be a child of God instead.

# 28

# The Sleeping Baker

*Their sleepeth all night (7:6 KJV)*

ONLY TWICE IN THE BIBLE do we read about bakers. The first time is in Genesis. Everyone knows the story of the chief baker who was hanged (Gen. 40). It may be that this baker was punished so severely because he was involved in a plot against Pharaoh's life. The second place in the Bible is this passage from Hosea.

Hosea's baker is only imaginary; that is to say, the prophet borrows an image from the baking business to make it clear what the evildoers in his day were doing up in Samaria. These evildoers are murderers who hatch a plot against their king and kill him. Was Hosea, perhaps, thinking of the unfortunate baker in Egypt when he compared the activities of the conspirators in Ephraim to what the baker does with the oven and the bread? It's very well possible.

In any event, it's important to remember that we're talking about an imaginary baker here. Hosea does not mean to make any adverse comments about the bakers of Israel. He is talking instead about those who broke the sixth commandment, that is, conspirators and murderers. There have been such people in all eras of history, and they're still around today, in many different forms–they kill without guns.

Some break the sixth commandment by *actually* injuring and killing people, while others break it through *hatred*. Both are guilty of the same sin, for whoever hates his brother is a murderer. Whether we kill others by piercing daggers or by piercing words and gestures, it is all the same from the scriptural point of view, for God regards all these things as murder. Thus, whether you're a preacher or a baker, a shoemaker or a truck driver, the important thing is to be on guard against such vile behavior as that of the baker in the example given by Hosea.

What about the baker anyway?

A few words are needed to clarify the reference to the baker, for the first seven verses of Hosea 7 are very obscure, as any reader can see. Even the most clever exegetes don't get much further than guessing about the real meaning. I don't propose to go into the details and offer guesses of my own. Instead, I will focus on the main point.

It seems more than likely to me that in this section, Hosea is describing the horrible practices of those who are guilty of murdering kings, for at the end of the section he declares: "They devour their rulers. All their kings have fallen" (7:7). We must bear in mind that much royal blood flowed after the rule of Jeroboam II, as king after king was toppled. Within a period of about 20 years, there were no fewer than six different kings on Israel's throne. The crown passed from one king to the next not for the usual reasons, but because of violence: each king was murdered by his successor, who was murdered in turn by yet another band of men bent on seizing power. Kings like Zachariah and Shallum did not rule long (half a year and a month respectively). That's how things went in those days.

Hosea now gives us a peek behind the scenes. He shows us how those plotters and assassins went about their work.

> By their wickedness they make the king glad,
> and the princes by their treachery (7:3).

One might suppose that what Hosea means is that the king won the throne in the first place through the deceit and wickedness of those henchmen, and that is why their wickedness makes him "glad." But what we read two verses later suggests another interpretation:

> They addle the king and leaders with wine and fumes
> as he mixes with these scoundrels (7:5 JB).

The occasion referred to here is probably a feast day, perhaps in honor of the king's birthday. The plotters seize on such a day as their opportunity.

"By their wickedness they make the king glad." In other words, they ply him with wine until he's in a good mood. They let him drink till he's drunk. The king, who knows nothing of their evil intentions, "mixes with these scoundrels." In an unsuspecting, friendly way, he spends time with the traitors who are plotting against him. These hypocrites each carry a concealed dagger, and soon the drunken king lies dead on the floor, a victim of their assassination plot.

These plotters know how to bide their time. They don't plunge ahead recklessly. No, they wait for the most suitable opportunity to make their move. Everything is pre-arranged. First, they wait for the day of the great festival. Then they wait for the king and his lords to succumb to the influence of wine. They take every precaution against the unexpected, against anything that might spoil their plans. Wait patiently! Bide your time!

But what about the baker? If someone were to ask how Hosea can compare those sly murderers to a solitary baker, he would get a simple answer: the similarity between them is their willingness to wait. Just like the baker, the plotters wait for the right time to carry out their plans. Only when the feast has ended, and the sun is about to come up do they make their move.

The baker cannot proceed with his work immediately. A baker in a hurry, a baker who doesn't have the patience to wait until the dough he has kneaded has risen, won't get anywhere. His bread won't turn out right. Therefore, the baker must wait. He does start a fire in his oven right away, but then he waits for the yeast to do its work in the dough. He sleeps while this is going on. His oven is also at rest–it smolders.

We must not make the mistake of thinking that while the oven and its baker are at rest, the process of making bread has stopped for a while. On the contrary, in the morning, the dough is ready, and the oven only needs a little more fuel to make it "blaze like a flaming fire" (7:6). Thus, waiting is an important part of making bread.

That's also how it is with the hatred of those plotters who enjoy murder. In a rapid series of metaphors, their hatred is compared first to the heat of the baker's oven (7:4, 6, 7) and then to the baker himself. But one thing is certain: just as the smoldering fire does not go out, and just as the sleeping baker is still involved in the process of baking and making sure to wake up at the right time, the hatred and enmity of the assassins do not die or disappear.

Don't draw any wrong conclusions from the calm way of waiting or their friendliness at the banquet table. Don't make the mistake of supposing that they've laid aside their enmity.

Their wrath is *smoldering*. Soon it will burst into flame again. They've only waited for the proper time. Their prey will not be allowed to escape!

If we read our passage from Hosea in this way, we can regard the gruesome machinations of these murderers as a prelude to the cross. Just as Israel *always* killed the prophets and slaughtered its kings, it didn't spare its highest Prophet and greatest King: "Shall I crucify your king?" asked Pilate (John 19:15). That's the necessary and inevitable outcome of this history. Who is to say whether Jesus himself may not have made the hearts of those two men on the way to Emmaus burn by explaining to them through an exegesis of Hosea 7 that those things had to happen as they did?

Like Isaiah 53, Hosea 7 includes traces of the blood of the cross–but not as clearly. Those kings of Israel could hardly be regarded as prefigurations of the Messiah king, but their murderers are definite prefigurations of the murderers responsible for the death of Jesus.

Didn't they nurse a hatred and enmity of Jesus in their hearts from the very outset? But they also knew how to bide their time. Their wrath slept, but it did not die, just as Hosea's baker slept as he waited. Continually they discussed how to get rid of Him, but they had to wait. "Let's wait until the great feast on the King's birthday," said the conspirators in Hosea. "Not at the time of the feast," said the murderers of the great

Hosea-Jesus. Yet it did happen after the time of the feast, for that was His hour. Then, "on the day of our king" (7:5), they laid their trap and made their cunning approach to Jesus.

The traitor, the one with whom Jesus shared His bread, is also present here in the form of the man with the mask. Judas betrayed the Son of Man with a kiss. The hatred that had smoldered for so long flared up and became a blazing fire as all cried together, "Crucify him! Crucify him!" It was the fire of this hatred that consumed Jesus–or rather, it made him the bread of life.

How do we benefit from Christ's sacrifice and death on the cross? Through Christ's death, our old selves are crucified, put to death, and buried with him, so that the evil desires of the flesh may no longer rule us" (Heidelberg Catechism, answer 43). That's how it goes with those who eat the bread of life and drink Christ's blood.

But as long as we remain mere observers at the cross and refuse to be crucified with Christ, our old nature will remain intact, and we will be *dominated* by the wicked desires of the flesh. We don't get around to laying aside our lust for revenge, and we let the sun go down on our anger. After sunset, we calmly go to sleep. We sleep all night long, and our hatred, anger, and desire for revenge sleep with us–but they do not die–not at all! The poisonous roots of murder, which destroy our own lives and the lives of others, are not destroyed–not at all! The baker sleeps all night, but in the morning, he wakes up. The jealousy becomes a flaming fire, and when the hour of wrath finally arrives, we see that we get our revenge.

Watch out for those sleeping bakers. If they have a score to settle with you, they'll get you sooner or later. Watch out for smoldering envy and wrath. Watch out for the lust for revenge. It smolders, but it refuses to die. It stays hot like a baker's oven, and its fire never goes out.

In church, we rejoice that the fire of God's wrath goes out, but the fire of *our* wrath is never extinguished–that would be asking too much! Then, we would have to deny ourselves in the least. Who wants to do that?

There's a world of unrighteousness in those sleeping, uncombated sins. Over here, I see someone with silent resentment smoldering within him. Beside him is someone harboring jealousy that never quite fades away. Over there is someone who's waiting for just the right moment to tell his neighbor off–in the hope of washing his ears instead of his feet. Every now and then, we hear an explosion as the fire of a quarrel suddenly flares up, only to go back to sleep a little later.

And if there's still a conscience awake here and there, if someone sees that these things aren't right and can't continue, there's always someone else to sing the old lullaby to the effect that things weren't any better in the old days when our fathers acted in the same way. If that doesn't work, you can always rely on the usual sleeping pill: just tell yourself that you "really don't have anything against him."

Then the baker will sleep again; he'll sleep all night; the baker and the chief baker are both asleep! They also have a dream. They dream about belonging to Jesus Christ while continuing to live under the dominion of the "wicked desires of the flesh." They dream about murdering their fellow kings, priests, and prophets (even if only through thoughts or gestures) while escaping the punishment they deserve.

But when the chief baker wakes up, he learns that he has been sentenced to death and is to hang on the king's day, that is, his birthday (Gen. 40:20–22). As on the day of the Great King, the eternal sentence of death will be pronounced on those who were not crucified with Him, who did not die with Him and were not buried with Him. Anyone who doesn't die before he dies will die, surely, when he dies.

Therefore, wake up sleepers! Don't let your anger sleep any longer!

I know, Lord, that I am very weak, and that my wicked desires are very strong. They will continue to seethe within me until the day of my death. Therefore, give me the assurance that when I fall asleep, it will not be a false rest. Don't let wickedness *dominate* my life but govern me through Your Spirit and Word. Through my faith in Christ, give me the strength to make my old nature die and be crucified with You.

# 29

# One-Sidedness

*Ephraim has become a cake half-baked (7:8 NEB)*

IT SHOULD NOT ESCAPE our attention that the prophet often uses the name *Ephraim* to refer to the nation of Israel. This is because Beeri's son is a prophet of *love*. He likes taking the name *Ephraim* on his lips, for it is an expression of God's fondness.

Jacob, driven by the Spirit of Christ, had already given Ephraim a greater blessing than Manasseh. Although Ephraim was younger, he was to be greater than Manasseh. That's just how it went in subsequent history: Ephraim was already a leader among the tribes of Israel. Therefore, *Ephraim* is a privileged name. In Jeremiah we read:

> Is Ephraim still my dear son,
> a child in whom I delight?
> As often as I turn my back on him
> I still remember him;
> and so my heart yearns for him,
> I am filled with tenderness toward him (Jer. 31:20 NEB).

What Ephraim did with that favored position we already saw from the somber history of the kings who murdered each other to win the throne. They returned God's love with a hatred Hosea compared to the fire of a baker's oven. That burning hatred consumed king after king.

Continuing to use the image of the fire, the prophet now compared Ephraim to a cake, a cake that the baker forgot to turn over: "Ephraim is a cake not turned" (7:8). That's indeed a sorry business, for we all know what happens to a cake if it isn't turned over. It's burned on one side and not done on the other. Thus, Hosea could just as well have said: "Ephraim is a cake that flopped."

Ephraim is good for nothing. We think, at once, of the words of the Savior: "if salt has lost its taste, how shall its saltiness be restored? It is fit neither for the land nor the dunghill; men throw it away" (Luke 14:34).

What Hosea is getting at through this metaphor can easily be made clear from the context. In the very same verse, we read the explanation: "Ephraim mixes with the nations" (7:8 JB).

Now, before we draw too many conclusions, we should remind ourselves that Israel was indeed located in the midst of many nations and had a calling with respect to those nations. God had placed this nation among the heathen nations so that it would be a "dew from the Lord" in their midst, as another prophet put it (Mic. 5:7). That was the one side.

On the other hand, the chosen people were called by the Lord to abide strictly and scrupulously by his commandments. Contact with other nations was not supposed to lead Israel to give up its unique, special position as the people of God. That was the other side. Thus, there was a task for Ephraim on both sides, and neither one was to be neglected in favor of the other. Both the earthly calling with regard to other peoples and the heavenly calling with regard to God would be carried out faithfully.

But now comes the catastrophe; "Ephraim is a cake not turned." It was burnt and dried out on one side, and cold and not done on the other.

It shouldn't take you too long to figure out on what side Ephraim was burnt. It's far from easy to get burnt on the heavenly side. The calling to seek the things that are above does not catch fire so easily. Normally, we wouldn't even consider the danger of getting too well done or being burnt on that side.

What Hosea tells us is that Ephraim mixes with the *nations*. Ephraim remained cold and half-baked on the side facing God, but on the other side facing the nations (i.e., the world) he got very hot. That's what Ephraim liked. He enjoyed joining in the activities of the other nations. Custom after custom was taken over from the heathens. Even their gods were embraced with rejoicing.

The most horrible practices in immoral forms of worship were given a warm reception by the chosen people in the promised land. Thus, God's exquisite cake was burnt and ruined. "Ephraim has become a cake half-baked" – that sealed his doom. He would have to be thrown out.

The awful thing was that no one realized this. The words of the prophet that follow immediately must be taken literally:

> Aliens devour his strength,
> and he knows it not;
> Gray hairs are sprinkled upon him,
> And he knows it not (7:9).

The background to the statement is that the nation's leaders, the politicians by profession, tried to make treaties with Assyria and Egypt. They regarded this as an eminently sensible policy, but the result was that Israel wound up in an even more dependent position. Very heavy payments were made to foreign powers, which undermined the nation's existence.

This made Ephraim look like an old man who had already lived out his life, an old man stumbling toward the grave. That's what Hosea meant by the "Gray hairs sprinkled upon him." Thus, Israel's end was getting closer and closer.

But what else could we expect if the baker forgot to turn the cake over? What is such a cake good for? Nothing!

A person whom God has tried in vain to change, who refuses to repent and doesn't want to be converted, is like a cake that flopped–a failure. We could say of such a person that he played with fire–sin is certainly a fire–and wasn't aware that the fire, whose heat warmed him nicely, would slowly, but surely scorch him and destroy him.

There are so many people who have succumbed to their own sins, people who have been burned to a crisp by the fire of their own passions. It's far from certain that someone who's on fire will be rescued at the last moment. Even if he is, he will carry scars from the fire around for the rest of his life.

Paul is a good example of this. After his conversion, he could never forget that he had persecuted the Church of the Lord and that he had let the fire of his hatred of Jesus the Nazarene scorch him. It always remained a dark blemish in his life.

The sin of one-sidedness, which Hosea sketched for us here, has always claimed its victims in the church as a whole. Many have fallen prey to it. Most of the time, this sin was not recognized as a sin and was not confessed. Instead, it was seen as something completely natural: everyone is one-sided and tends to go to extremes. Yet there are great dangers in this attitude, as the example of Ephraim demonstrates.

Who is to say how much the church in our era has already "mixed with the nations" and has been burnt and disfigured on the side facing the world? This may very well have happened without anyone noticing it. The sin of conformity to the world advances by peaceful infiltration. One concession after another is made to the world–for the most beautiful of reasons. The process of scorching has probably advanced further than even the greatest pessimist realizes. Not even our holiest institutions are safe! Is today's Ephraim a useless, half-baked cake?

The dangers don't come only from the world side. This sin moves in all sorts of areas and insinuates itself everywhere. Everyone knows that God has created man with both *intellect* and *feeling*, and that there is a place for both in the church and in worship. But sinful, one-sided man now comes along and sets one of them aside.

For some people, *feeling* is dominant. They don't want to hear anything about the place of intellect in the life of faith, for intellect represents the letter, which kills. Doctrine is something that we should get rid of as quickly as possible.

If the church follows this path, its ship is in danger of capsizing in the deep waters of mysticism or running aground on the dangerous reefs. Experience then becomes the determining factor. Ephraim burns on the side of mysticism, like a cake that the baker forgot to turn over.

But we must be careful not to close our eyes to the opposite form of one-sidedness, namely, the great danger of intellectualism. Those who choose this path leave room only for the *intellect*.

This form of one-sidedness is often presented as the truly Reformed outlook. That's a shameful mistake, for it overlooks the fact that the Reformed symbols and statements of doctrine contain an element of genuine mysticism. Making this mistake is like becoming "more Catholic than the Pope."

According to the Heidelberg Catechism, I can *feel* or *experience* the beginning of eternal joy in my heart (Answer 58). That's something for intellectualists to think about. They turn God's mysteries into puzzles that we must solve. The church of the Lord becomes as chilly as the inside of a freezer. For them, too, Ephraim is a cake that has not been turned over– he's useless. Even if I *knew* all the secrets and mysteries but had not love, I would be nothing.

This sin of one-sidedness takes on its ugliest form in relation to the grace of our Lord Jesus Christ. We are saved by grace alone—not by works or by keeping the law. But even though the Scriptures proclaim that good works will not save us, we must remember that faith without works is *dead*.

Anyone who thinks he doesn't need Christ since he'll save himself through his good works is in for an unpleasant surprise. An equally unpleasant surprise awaits those who labor under the illusion that the process of sanctification can take place in their lives without good works, and that they can calmly continue to live as trees that bear no fruit.

The barren fig tree is cut down and cast into the fire. The cake that has not been turned over will also be thrown away—it has no taste! Let's think carefully about the necessity of conversion.

# 30

# Unheard Prayer

*I wanted to redeem them, but they tell lies
about me (7:13 JB)*

Hosea 7 is a chapter full of comparisons. To what shall I compare this generation? The prophet has no difficulty finding an answer. He takes one example after another from daily life to expose and illustrate the stupidity of his contemporaries. The Israelites do not survive Hosea's attack unscathed, for he tells the unvarnished truth.

We have already discussed the sleeping baker and the half-baked bread. Now follow a pair of comparisons drawn from military life and the animal world respectively.

In the last verse of this chapter, Ephraim is compared to a "treacherous bow." What Hosea means is a bow that bends too easily. Whenever the bowman uses it to shoot an arrow, he misses the target. This is not his fault, nor is it the fault of the arrow. The problem is the bow, which is simply too slack.

God is like the bowman in that He is disappointed in His people again and again. He thought He would be able to accomplish a great deal with Israel and make good use of him in the "holy war," but His plans come to naught. Israel turned out to be useless. What can be done with a useless instrument? We throw it away. Thus, we read:

> Their leaders will fall by the sword
> because of their arrogant talk,
> and how they will be laughed at in the land of
> Egypt (7:16 JB).

No doubt the leaders of whom Hosea speaks are Israel's politicians, who made a treaty with Egypt to defend Israel against Assyria. The Egyptians laugh boldly and scornfully about the fate of those leaders of Israel, but they laugh too soon.

Hosea's other example comes from the animal world:

> Ephraim is like a dove,
> silly and without sense (7:11).

Israel believed he was very sensible indeed. The two great powers of that time were Egypt (to the south) and Assyria (to the north). Both cast longing glances at Palestine. Israel thought that the sensible thing to do would be to remain friendly with both, and therefore he fluttered from the one to the other like a senseless pigeon. But any political move that doesn't take the Lord into account is foolish, however sensible our calculations might appear to be.

Ephraim's foolish wisdom or wise foolishness was that he trusted in man rather than God. Israel's politicians regarded themselves as clever operators, believing that they combined the cunning of the snake with the innocence of the dove. But Hosea informs them that this innocence is really stupidity, for their approach is bound to lead to trouble.

Things were bound to go wrong, for the Lord is a jealous God who will not watch indifferently when Israel begs the great military powers for help instead of turning to Him. This flying dove will fly right into trouble: "Wherever they turn, I will cast my net over them" (7:12 NEB).

One might conclude that Ephraim no longer needs to pray, for putting one's faith in the great powers is incompatible with seeking shelter in the power of the Lord. Praying a genuine prayer means not fixing your hopes on creatures but pinning them on God alone. The difference is absolute.

One may have ambassadors or representatives at the courts of various earthly rulers and maintain diplomatic relations with a number of countries, but it is not possible to dwell both in Egypt's courts and in God's courts. We must choose one or the other. Fixing our hopes on people is incompatible with fixing our hopes on God. Our eyes cannot be fixed on the heavens above and the earth beneath at the same time.

Anyone who goes on praying when his mind is occupied with earthly factors is putting an "as if" at the beginning of each prayer. Such a prayer is not worthy of the name, for prayer is an absolute, unconditional surrender to God. When we pray, we *close* our eyes. This is more than a mere custom, for one of the things it symbolizes is that the person praying no longer sees anything or anyone around him. His attention is fixed on the unseen world as he surrenders himself in blind faith to the Lord.

Now, Ephraim would be quick to tell you that he had *not* stopped praying, but we must ask ourselves what this praying really amounted to. It was mere form without content, appearance without substance. Ephraim's prayer was a *lie!*

This is the meaning of Hosea's blunt judgment; in the name of the Lord, he reproaches Ephraim for *lying* about God. The Israelites recite prayers and say all the right things, but their words come from their mouths and not from their hearts. Their hearts are in the palaces of Egypt and Assyria; they are not bowed down before God's throne in His great palace. This purely formal religion of falsehood is condemned in even sharper terms as Hosea comments on these prayers:

> They do not cry for me from the heart,
> but they wail upon their beds (7:14).

That's what God is angry about. It's one thing to act like a silly and senseless dove – that's foolishness. But it's quite another to pray without offering yourself, without surrendering your heart – that's godlessness.

Prayer must always involve the heart, the very center of our being. The first condition for prayer pleasing to God, prayer that will be heard and answered, is that we call upon Him with our hearts rather than just our lips! God loves truth – not lies. A prayer that dribbles out of our mouths but does not issue from our hearts is a useless waste of time. Without the heart, prayer has no substance; it is a pathetic, impotent, dead lie!

If Israel had abolished prayer completely, he would, at least, have been consistent and honest. Those who do not pray at all are not guilty of the hypocrisy engaged in by those who pray with their lips alone. All that "wailing upon their beds" makes things worse instead of better. The Israelites were taking the name of the Lord in vain, and their praying was really cursing.

There is no greater sin, no sin that makes God more angry, than calling upon Him with our lips while our hearts are far from Him. That sin dishonors His name and is punishable by death.

Because I know that every prayer that does not proceed from the heart dishonors God's name and rings in God's ears like a curse, I would not dare answer the question of whether there's more swearing going on in an army barracks than in the church. Suffice it to say that there is a great deal of swearing in the church.

In our supposed holy places, we are really cursing piously. Unfortunately, Hosea's complaint about "wailing upon their beds" and telling lies about God is all too relevant in our time. In front of me in the church is someone who thought long and hard before deciding to come to church this morning. In a way, he would have liked to stay home, but he figured it would be just as boring as going to church. Thus, he decided to come. And now he joins the rest of the congregation in singing that he's gripped by a strong desire to enter the Lord's house. He's telling a lie!

Over there sits someone with a heart full of venom. Listen to his prayer: "forgive us our debts, as we have forgiven our debtors." That's a lie! I also see a butcher who worked like fury all week long to earn a living and even complained to the elders of the church who called on him that he would simply have to close up shop if his fellow church members did not buy meat from him. Listen to his prayer: "Give us this day our daily bread." That prayer means that we are not to trust in creatures but in God alone. He's telling a lie too!

There are so many useless, ill-considered, purely formal prayers pervaded by lies and deceit. We sing so many psalms and hymns in church without ever stopping to think just what prayers they contain. There are so many places of prayer that are offensive to the Lord. He tells us: "Spare me the sound of your songs" (Amos 5:23 NEB). He simply won't listen to them.

The most obvious conclusion to draw is that we shouldn't pray at all, but that's the logic of hell. Satan certainly knows how to talk pious language. He says to you: "The most important thing is not to be a hypocrite. If you must choose between a religion of custom and no religion at all, choose the latter. Stop going to church and stop praying if you don't strongly favor these activities in your heart." The murderer from the beginning suggests this because he would like nothing better than to completely cut off prayer, which is "the breath of the soul." But this advice from hell is false.

Heaven's advice is not to dispense with prayer but to change your way of praying. Don't pray only with your lips; make your prayers come right from your heart. Actually, that is more than advice: we are *commanded* to pray this way. It is a command which the Lord God gives to Israel: "call upon me in the day of trouble; I will deliver you" (Ps 50:15).

"I will deliver you," says God. Thus, He will hear our prayers. The Lord is always ready to redeem us and help us, but we make it impossible for Him, for we do not pray. (Those "pious" mutterings of ours are not worthy of the name *prayer*).

Our prayers will not be heard, Hosea explains, for the simple reason that they are not real prayers. There's nothing for God to hear. As soon as *one* true prayer for help and deliverance penetrates to heaven, we'll see that the Lord is quick to come to our aid.

This is part of the answer to the riddle of "unheard prayers." *We* sometimes complain that God doesn't hear our prayers, but *God* complains that there are no prayers to be heard. We're still sinful enough to try to pin the blame on God, but the Lord rightly points the finger at us. The fault lies not with the one who hears prayers, but with those who send them up. The change needed is not that God must learn to be a better listener. The change must be in us: we must learn to pray. God won't hear and answer us until we learn to pray properly. He'll wait until we finally learn to pray from the *heart*.

What's wrong with our prayers as a rule is not that they're not solemn enough–for we're nothing if not solemn–or that they're not numerous enough–for we take pride in praying often–but that they're not deep enough, that they don't come from the heart. A prayer that ascends to the heights must come from the depths. Such a prayer is not like a soap bubble that bursts after a brief moment; it goes straight to heaven and reaches the ears of the Lord of hosts.

Therefore, let's all repent and change our way of praying.

# 31

## Sensible Asses

*...a wild ass wandering alone; Ephraim has hired lovers (8:9).*

MAN MAY BE WISE, but there are still a few things he can learn from dumb animals. The lessons he learns from animals usually put him to shame. Solomon advises the sluggard to consider the ant, for the ant can teach him a thing or two. Isaiah points out:

> the ox knows its owner,
> and the ass its master's crib;
> but Israel does not know,
> my people do not understand (Is. 1:3).

Jesus also taught the doubtful disciples a lesson by pointing to the animal world: "Look at the birds of the air; they do not sow and reap and store in barns, yet your heavenly Father feeds them" (Matt. 6:26 NEB). In the same way, Hosea tells his contemporaries that they could learn a lesson or two from the ass!

Now, the ass does not enjoy a reputation for high intelligence. That's why a person lacking in intelligence is often called a "stupid ass" by someone who fails to control his tongue. But the prophet turns things around. He seems to think that if asses could talk–remember Balaam's ass–they might well say to each other in moments of anger: "You stupid man!"

Whatever other people may say about asses, Hosea knows that, in one respect, their behavior is certainly to be preferred to that of man. Thus, Ephraim could well learn a lesson from the asses. When we compare man and asses, the asses come out on top, Hosea tells us. The wild ass keeps to himself, while Ephraim tries to buy love.

This comparison between Israel and those sensible asses, a comparison in which Israel comes off so poorly, needs some further explanation. We see this as soon as we look up this text in different translations of the Bible. Some translations assume that when Hosea refers to a wild ass, he means to equate *Assyria* with a wild ass. Other translations make *Israel* a wild ass for running to Assyria.

The question is how three short sentences are related. In the Revised Standard Version, we read:

For they have gone up to Assyria,
a wild ass wandering alone;
Ephraim has hired lovers.

It seems to me that we should read the second line as an independent sentence. Hosea is telling us that the wild ass wanders alone – but Ephraim hires lovers.

The point Hosea wishes to make in connection with these wild asses is that they live by themselves on lonely plains. They do not seek *each other* out, but they avoid man. They are deathly afraid that man will rob them of their freedom, feeling instinctively that man is their enemy. Thus, it is their love of freedom and their fear of men that make them so sensible and keep them away from man. The wild ass keeps to himself.

What about those 'wise' leaders of Israel, those cunning politicians? With all their cunning, Hosea points out, they are not as sensible as wild asses who act out of instinct. These leaders choose to break out of the isolation that gives them safety: "They have gone up to Assyria." They are not afraid. They dare to venture into the presence of those who are plotting against them, who plan to rob them of their freedom! They're running into death's arms!

But that's not what these wily characters meant to do. They thought they could make a treaty with Assyria, and therefore they came to the Assyrian court bearing all sorts of gifts, hoping to win the friendship of the Assyrians, hoping to buy their love. Ephraim had an adulterous friendship in mind, but he did not understand that he would be crushed in the powerful arms of his Assyrian lover. That so-called "treaty" with Assyria was to lead to a complete annexation. Ephraim would be incorporated into Assyria, and his independent existence would come to an end.

Cunning Ephraim runs right into the arms of his mortal enemy. That's what happens when man considers himself wiser than God—when, in fact, he's not even as wise as an ass.

God had declared that Israel's isolation was its strength, and that Ephraim was to keep himself, just like the wild ass. Ephraim's reply was: "Only an ass would live like asses live." In other words, who would be so foolish as to pass up the chance to make friends with mighty Assyria? Therefore, Ephraim broke the chains of his isolation—and was bound. He wanted to become strong and free—but he became a slave. He looked to Assyria for friendship—and met an enemy.

We all know the old story of the Garden of Eden. Man sought friendship with satan—and found out that satan was a murderer from the beginning. He attempted to leap toward the heavens in order to be like God—and fell flat on his face.

If only Ephraim had been as sensible as an ass! Sin had made us not only wicked but also stupid. Ephraim was not the first one guilty of such stupidity, nor will he be the last. We can calmly say that the great sin—or great stupidity—of the church today is that it is not *afraid* anymore.

There is, of course, unjustified fear without a proper basis. When the believer is afraid that he won't be saved after all, or when he worries about all sorts of details in his life here on earth, his anxiety represents a lack of faith in God's promises. Then, there is reason to ask: "Why are you so afraid? Have you so little faith?"

But there is also a justified fear that we should not try to eliminate. Just as the wild ass is afraid of man and, therefore, stays away from human habitations, the Christian must live in deathly fear of his mortal enemies who seek his life every day, namely, the world, satan, and the sin in our own heart.

Why would God urge us so strongly to stay away from them if they were not capable of harming us anymore? The struggle against sin is no puppet show. Those who underestimate their deadly enemies or don't take them seriously will find themselves in deep trouble.

The struggle is a matter of life and death. There is no room for overconfidence. Fleeing is an indication not of cowardice but of courage. In this case, fear is not weakness but strength. Blessed is the man whose fear does not vanish and who knows what it means to work out his salvation with *fear* and trembling. This deadly fear can be read on the face of the person who prays: "Lead us not into temptation, but deliver us from evil."

It's not a question of underestimating our own strength when we ask God for help in resisting evil and staying away from it. We must realize and confess that we ourselves are weak and do not possess the power to resist, and also that our deadly enemy (i.e., the world, the devil, and our own flesh) never leave us in peace. Therefore, we must seek strength in the power of the Holy Spirit, so that we will not succumb in this spiritual struggle.

For many people, such fear represents a standpoint and attitude which they left behind long ago. "*We* are not afraid! We don't fear *the world!* That talk about strength in isolation is hopelessly old-fashioned. That's no way to live in the twentieth century. Therefore, we'll allow ourselves a few excursions into the world's territory, a few exploratory journeys. After all, what could be wrong with that?"

Most of the inhabitants of the Kingdom of God are to be found in the broader areas, where there's ample opportunity for smuggling. It is no longer widely believed that the world is a sinking ship that we must flee if we wish to save our lives. The result of our friendship with the world will be the same as the result of Ephraim's friendship with Assyria–annexation!

There are more Christians who have already been co-opted into the world than you might suspect. We abstain from certain worldly forms of entertainment, but for the rest, the way of life of many church people is indistinguishable from that of their unbelieving neighbors, as we already saw when we discussed conformity to the world (Chapter 27).

Our good friend, the "world," is busy crushing the "life of faith," and in this, he unmasks himself as our mortal enemy. Our failure to see this gives Hosea reason to make the somber remark that there are indeed animals more sensible than people–for example, asses. Asses know enough not to stray too far from their own territory.

We are not afraid of the *devil* either. In theory, we all profess to believe in the existence of devils, but in practice, we seem to regard them as legendary figures. We take them into account so little that we let them dance their joyful dance undisturbed, all around us, as we attend meetings, call on our friends and relatives, and participate in the life of the church. The Heidelberg Catechism points out that gossip, slander, and condemning someone without hearing his side of the story are all *works of the devil*, but it doesn't look as though the devils who occupy key positions on our tongues, in our ears, and in the pews beside us are being engaged in a bitter, life-and-death struggle.

We all know the famous story of Martin Luther throwing an inkwell at the devil. Some scholars dismissed the story as a legend, which it may well be, but it certainly wouldn't be a bad idea to throw a few inkwells at the devil today, for much of the devil's work is done with pen and ink.

In other words, learned authors also have something to learn from wild asses. The wild asses stay away from men, but there are seemingly wise people who do not stay away from devils. If only they could have a word with those wild asses and learn something about sensible fear!

We are not afraid of *ourselves* either. A reformed Christian should know that he must fear his own sinful nature above all, for that sinful nature is even more dangerous than the world and the devil put together. Our sinful nature is a traitor *within* the fortress. We're our own worst enemies, but we don't realize it. And we're not asses either.

If you read our Christian magazines and weeklies carefully, you'll get the unmistakable impression that the Christian segment of our population is far superior to the rest. You may not read those exact words, but that's what it boils down to.

How could we ever be so foolish? Can't we see how much we fall short of the ideal of Christian living? Is the confession that we're all "miserable sinners" nothing more than a pious phrase? The more we get to know ourselves, the more we turn away from our sinful natures in disgust and become afraid of ourselves. This also makes us willing to put the old nature to death. But as long as we remain infatuated with ourselves, we will still have a great deal to learn from those sensible asses!

Hosea tells us that the wild asses keep to themselves. But what is Ephraim up to? Ephraim tries to buy love. That's the striking difference between man and beast, as Hosea sees it. Here again, the puzzling language of the Bible contains a timely lesson for us.

# 32

# Sowing and Reaping

*For they sow the wind,*
*and they shall reap the whirlwind (8:7).*

A SUITABLE HEADING for the eighth chapter of Hosea would be: "Those who refuse to listen will learn the hard way." The prophet comes back to this point repeatedly.

We have already seen that Ephraim had much too high an opinion of himself, and that Hosea hoped Ephraim might learn from the wild asses that isolation is still the safest policy to follow. By breaking out of his isolation and embracing Assyria, Israel had run into the arms of his mortal enemy and dug his own grave.

Israel thought he was on good terms with his chief ally, and that the treaty was a clever political move. Yet things did not turn out as he expected:

> Israel is now swallowed up,
> Lost among the nations,
> a worthless nothing (8:8 NEB).

Israel had become an old piece of junk thrown on the rubbish heap–something that wouldn't even interest a junkman. In short, Israel committed national suicide.

This idea is now further explicated by way of a farming metaphor. Hosea does so in a text that has become a popular proverb: he warns that those who sow the wind will reap the whirlwind.

The idea behind this proverb is not just that the deeds of men have their own inevitable consequences. More particularly, Hosea is telling us that as a rule, the consequences are much greater than the deed itself, just as a whirlwind is much greater than a wind. The whirlwind is God's path above the clouds of the heavens. It's *twice* as strong as the wind.

We sometimes point out that small things lead to great things: great oaks from tiny acorns grow! That's also what the Savior taught us when He spoke of the seed that fell on good soil and produced rich crops–some thirtyfold, some sixtyfold, some a hundredfold. The one seed becomes a great family with many members, just as Jacob had only a staff in his hand when he crossed the Jordan but later became two companies (Gen. 32:10).

In just this way, Hosea warns us, we'll reap a whirlwind if we sow a wind. In other words, we'll get much more than we bargained for. We'll get a frightening increase, for the whirlwind is a catastrophe that destroys the harvest and the reapers as it dashes all our expectations to bits.

It's hard to attach any hope or optimistic expectations to this text. A whirlwind is *always* frightening, but even the *wind* can give us problems. The wind, as such, is a blessing, but it's not a help when it's time to sow the seed. Anyone who goes out to sow when a strong wind is blowing is a fool.

In this context, the wind symbolizes all that is vain, useless, and worthless. The seed used by Israel was good for nothing, and this was reflected in the harvest. Thus, both seed time and harvest were a disappointment. The seed was no better than the harvest, and therefore we are led to conclude that the one who sowed the seed wasn't worth much either. The sower was the real cause of the failure all along the line.

If we leave the negative factors out of the picture for a moment, we see something encouraging in the fact that the harvest far exceeds what was planted. We see that what we bring into our barns is greater, as a rule, than the man who sowed his seed with tears in his eyes had dared to hope. A handful of grains scattered on top of a hill sometimes yields such an abundant harvest that the dry field appears to have been remade into one of the fruitful slopes of Lebanon, where the wind sighs as it passes through the long grass. That's the kind of harvest we get.

But appearances are often deceptive. The Lord of the harvest sends many of us out to sow. He sends parents at home, teachers at school, office bearers in the church, and missionaries in heathen areas. But all these people are inclined to get discouraged, asking to see the results of their labors. Sowing the Word looks like a hopeless undertaking at times. Week after week, the Word is broadcast, but where are the results?

We sometimes get impatient with government bodies and complain that they leave things just as they are. But are we any different when it comes to preaching and the church? Before, during, and after the sermon, we remain the same. Our longstanding quarrels smolder on, and the sinful elements in our character do not change. We remain unmoved and stay seated right where we are.

It's fine to mouth the doctrine about crucifying and burying our old nature. We love to hear a beautiful, stirring sermon about Paul and Felix. Felix was certainly a hard and impenitent heathen, sending Paul away at just the critical moment when his conscience was pricked by Paul's remarks about justice and self-control and the judgment to come. Felix didn't change; he stayed just as he was. Paul could well have asked to see the results of his labors. What a hopeless, hardened sinner that Felix was!

After congratulating ourselves that we are not like Felix, we still manage to dodge the Word's demands by letting everything stay just as it is. The one leaves things as they are in the field, and the other leaves things as they are in his business.

In any event, Paul's sermon was much too moralistic. He was asked to preach about faith in Christ, and he should have done so in a Christocentric way, emphasizing the covenant instead of talking about the "virtues" of justice and self-control! If Felix had only known a bit more about doctrine, he could have hidden his unwillingness to repent behind a certain kind of sermon criticism. He could have said, "We don't hear the kind of sermon today that we used to hear." Then, things would still be left just as they were. Thus, things don't look so bright with the harvest.

When you think about it, though, the sower really doesn't need to ask about the harvest. A sower goes out to sow–not reap. That's his only calling. He goes out not to gather the fruit but to broadcast the seed. That's all he has to do–but he must do it obediently.

As long as we do not sow the wind, as long as our preaching is not all wind, there will be a harvest–but it may come after the preacher's own time. It may happen that the sower, who would have loved to see the fruit, has already closed his eyes in death by the time the seed germinates. A later generation may then carry into the barn a large harvest that they have not sown.

One sows and another reaps, but it is God who gives the increase—an increase that more than repays our labors. This is certainly an encouraging thought for those who sow the seed obediently with tears in their eyes.

I have already pointed out that Hosea's statement about the wind and the whirlwind, a statement which shows that the seed is really no better than the subsequent fruit, has negative implications in the context in which we find it. The meaning intended is clear enough: we will reap what we sow!

Israel lived a wicked life. Perhaps *wicked* isn't the right word. Let's just say that it was an idle life, a useless life, as insubstantial as the wind. (I'll come back to this later.) Hosea then points out that the result of such a life will be useless, idle, and insubstantial too. The deeds of the Israelites will return to haunt them just as surely and inevitably as the seed grows and swells to form the harvest. In this case, the harvest will be a "whirlwind," a destructive force that will blow them right off the earth.

Later came the great whirlwind of the "exile." If Israel emerged from that whirlwind torn and battered, bobbing as a badly damaged boat on the sea of the nations, whose fault was that? Are we to attribute the catastrophe to the power of the heathens or to unshakable destiny?

Are those wandering Jews slaughtered innocents? Are they martyrs among the nations? No, not at all, Hosea warns. What happened to them resulted from their own deeds. They reaped what they sowed. It was the inevitable consequence of how they lived. They themselves prepared the way for it. They sowed the wind and reaped the whirlwind!

It's a tragedy that many an individual and many a nation has helped dig its own grave–sometimes even in a festive mood. Many a man has been lashed with a whip made of his own sins. The consequences of our sinful deeds are not proportional to those deeds but often turn out to be disproportionately large, just as the whirlwind is much fiercer than the wind. We didn't want such an outcome or even realize what would happen, even though we should have known, for Hosea made this clear a long time ago.

A text like this should not be reserved for Communists and revolutionaries and people of that sort. Sometimes we're too eager to throw such texts at them. We see how a revolutionary regime destroys itself when its citizens are locked in a bitter civil war and the evil spirits released can no longer be contained, and we say to each other, "Those people over there are reaping just what they sowed."

We must learn to apply this text to *ourselves* in a concrete way. Think of all the parents who recognize the sins of their youth–and perhaps even of their advanced years–in their children, and in increased form at that, a form that turns into a whirlwind that destroys young lives. The father was still able to hold his ground–against the wind. But the son is swept away–by the whirlwind!

There are parents who have not taken the trouble to bend the young branches while they were still tender and pliable. Before long, their sons and daughters became independent adults going their own way. Then, the whirlwind of revolution sweeps through the family. The father cautions that children are now too old to be led by the hand, while the mother sighs dejectedly about "young people today." Both parents flee from their responsibility and forget that they are reaping the fruits of their own sin. They have sown the wind and are reaping the whirlwind.

I'm sure you can think of many other ways to apply this text. The proper general application is: make sure you proceed carefully. The results of your sin will not affect you alone. Sin's unwanted growth spreads surprisingly quickly. The harvest may mean your own destruction. It's entirely possible that you are the one responsible for those "storms" about which you complain and in which your house may perish. We reap what we sow.

As I promised earlier, I will now comment on that "wicked" life of Israel. When we speak of people leading "wicked" lives, we normally think of prostitutes, tax collectors, and other such flagrant offenders. This would allow "nice people" like you and me to remain out of the picture and say to themselves, "This has nothing to do with *us*. The whirlwind won't sweep across *our* land." Therefore, we would do well to pay attention to what Hosea says to Israel here.

Hosea reproaches Israel for sowing the "wind." This accusation must be seen not so much as a matter of (positive) transgression as of (negative) omission. The wind represents that which is idle, meaningless, without substance. The life of those Israelites was an idle game; it was all show. It was not something real and serious that one could take hold of. Try grabbing the wind sometime. When you open your hand, you'll see you have nothing. Their life was like a mere wind; it was hollow, empty, insignificant.

This casts a new light on our text. For now, the storm blows not only in the direction of evildoers but also toward those people full of hot air who waste their time hanging around shooting the breeze instead of helping with the work of God's Kingdom. Now a howling storm comes at them to sweep away all their hollow activity because their life was filled not with Christ, but with their own laziness and small talk and squabbling.

Perhaps some of these people are filled with genuine industriousness, trying to find their own way bravely, but without the strength and joy and peace that Christ brings. Not only feeble and useless lives but also some stalwart, active lives are judged by God to be less than full. They are hollow and empty wind. They have sown the wind and reaped the whirlwind.

Jesus Christ, who is both the great Sower and the great Reaper, has also sown the wind in the church–the wind of Pentecost–so that the whirlwind of an enthusiastic faith will result in a mighty power that the world will be unable to resist.

# 33

# A Hostile Audience

*Ephraim watches the prophet's tent,*
*traps are set for him on all his paths,*
*in the house of his God enmity awaits him (9:8 JB).*

HOW DID THE PROPHETS preach on feast days? Hosea 9 answers this question for us, for it records an address given by the prophet on one of the holidays. That it is indeed such an address is evident not only from the initial admonition not to rejoice too loudly but also from verse 5, where Hosea asks sarcastically what the Israelites will do on the day of the festival when they are in exile (vs. 3 and 6) and there are no more threshing floors to dance on and no more wine vats to drink from.

The reference to threshing floors and wine vats makes us think of the feast of tabernacles combined with the harvest feast. At the moment when everyone is filled with the joy of the feast, Hosea appears on the platform. He is applauded. The orator of the festival has arrived! He will now give an inspiring address or at least bring the festival to a thundering conclusion with his words. Everyone strains to hear as the man of God prepares to speak. But the address he gives on this day, which is a special day for the people of the Lord, is a very strange sermon indeed.

The least he could have done was to begin by saying what a great and glorious day it was. Surely, he could have exhorted the people to rejoice. But Hosea quickly sobered all the revelers by crying out: "Rejoice *not*, O Israel!" (9:1). He advised them to end their festival as quickly as possible, and he completely denied that the day might have some redemptive significance. Instead, the prophet of doom spoke of nothing but misfortune:

> Threshing floor and wine vat shall not feed them,
> and the new wine shall fail them (9:2).

Things are bound to go wrong. But that's not all:

> They shall not dwell in the Lord's land;
> Ephraim shall go back to Egypt,
> or in Assyria they shall eat unclean food.

> They shall pour out no wine to the Lord,
> they shall not bring their sacrifices to him (9:3–4 NEB).

Thus, the worship ceremonies in the "instituted church" will fade away into a golden age long past. The Israelites will have just enough bread to satisfy their hunger, but there will be none left over for use in the House of the Lord, which will no longer exist anyway:

> For their bread shall be for their hunger only;
> it shall not come to the house of the Lord (9:4).

The prophet spoils all the fun, as we see once more how coldly an effectively prophets break spells and shatters moods. When everyone is rejoicing, they weep. When the multitude rejoices in timely help and deliverance, they pile one threat on another. They call upon the people to beat their breasts at the very moment when they feel like playing the flute.

I don't suppose the brothers applauded when Hosea said amen. We don't do that after sermons either–neither with our hands nor with our hearts. On the contrary, the people in that hostile audience would like to have killed Hosea as they stared at him with eyes full of hatred. That scoundrel, that prophet of doom, even had the nerve to conclude his sermon by declaring:

The days of punishment have come;
the days of recompense have come (9:7).

Yet he also gave voice to what the Israelites were thinking in their hearts:

The prophet is a fool,
the man of the spirit is mad (9:7).

Is Hosea the only preacher in the Bible accused of insanity? That's the kind of sermon the prophets preached on feast days!

Hosea did not restrict himself to the "what" question: he also went on to the "why" and "wherefore." He pointed to the cause of the misfortune he prophesied–Israel's iniquity. Hosea declared that the punishment would come "because of your great iniquity and great hatred" (9:7), referring to a hatred and enmity which the Israelites directed not so much against each other as against God.

But how could Hosea talk about hatred and enmity? Didn't the Israelites regularly bring abundant offerings? Didn't they observe the feast days of the Lord scrupulously? The very day on which Hosea made this comment proved it. What a nation Israel was! What enthusiasm!

Hosea, you must try harder to be fair! No one denies that there are little things wrong here and there, but surely the accusation of *enmity* against God cannot be made to stick. Haven't these Israelites, who are so faithful in discharging their duties, shown that they are on very *good terms* with the Lord? What's your answer to that, man of God?

Indeed, what could Hosea or anyone else say in response? When someone believes he is a friend of God and is generally taken to be one by other people, it's difficult to show him that he's wrong, that he is actually an enemy of God. We usually seek God's enemies *outside* the church, but there are plenty of them to be found *inside* the church as well.

Let's own up to this once and for all. When Paul talks about "*enemies* of the cross of Christ," does he mean murderers and thieves and revolutionaries? No, he's simply talking about people with their "minds set on earthly things" (Phil. 3:18–19). That's a frightening thought! Those drab and unexciting Christians who can find it as easy to say a prayer as to drink a cup of coffee are the enemies of God!

The superficial masses of people who have no notion of what it means to raise our hearts to heaven, who do not return from the heights of prayer with a shining countenance, as Moses did, who never talk about anything except the events of the day, who live by the principle that everyone should look out first and foremost for himself–they are the enemies of God. The people who are frightened at the thought of crucifying their old, egocentric nature on the cross are enemies of the cross of Christ, Paul announces in tears. Hosea is in full agreement with him.

What was wrong with Hosea's worship ceremonies was not their regularity. The problem was rather that they had assumed a worldly–and therefore heathen–character (9:1). That's why Hosea spoke of enmity against God.

Our text for this chapter gives us a second indication of the magnitude of Ephraim's enmity. Yet the text is not entirely clear. Different Bible translations come up with entirely different versions. In the King James Version, we read: "The Watchmen of Ephraim was with my God: but the prophet is a snare of the fowler in all his ways, and hatred in the House of his God." The confusion about this text has to do with the watching going on.

The purpose of the watchmen is not to guard Ephraim. No, Ephraim himself is doing the watching, and he has a hostile, negative purpose in mind:

> Ephraim watches the prophet's tent,
> traps are set for him on all his paths,
> in the House of his God enmity awaits him.

We must understand this text as follows. Instead of listening humbly to the Word of the Lord, the Israelites hope to find something in the words of the Lord's prophets to use against them. Thus, the prophet sees traps set for him everywhere. Even when he speaks in the House of God, he knows he faces a hostile audience.

What kind of audience was Hosea preaching to that day in the church at Bethel? Was it a submissive audience ready to bend to the demands of the Word of God, or was it a hostile audience eager to hear words that could be used against the prophet? Hosea gives us the answer in this text.

Those seemingly pious people had not come to the holy place to listen to what God had to say to them through the mouth of His prophet. They listened instead in the hope that Hosea would say something to get himself into trouble, in the hope that he would lay himself open to criticism. Thus, their mood was definitely hostile. That's the kind of flock that Hosea, Israel's shepherd, had to care for.

Actually, the flock was not made up of sheep, or even goats; it was a pack of bloodthirsty hounds that growled threateningly whenever anyone came too close. Those Israelites were the kind of people who fly off the handle as soon as they hear a comment that rubs them the wrong way, people who are not even afraid to attack the preacher. Watch out what you say in such a company, Hosea!

The beautiful thing is that the prophet ignores it all completely. All he wants to do is to bring the Word of God, and therefore, he does not take the animosity personally. He sees it as directed against the One who sent him. Ephraim's enemy, ultimately, is God–not Hosea.

This hostile attitude towards preaching is much in evidence in our own time. If we were hostile toward *each other* only, that would already be bad enough. We live in a Christian fellowship and as members of a church community. Within these circles, we sometimes feel a great deal of hostility. We sometimes get the feeling that we are surrounded by spies rather than brothers. We are watching carefully on all sides. If we make a public speech or publish an article somewhere, we can count on it that several of our fellow believers will attack us as viciously as hyenas if they find anything whatever to question.

Schiller's comment about women acting like hyenas can also be applied to men. Some more recent exegetes explain the beasts against which Paul fought at Ephesus (see I Cor. 15:23) in figurative terms. In other words, the "beasts" of which Paul spoke were people who were opposed to the gospel. Given the situation in our time, I am more inclined to agree with this interpretation. There are also people who interpret the Apostolic command to teach and admonish one another as meaning that we must run some sort of espionage network to keep track of what everyone is doing. We then report to each other over coffee: "Did you hear about so-and-so?"

What should worry us even more is that some Christians are hostile to God Himself and go to His house not so much to listen as to find fault. They do not ask themselves what God is saying to them. They're more interested in the idiosyncrasies and shortcomings of God's message bearers. They're not moved by a strong desire to hear the message of salvation, but they're curious about the preacher's "theological" tendencies. They listen carefully to see whether he puts enough emphasis on the covenant. They keep track of how much time he spends on exegesis and application respectively. They discuss his talents and abilities, and they complain if he consults his notes too often.

It was once the custom for the elders of the church to meet after the service and pray, so that all might ponder further the truth just proclaimed from the pulpit. In churches today, the jackals are already busy tearing the sermon apart before the preacher has finished, with the result that not even a piece of an ear is rescued from the lion's mouth, to borrow an expression from another prophet (Amos 3:12).

Thus, Ephraim is hostile to the Word of God proclaimed in church. It's too bad that Ephraim doesn't direct that hostile attitude toward the devil instead. The devil is certainly ready to pounce on him at the first opportunity, and he will surely devour him if Ephraim does not soon repent of his hostile attitude toward God's messengers and learn to listen obediently and submissively.

# 34

# A Horrible Prayer

*"Give them, O Lord—what wilt thou give them?
Give them a womb that miscarries and dry
breasts" (9:14 NEB).*

IT CANNOT BE DENIED that Ephraim's life was nothing to be proud of. Hosea reminded the Israelites just how bad it was by drawing their attention to a shameful episode in the past:

> Like grapes in the wilderness,
> I found Israel.
> Like the first fruit on the fig tree,
> In its first season,
> I saw your fathers (9:10).

Just as the heart of the gardener swells with happy expectation when he looks at the first young fruits of what he has sown, so the Lord–speaking now in human terms–had high hopes for the people He had led out of bondage with His outstretched arms.

The chosen nation, which was descended from Abraham and had enjoyed so many favors from God, had every reason to sing His praises. The prospects for the future were bright. The small shoot planted by the Lord's own hand was intended to bear much fruit. The branches in the vineyard, tended by God Himself, would hang low because of all the grapes growing on them. The joyful band of people who left their footsteps in the seabed was supposed to become a large nation that would love and serve the Lord throughout the generations.

This expectation was bitterly disappointed. The stirring events of the past did not seem to make much of an impression on the Israelites. The nation that sang that it would not forget a single one of God's benefits could hardly remember one.

The trouble already began on the journey between Egypt and the promised land when God gave the Israelites a rich demonstration of what He could and would do for them. For 40 years, Israel caused God disappointment instead of pleasure. As a result, only two members of the generation that had seen all those wonders were allowed to enter Canaan. The others perished in the wilderness.

As soon as the Israelites came into contact with people who worshiped Baal, there was trouble. Hosea reports:

> They resorted to Baal-peor
> And consecrated themselves to a thing of shame,
> And Ephraim became as loathsome as the thing he loved
> (9:10 NEB).

If this were an isolated incident, we could let it pass. But the quest for idols became epidemic. From the beginning of Israel's history as a nation right up to the time of Hosea, the constant unfaithfulness to God continued. Time and again, Israel turned his back on God and embraced idols. Thus, Hosea was talking about a long, sorrowful history of unfaithfulness to the Lord. Ephraim was indeed in a sorry state.

It's incomprehensible that things could have gotten that bad! But it's no less incomprehensible that Hosea, the prophet of the Lord, should respond to this cancerous national sin with such a horrible prayer as we read in the text for this chapter. This prayer is not something we get over quickly and easily.

Actually, Hosea's prayer is even more abnormal than Israel's sin. As far as Ephraim's constant unfaithfulness is concerned, we can shake our heads and wonder how it's possible. But when we look at our own lives, we see that we're doing the very same thing. Yet, we certainly don't pray the way Hosea prays here.

Listen to how this man of God prays: "Give them, O Lord...," he begins. At least there's one person in this frivolous crowd of people singing and dancing around the wine vats[13] who still knew how to intercede with God for those poor people.

"Give them, O Lord...." At last! Someone is on his knees to lead us in prayer, stretching out his hands toward heaven and pleading for this people headed for destruction, this people he loves so much.

"Give them, O Lord...." This prayer of thanksgiving comes after the sermon. But then the preacher on the pulpit falls silent. He hesitates in his prayer. He can't go on. Maybe he wants to think carefully about just what he should ask for on behalf of the people.

All the people listen in suspense. What heavenly benefits will the prophet demand from the Giver of all good gifts as he folds his hands in prayer and throws his whole being into the supplication? "What wilt thou give them, Lord?"

The Lord has so much to give them! Should Hosea ask the Lord to give them a new heart so that they will walk in His ways? Should he ask God to forgive them, for they know not what they do?

---

13. This scene probably took place at the same Feast of tabernacles at which Hosea preached the "sermon" discussed in chapter 33.

We all sense that Ephraim needs forgiveness even more than he needs bread. Come on, Hosea, appeal to God's grace! Beg God to be merciful to your people. We all listen anxiously.

"Give them, O Lord–what wilt thou give them?" Then a frightening curse comes from Hosea's mouth as he leads the Israelites in prayer: "Give them a womb that miscarries and dry breasts"!

In Israel's part of the world, that was the worst curse of all. It meant a nation's *death*. Hosea was asking God to curse Israel with the worst punishment he could think of. Wipe them off the face of the earth! That's what Hosea prayed after preaching his sermon.

The sermon was full of judgment, and the prayer was an awful curse. Hosea's hearers were crushed, and we, too, are amazed. We ask ourselves how it is possible for a nation to sin so much. In even greater amazement, we ask ourselves how a national religious leader could utter such a curse. How would you like it if you heard such a curse on Sunday morning after the sermon?

Psalms and prayers containing curses are common in the Bible. Think of the poet of Psalm 104, who cries "Praise the Lord!" at the thought of sinners being wiped off the face of the earth, and the exile who says to Babylon:

> Happy is he who shall seize your children
> and dash them against the rock (Ps. 137:9 NEB).

The people being cursed in such passages are the heathens, the enemies of God's people, but Hosea now pronounces a curse on his own people. That's what makes it all the more mysterious.

We might be inclined to think here of the wrath rising in Hosea's own soul. We might then argue that seeing so much godlessness at one of the Lord's feasts is what made Hosea pronounce this curse on his people, and that later he was sorry he had let his feelings get the better of him. But respect for the Scriptures quickly shows us that such a view is untenable.

Equally untenable is the view that we are dealing here with a typical example of Old Testament wrath. The New Testament, according to this view, contains none of this wrath, for Christ replaced wrath and curses with love and blessing. But this opposition between wrath and curses, on the one hand, and love and blessing, on the other, is purely imaginary. From the mouth of Christ Himself came some dreadful curses. Praising the Lord for the destruction of the godless is not just something an Old Testament "zealot" would do. Those who are in heaven will praise God when Babylon finally falls, and the blood of the Lord's servants is avenged.

Furthermore, Hosea's words have nothing to do with any *personal* desire for revenge. He was motivated only by love for God and concern for His honor. Hosea wasn't trying to pay anyone back. His desire was simply that God be praised for all He has done. Godlessness stands in the way of such praise. Sinners are out of tune with the song of God's creation; they are bloody stains on His white garment, brutal destroyers of His work of art, intruders in His house, priests of Baal before His altar.

Tell me now–if God's honor means something to you, can't you at least *understand* Hosea's prayer that anything standing in the way of His glory be swept aside, destroyed, cursed, even if it turns out that His *own people* are standing in the way?

I don't believe it was easy for Hosea to pray this prayer, for he loved his own people dearly. Who can pray that what he loves to be cursed and destroyed? But Hosea loved his God even more than he loved his people. There must have been a tremendous struggle going on in his heart–that's why he paused and hesitated–as to which love would win out.

At God's command, Hosea was ready and willing to prophesy that his people would be destroyed–and that's amazing in itself. In fact, he became so obedient and sensitive to God's purposes, so eager to do God's bidding, that he *begged* for the destruction of his people. How, then, can there be any talk of lovelessness or a desire for revenge here? The curse, expressed in this prayer, results from the love in Hosea's heart, a love for God, a love that is so deep and intense that it goes beyond all human understanding.

The curses in the prayers and psalms of the Old Testament would not seem so mysterious if we were not such poor Christians who take so little interest in God's honor. The great question of our lives should be not whether we *understand* this prayer of Hosea but whether we can join in it, whether we, too, can make the request that Israel be cursed. To pray such a prayer would be to pray *against ourselves.*

Someone who is spiritually healthy always thinks well of others but poorly of himself. He recognizes that he himself is the godless sinner, the one who sings out of tune with the others, the one who is out of place. *I* am the man or woman who stands in the way of God's honor.

This is what leads to that horrible prayer, the prayer for my own destruction, the prayer that my old nature be put to death and buried and wiped off the face of the earth, the prayer that my old nature be *crucified*, even though death on the cross is cursed by God. I must pray for a curse!

Anyone who is willing to recognize how much he still loves *himself* and how much he is still attached to his pet sins will not be able to pray this prayer easily and gracefully. He will stumble and hesitate, just as Hosea the prophet did. The words will not issue from his mouth easily. Such a prayer becomes an intense struggle, in which self-love and love for God fight it out.

Do any of us ever pray for the strength to be hard on ourselves? How many of us could get through such a prayer? How many of us could pray: "Give me, O Lord—what wilt thou give me? Give my sinful nature a barren womb"? Who would emerge victorious from such a prayer, as "Israel," as a ruler subjecting himself to God's will? Who cries out with Paul: "Wretched man that I am! Who will deliver me from this body of death?" (Rom. 7:24).

Only the horrible curse that rested on our Lord Jesus Christ can make us understand the horrible curse in Hosea's prayer. It is only through *His* power that I can pray for a cursed death for myself.

The reason we're not "alive" enough is that we are not sufficiently willing to "die." The reason we don't fight sin to the death is that our prayers are too smooth and contain no pauses and hesitation. May all who can grasp these paradoxes learn something from them and understand the reason for Hosea's horrible prayer.

# 35

# The Love of Monuments

*Israel was a luxuriant vine*
*yielding plenty of fruit.*
*The more his fruit increased,*
*the more altars he built;*
*the richer his land became,*
*the richer he made the sacred stones.*
*Their heart is a divided heart;*
*very well, they must pay for it:*
*Yahweh is going to break their altars down*
*and destroy their sacred stones (10:1-2 JB).*

THE TENTH CHAPTER OF Hosea is made up of three parts. Each one begins by pointing to a particular sin and ends by announcing a judgment. The three parts are verses 1–8, 9–10, and 11–15. Anyone can check this in his own Bible.

In the first of these proclamations of judgment, we hear a familiar statement:

> So they will say to the mountains, 'Cover us,'
> And to the hills, 'Fall on us' (10:8 NEB).

Jesus declared that when Jerusalem is destroyed, the unrepentant Jews will voice the same vain hope (Luke 23:30), and John heard the same heart-rending cries on Patmos when he had his vision of the final judgment (Rev. 6:15–17). This ominous repetition makes it clear that this sinful, recurring flaw is leading these frightened souls to voice such a prayer, a prayer that remains unanswered because it comes too late.

It's very important for us to discover just what this sin is in which generation after generation seems to be caught. It is a sin about which our consciences don't complain much—and that makes it all the more dangerous. Hosea points to this sin when he warns the Israelites against an excessive love of monuments: we read in our text that "the richer the land has become, the richer he made the sacred stones."

What was the problem with Israel? We know that God had been good to Israel—shamefully good. This does not come out clearly in the King James Version's rendering of our text, where we read that Israel is an "empty vine" that brings forth fruit.

The vine that the Lord Himself had planted was no empty vine; on the contrary, it had survived a long, long time and had grown large and strong. Especially in Hosea's day, during the rule of Jeroboam II, it was a pleasure to see how full the wine vats were. There was plenty of reason to celebrate a harvest festival. (Hosea's sermon, recorded in chapter 10, may also have been delivered at the harvest feast which I mentioned in the two preceding chapters.)

Thus, the Lord never got tired of giving Israel generous gifts. Of course, one might argue that the Lord was rich. The cattle on a thousand hills were His. His generosity toward Israel did not make Him any poorer. But the wonder of God's generosity was that He filled the wine vats of people who forgot all about Him; that's incomprehensible goodness!

What did Israel do with those gifts of God? The prophet informs us in the first place that he built many altars–so that he would have a place to offer his sacrifices, of course. Hosea declares: "The more his fruit increased, the more altars he built" (10:1).

"What's wrong with that?" you may ask. Does the man of God have to complain about everything? Is Hosea one of those prickly critics who's never satisfied, one of those unpleasant people with whom you can never win? If you don't build altars, he's angry. If you build a lot of altars, he's still unhappy. It seems to me that the profusion of altars in Israel would put many nations to shame. Isn't it only to be expected that the number of altars should correspond to the abundance of the gifts?

Usually, it's just the other way around: countless blessings and no altars. God is overwhelmingly good, but no offerings are brought. Israel's example here could certainly put many couples to shame on their wedding day, as they spend their money freely on food for the reception and elegant clothes for the ceremony. What about the bill? There's nothing to worry about. You only get married once!

But where is the altar, and where is their thanksgiving offering? That's the riddle we might pose at the wedding reception–following Samson's example–or perhaps at other festivals and anniversaries. We take care of God with a few pious words printed on an invitation card or a program: "We wish to thank God...." My question is: Have you actually done it yet, or are you still at the wishing stage?

Now then, Israel is much better in this respect. Israel did build altars, a great many altars, and he certainly was not ungrateful. Instead of praising the Israelites for this, Hosea castigates them. It's certainly a strange business!

The second thing Israel did with God's gifts was to build monuments. "The richer his land became, the richer he made the sacred stones," the prophet tells us. Thus, in addition to all the altars (religion), Israel also devoted a lot of attention to the care of monuments (art). Israel was a religious nation, a nation that lived close to its altars, but in those days, it seems to have reached the realization that art must not be neglected.

Therefore, official attention was devoted to establishing and caring for monuments–the "sacred stones" of our text.

No doubt you know all about such sacred stones set up as memorials (Jacob had established one of them), stones with "Ebenezer" or some such message carved into them. Wasn't it a pious practice to care for those stones faithfully? Not only were they cared for, but they were also improved and restored. The rough stones, set up by the fathers, were turned into beautiful pillars in which Israel's ties to the past were made permanent and concrete. Alongside the old monuments, many new ones were erected, with even more beautiful and edifying inscriptions.

Now, Hosea, what could you possibly have against that? The Israelites could have thought of worse ways of spending their money. Suppose they had built brothels or gambling casinos instead.

No, Israel was careful in this respect. The money was not squandered or wasted on liquor. Large sums of money were made available for altars and monuments, religion and art, the church and scholarship. Through his words and deeds, Israel demonstrated that he attached great importance to preserving cultural objects. Wouldn't Hosea's sharp critique have the effect of hampering or even destroying those praiseworthy practices?

According to Hosea, the Lord had nothing against altars and monuments as such. Yet he declares that He will destroy their altars and their sacred stones. Why? Hosea tells us why. Their heart is "false" (as we read in the Revised Standard Version) or "divided" (as the King James Version has it).

At this point, we'll ignore the fact that the worship at Bethel was sinful and shot through with heathen customs and practices. But even if that were not the case, the altars and monuments still would not please God because the people did not have their hearts in it. They just had to understand the simple truth Paul taught the Romans when he declared that God's kindness is meant to lead us to *repentance.*

Kindness is one of the means God uses to get us to turn to Him again. Sometimes He chastises us, and at other times, He tries to win us with kindness. We bask in His kindness as a sleeper wakes up in the morning sunshine.

Israel didn't understand that. The Israelites kept building altars and monuments, but they did not repent. They did not devote their hearts fully to the Lord their God. What would the Lord want with altars if His people do not offer their very selves as living sacrifices? Why would God care about the restoration of monuments bearing images from the past if we don't bother restoring God's image in us? The Almighty will sweep all the altars away and destroy all the monuments.

Thus, we see that serving the Lord isn't quite as easy as it sometimes looks. We should not be so foolish as to suppose that we can deceive God with pomp and ceremony. Erecting monuments simply isn't enough.

Of course, we are very good at it by now. We put an announcement in some church magazine, and under it, we place the word *Ebenezer*. At our wedding anniversaries, we declare that the Lord has guided us for 20 or 25 or 40 years, in the hope that this bow in God's direction will sanction our worldly celebration. If there's anything left after our feast, we have it sent to the poor people of our church–if we remember in time.

These are some of the monuments we erect in praise of the goodness of our God and Father, who showers us with His blessings and looks after us better than any earthly father– "The richer his land became, the richer he made the sacred stones." But if God's goodness does not lead to an "improvement" in our lives, if it does not lead to repentance, the monuments become an albatross around our necks. People devoted to God, people who are living monuments to God's faithfulness, are worth much more than the most exquisite monuments of marble, granite, or carved wood.

The better things go for us ecclesiastically, the richer we make our sacred stones. Our modern cathedrals and churches are much more beautiful than the meeting places in which our fathers had to worship in the days when the church could not worship freely. Today, we remember those days by publishing books about them and erecting monuments to them. But Paul speaks of the church as "a letter that has come from Christ, given to us to deliver: a letter written not with ink but with the spirit of the living God, written not on stone tablets but on the pages of the human heart" (II Cor. 3:3 NEB).

Thus, the church is to be a living reminder of Jesus Christ and a daily advertisement for His name. Do we live up to that ideal?

I hope that no one will draw the conclusion–for the heart is more crafty than any other thing–that because the Lord wants a broken and contrite heart as a sacrifice, there is no need to lay anything else on the altar. It's not a question of either/or: the Lord wants *both* kinds of offerings. Sacrifices must be laid on the altar, and monuments must be erected–as long as they are erected by Christians who are living monuments themselves, whose hearts are devoted to the service of the Lord in undivided loyalty.

The life of our Lord Jesus Christ was a life of love and sacrifice, and we "remember" it regularly when we celebrate communion. It is only in communion with Him that the improvement of altars and monuments will keep pace with the improvements in our lives, as we become conformed to the image of God's Son.

# 36

# Standing Firm

*Since the day of Gibeah Israel has sinned;*
*there they took their stand in rebellion*
*(10:9 NEB)*

IT SHOULDN'T SURPRISE US that Hosea draws a parallel between his own days and the days of Gibeah. In Judges 19, we read what happened long ago in Gibeah. We all know how the author of Judges appended a few chapters to the book telling how things went when there was no king in Israel and every man did what was right in his own eyes. The story of Micah (ch. 17–18) is typical of the *religious* anarchy of the time, and the *ethical* degeneration is illustrated by the multiple rapes of the Levite's concubine, which led to her death (ch. 19–21).

It was the tribe of Benjamin that was guilty of this outrage. Jacob had already seen that there was something beastly about

Benjamin, for he prophesied: "Benjamin is a ravenous wolf" (Gen. 49:27). Thus, immoral inclinations were present in Benjamin from the beginning.

If Benjamin had only followed the Lord's command and driven out the inhabitants of Canaan, whose moral standards had sunk so low, the incident at Gibeah might never have occurred. But Benjamin, like the other tribes, did not obey this command of the Lord

Now, no one can say what may happen if the fire gets too close to the fuse. Surely, we should expect a raging fire at the very least. Benjamin's atrocity at Gibeah reminds us of Sodom.

The Lord could not let such a deed go unpunished. The horrible sin led to an armed conflict with other tribes. In the ensuing struggle, Benjamin was so badly defeated that it barely escaped complete eradication. Only 600 men managed to survive by hiding in the rock of Rimmon. That was the story of Gibeah.

Hosea now reminds his contemporaries of this story: "From the days of Gibeah, you have sinned, O Israel" (10:9). But this is not the first time the prophet refers to this story. Earlier, he had said: "These men are steeped in corruption as in the days of Gibeah" (9:9 JB).

Hosea's purpose in drawing attention to this historical parallel was not to argue that the ethical degeneration in his own time was progressing as rapidly as that of the days of Gibeah. It was true, of course, that moral standards were not especially high, as Hosea's contemporary Amos also pointed out. Even at the festivals of sacrifice, strange things went on; temple prostitution was by no means unknown in Israel. But we remember that from the beginning, Hosea placed Israel's decline in the context of (spiritual) adultery. Israel had broken the marriage bond with the Lord by serving idols–that was unfaithfulness, whoring, turning away from God. This unfaithfulness was still Hosea's concern when he pointed to the atrocity at Gibeah as typical of the religious and ethical decline of the people: "From the days of Gibeah, you have sinned, O Israel."

Hosea then goes on to ask: "Shall not war overtake them in Gibeah?" What the prophet means is that his contemporaries will become involved in the same sort of struggle as the inhabitants of Gibeah long ago, and that they will suffer the same kind of fate because of their godlessness. The same sin will lead to the same punishment. We are then told what the punishment will be:

> "I shall come and punish them.
> The nations will muster against them
> to punish them for their double crime" (10:10 JB)

By this "double crime," Hosea probably means the two golden calves at Dan and Bethel. And the nation referred to is no doubt Assyria!

This is the second time in the tenth chapter that Hosea speaks of sin and punishment. Yet this is hardly tiresome repetition on his part. The first time was when the prophet sounded his warning about monuments. (See the preceding chapter on the division of Hosea 10.)

Sin takes on many forms. We could compare it to a many-headed monster. Thus, when the prophet of the Lord now focuses his spotlight on Israel's sin again, it shines on something different. At the bottom, it's really the same sin, for in the final analysis, all of our many sins represent variations on one and the same theme. But the side of sin Hosea now points to is *stubbornness*: "From the days of Gibeah, you have sinned, O Israel."

This is a very grave statement indeed, for it shows us the worst thing about Israel's sin, namely, that it is deeply rooted. Israel's sin is one continuing line; it is a crease that is never ironed out. One cannot with a free and clear conscience say that Israel fell into sin because of its "weakness." Falling into sin through weakness is certainly a serious matter, but the church teaches that when we sin out of weakness instead of willfully, we can still count on God's grace, for we have an eternal covenant with God.

Israel was also a party to such a covenant. The Lord was most merciful to His falling, stumbling children. If Israel's waywardness had been a matter of falling into sin because of weakness, we can rest assured that the repeated somber threats of judgment would not have been made. Then we would hear: "Comfort, comfort ye My people, says your God." Then we could sing: "Though your sins be as scarlet, they shall be as wool."

But that's not how things were with Israel. The Israelites continued in their sin– "Since the day of Gibeah," declares the prophet, using strong language, "they took their stand in rebellion." They refused to change their position. These Israelites knew what it means to stand firm.

Now, standing firm can be a good thing to do. Firmness of character is a desirable quality. Blessed is the man who stands firm for his principles and is not blown about by every wind of doctrine. That man is a pillar in the church. Blessed are those who will not budge. But cursed are those who will not budge from their sin.

The firmness of the Israelites was of the latter variety. They did not just remain mired in their sin: they stood firm in it. They were immovable. They dug in their heels and refused to give an inch. You know the type. They were stubborn as mules, steadfastly refusing to bend. Although they knew better, they clung to their sin. The Israelites would not and did not say goodbye to the sin of Gibeah. They had no idea what it means to crucify and bury the old nature, and if they had known, they would not have been interested. It was so much more enjoyable to go on living as they were. Theirs was indeed a sorry situation.

Those who sometimes fall into sin through weakness have the assurance that their sin will be forgiven. But all who *choose* to live in sin are in a perilous position. If they participate in a communion service, they eat and drink judgment to themselves. Although the communion service is intended to remind us of the greatest of all acts of love, it contains the element of judgment just as the warnings made by the Old Testament prophets do. Jesus Christ stands firm *against* sin, just as these Israelites stood firm *in* their sin.

This "standing firm in sin" is an ugly phenomenon to which we should devote some careful attention. I sometimes get the impression that this standing firm has assumed enormous proportions in our time. The church, the army of Jesus Christ, is a *militant* church. It is engaged in a struggle, but it does not always fight against what it should combat, namely, sin.

The church is all too enamored with the command, "At ease." Everyone remains exactly where he was, and we see little evidence of any conquest of sin or progress in sanctification. Many of these soldiers are no farther at 50 years of age than they were at 20. Perhaps they have become office-bearers in the church in the meantime, but for the rest, they're standing firm.

There are some whom we might excuse because their lives are a brilliant illustration of a doctrine that the church confesses: "In this life even the holiest have only a small beginning of this obedience." Really? That's a lie.

Don't be so startled! It's not a lie that even the holiest among us make no more than a "small beginning," but this truth becomes a half-truth and, therefore, a lie if it is taken out of context and separated from the sentence that follows it: "Nevertheless, with all seriousness of purpose, they do begin to live according to all, not only some, of God's commandments" (Heidelberg Catechism, Answer 114).

The "holiest" among us are not the ones who take the earlier sentence out of context and try to use it as an excuse to yield to the flesh. Those who misuse this sentence don't want to be among the "holiest." The punishment and condemnation of these "unholy" people will be all the more severe because they "stood firm."

Others are surprisingly quick to point out that man is human and always remains "all too human." They certainly didn't get that from the Bible! I thought I read in the Bible that a believer, someone who reforms, becomes a different person. Those who were once sinners are washed and purified. New powers are at work in the converted man, for Christ lives in him.

Didn't Zacchaeus become a different man? Was he able to continue his former life of deceit? Did he stand firm? It doesn't look that way. The Spirit of God that renews the face of the earth also renews the face of the church: our attitudes change, and we learn to speak differently. Our habits change, and we spend our time in new and different ways. Once *Christ* begins to live in us and we are renewed according to His image, people no longer recognize us.

It's frightening to see that even reformed Christians remain just as covetous, just as spiteful, just as conceited, just as malicious, just as slothful, day after day, year after year. Does the gospel perhaps come to us in words, but not in power? We who are guilty of failing to progress like to point to the past. "Weren't our fathers just like us?" we ask. "Didn't they fight like cats and dogs? Wasn't the church constantly embroiled in quarrels?"

The answer to all these questions is yes. That's why Hosea reminds us of Israel's sin–not by way of excuse but to make the charge even more grave: "Since the day of Gibeah Israel has sinned; there they took their stand in rebellion." Thus, there was nothing for Israel to do but repent.

Of course, *we* don't need to repent immediately of such gross and horrible sins as the atrocity at Gibeah, for that sort of thing makes our neatly groomed hair stand on end. But we do need to repent of some deeply rooted habits that we have not only come to tolerate but have even granted a measure of approval, habits rooted in the old self that we must put behind us, habits that obscure the light of our candle and make the good salt lose its taste.

Christ is the only avenue making such repentance and conversion possible. Therefore, we must pray that He will let us grow and blossom in Him, for He is the true vine. Unless His power flows in our lives, we are doomed. Only Christ can and will make us fruitful. When He does, we will learn what standing firm really means.

# 37

# Favourite Activities

*Ephraim is a well-trained heifer
that loves to tread the threshing floor;
very well, I myself mean to lay the yoke
on that fine neck of hers,
I am going to put Ephraim in harness,
Israel will have to plow,
Jacob must draw the harrow (10:11 JB).*

AT THE END OF HOSEA 10, Israel's sin is given a name for the third time. Once again, the prophet tells us what the punishment for this sin will be.

To make his point as clear as possible, he chooses a farming metaphor, for Israel was very familiar with farming. He uses this metaphor to condemn Israel strongly: "You have plowed iniquity, you have reaped injustice" (10:13). What Hosea means is this: just as the farmer's time is almost completely taken up with plowing and reaping, Ephraim's life consists of little but wickedness and iniquity. As a result, Ephraim takes pleasure in eating the fruits of his labor, i.e., "lies" (10:13). Israel's entire life as a nation is cancerous and rotten to the core.

Thus, it shouldn't surprise us that Hosea calls for a total renewal of life. He tells the Israelites:

> Sow for yourselves righteousness,
> reap the fruit of steadfast love (10:12).

To do this, the Israelites need a new field, for if they "sow among thorns," as Jeremiah puts it (Jer. 4:3), that is, in a field where the weeds have not been rooted out, the young plants will quickly be overcome by weeds. Hence, Hosea's advice is: "Break up your fallow ground," by which he means that they are to look around for an entirely new piece of land. In other words, there must be changes not only in how they sow and reap, but also in the land. The message, expressed in this series of metaphors, is clear.

When we talk about conversion, we mean that the whole person must be changed. The converted person must change not only in his *conduct* but also in his *thoughts* and *attitudes*. The change must affect not only how others see him, but also what lives in his *heart*. The heart is the ground, the field, the fallow land of which Hosea speaks. The heart is the basic issue at stake. The psalmist declares:

> I will run the course set out in thy commandments,
> for they gladden my heart (Ps. 119:32 NEB).

The psalmist is right. First comes the heart, and then the feet. If the mainspring of your watch is broken, it won't do any good to play with the hands. The heart of your timepiece must first be repaired, and then the hands will start to move again too. Likewise, your heart must change first if your life is to change, for out of the heart flow the springs of life. That's why Hosea did not talk to the people just about sowing and plowing but also mentioned the importance of the land.

Israel was not interested in such change and repentance. Hosea argued that "it is time to seek the Lord, that he may come and rain salvation upon you" (10:12), but Israel let God's grace slip by unclaimed. Therefore, the punishment of which Hosea spoke was unavoidable.

Hosea makes this punishment known in two ways. In the first place, he shows *how* it will actually come: "All your fortresses shall be destroyed, as Shalman destroyed Beth-arbel on the day of battle" (10:14). We don't know who this Shalman was, nor do we know just where Beth-arbel is. But that makes no difference. Hosea's contemporaries knew. That particular incident lived on in their memories as a horrible bloodbath in which "mothers were dashed to pieces with their children." That's what will happen someday, Hosea warns.

Even before this, however, the prophet uses an interesting metaphor to describe the coming judgment. This metaphor is also borrowed from farming. Ephraim is compared to a "well-trained heifer that loves to tread the threshing floor." The important point to bear in mind here is that treading the threshing floor was easy work. No one would think of it as a difficult or demanding task. The ox on the threshing floor didn't need a yoke and could eat as much as it wanted, for the Mosaic law forbade muzzling an ox on the threshing floor. Compared to the heavy work that oxen had to do when they got older and stronger (i.e., pulling a heavy plow through the furrows and bearing a yoke around the neck), the work on the threshing floor was truly a pleasure. There was hardly a place where an ox would rather be. That's why Hosea declares ironically that Ephraim is a heifer that *loves* to tread the threshing floor.

Israel loved the life of luxury it led during the prosperous days of Jeroboam II. The Israelites had also lived through other, less prosperous times. Was there anyone who didn't know about the old days when Israel was weighed down by the hard labor of making bricks, when it had a heavy yoke around its neck as it complained about its fate? Fortunately, that was all part of the gray and distant past. The slave of an earlier era had become a cultivated gentleman and no longer had anything to fear from others. He was well off.

The life of luxury definitely agreed with Israel. It was a life of great enjoyment, of eating without being muzzled, of sitting in the shade of a fig tree. These were all favorite activities: "Ephraim is a heifer that loves to tread the threshing floor." But the Israelites had no interest whatsoever in heavy labor. They simply didn't want to *repent*.

In this respect, things haven't changed much. There are all sorts of easy jobs that we do willingly and with pleasure, jobs that we count among our favorite activities. We even find such jobs within God's Kingdom. We serve on committees and work for societies of which we are members. Of course, not all of that work is enjoyable, for it usually means spending many evenings away from home and putting up with opposition and criticism. But, like the ox on the threshing floor, we are not muzzled either. Praise will not be completely withheld from the faithful workers in the Kingdom of God, and when one of them reaches a milestone or anniversary of service, he is suitably honored.

We love that work on the threshing floor. And it's one of the easier jobs around. The heavy work of repentance and conversion is another story entirely.

In a certain sense, it's much easier to be a faithful committee member than to be a follower of Christ, a follower who takes up Christ's cross and denies himself. It's easier to attend church twice every Sunday than to turn the other cheek twice each day. It's much simpler to sing in a hymn that we are God's servants than to actually serve our brother and wash his feet. There are people who call themselves "servants of God" but act as tyrants toward others.

It's understandable that we love to do the lighter work on the threshing floor, that we enjoy and relish it. But the important thing is the heavy work of repentance and conversion. Doing this work means admitting regularly that I was wrong. It means denying myself. It means allowing myself to be muzzled. It means keeping silent when a wrathful heart wants to spit out something spiteful. It means bearing a yoke willingly–the yoke of Christ (which is easy, in any event). We do not engage in these difficult activities gladly and with pleasure.

The time spent on the threshing floor was a time of luxury for Israel, as we saw. The Israelites had come a long way. They were not muzzled anymore, and they could even make their influence felt in international relations.

It can hardly be denied that we are living a life of luxury as far as the church is concerned. Don't we have it made? There are no legal barriers to the preaching of the Word. Preachers are not muzzled, and the church is not subject to the yoke of government. In church each Sunday, we even thank God for all these blessings.

Furthermore, the Christian segment of the population has some influence in public affairs. Christians occupy important positions in society and government. The public is aware of their achievements in scholarship and other areas. The Christians are no longer at the bottom of the heap, as they have been in times past. When we look back and see how far we've come, we hardly recognize ourselves.

But the prosperity of the church is not always an indication of spiritual health. Prosperity brings some definite dangers in its train. That's always the case. It certainly applies to material riches. Once in a while, we still hear someone say that it's very hard to hold onto your faith if you're poor and unemployed, but let's not forget what Jesus said: "It's easier for a camel to go through the eye of a needle than for a rich man to enter the Kingdom of God." The church's prosperity may well be its downfall.

For Ephraim, in any event, the time of luxury was a very bad time: religion became a matter of mere externals, and Israel, as a whole, assumed an increasingly worldly spirit. Therefore, God declared:

I am going to put Ephraim in harness,

Israel will have to plow,

Jacob must draw the harrow.

Thus, the punishment fits the crime. God, the heifer's owner, will harness her to pull the plow. Evil days will follow the time of prosperity and luxury. Israel will go into exile. Because she doesn't want to listen, Israel will have to learn the hard way. Israel will have to learn that we don't serve God just by having fun. God wants us to repent.

Many a mouth that was used to eating a lot had to be muzzled. Shoulders, accustomed to luxury, had to get used to a yoke. The church that forgets its real purpose during prosperous times will also have to bear the yoke of which the Book of Revelation speaks in such frightening terms.

God lays the yoke upon us not because He is a brute or a tyrant but because He wants the ox that loves the threshing floor, this stupid animal that no longer knows its owner or its master's stall, to be with Him in heaven. Sometimes our temporal welfare has to be sacrificed to our eternal welfare. He who wants to save his life must lose it.

He who has ears to hear, let him hear what the Spirit says to the churches: "*Repent*, for the Kingdom of heaven is at hand."

# 38

## Exodus

*When Israel was a child, I loved him, and out of
Egypt I called my son (11:1).*

IN SACRED HISTORY, we see the nation of Israel grow from childhood through youth to manhood. The cradle of the most remarkable people was Egypt. Hosea now reminds Israel of his earthly youth: "When Israel was a child, I loved him." The childhood years were spent in the wilderness; that's where Ephraim learned to walk (11:3). When he could go no further, God carried him in His arms.

The child of the wilderness grew up; he became a young man whose pride was in the strength he displayed as he drove his enemies out of Canaan. In Hosea's day, this youth became an adult. Ephraim had really grown up; he was now a force to be reckoned with. Ephraim had become a magisterial figure who preferred not to be reminded of his humble origins.

That's exactly why Hosea now reminded this upstart of his past. He didn't do so for the fun of it, or to tease Ephraim, or to laugh at him; he did it to prick his conscience, to bring him to conversion if possible.

Remind a stumbling sinner who has shamed his father and broken his mother's heart about his childhood years, the years when his mother told him about the Savior and prayed with him. He would have to be hard-hearted indeed not to be moved. But that's just what happened in Ephraim's case. He became a man not only in appearance and strength, but also in sin. He became so independent that he thought he didn't need God anymore. He had forgotten all about God.

"Now listen for a moment," Hosea says. "Don't you remember how things used to be? Don't you remember God's fatherly and motherly concern about you? Don't you remember how God loved you when you were a child? It was your 'Father' who made you what you are today. You didn't fight your way to freedom; God brought you up out of Egypt as his son. He *called* you out of Egypt. All that tugging on the slave's chain did you no good, but one powerful word from the Lord was enough to break your fetters."

Hosea was talking about the time when God sent Moses to Pharaoh with the words: "Israel is my firstborn son. I have told you to let my son go so that he may worship me"

(Ex. 4:23 NEB). Now then, if these references to Ephraim's childhood don't break his heart and send him home again like the prodigal son, Ephraim must be a hopeless case!

Hosea says it simply: "Out of Egypt I called my son." Yet it must have been a glorious exodus indeed. The Israelites numbered more than 600,000 people, not including the children. There were a lot of people who had mixed with the Israelites and left Egypt with them. And the Israelites took livestock with them–cattle and oxen. They also took plunder surrendered by the Egyptians–clothing and many silver and gold objects. No, it was not a humble departure but a royal exodus. We read: "And the people of Israel went up out of the land of Egypt equipped for battle" (Ex. 13:18).

No doubt the One seated in the heavens laughed at the sight. Not only was Egypt forced to let God's children go, it even had to provide the weapons with which Israel would later destroy Amalek, another enemy. Egypt, likewise, provided the wisdom and learning that made it possible for Moses to record God's deeds, just as the ancient world later provided the language that would make it possible to preach the gospel to all nations.

God's enemies are always forced against their will to help build up His Kingdom, even though they mean to destroy it. The way God leads his church in the world is glorious! Israel's exodus proved that. Protected by a pillar of cloud by day and a pillar of fire by night, the chosen people of the Lord started out on their journey. The Lord gave them the land of the heathens, as Israel became heir to all that the nations had built up in Canaan.

Why did Israel receive all those benefits? Why did God love Israel as a child and pamper him? Why was this nation of slaves like a procession of princes? Was Israel such a lovable and winning child?

Not at all! As a child, Ephraim was already obstinate and hard to manage. We've heard all about that! God loved this child because of *the* child, because of *Christ*. God considered the face of His Anointed—and not the sins of Israel. His wrath was cooled by Christ's intercession.

Actually, Christ was already in Israel while Israel was still in Egypt. Christ was in the loins of Ephraim. Each attack on this nation failed because Christ was within it. Could God let His holy child Jesus drown in the Nile? That was what Satan had in mind.

Satan didn't care about the Jewish children as such, for *they* would do him no harm. But he was afraid of the unborn child Jesus. That's the one he hoped to smother at birth in the water. But he didn't succeed, for God was watching over His child. Because of the child Jesus, Israel's children were sacrosanct and inviolable.

The exodus took place for the sake of Christ. Christ, still contained in the loins of His fathers, had to get out of Egypt, and so He took them with Him when He left. The exodus of the children of Israel was a consequence and fruit of the exodus of the child Jesus from Egypt.

At the Red Sea, Jesus already delivered and saved His people. Just as God was willing to spare Sodom and Gomorrah for the sake of a few righteous people, Israel was safe because of the righteous one in its womb.

Thus, we should not assume that Jesus was first called out of Egypt when He returned from there to His own country as a baby in the arms of Joseph and Mary. Long before His birth, He was already called out of Egypt–accompanied by the bones of the other Joseph!

The claim that Christ himself came out of Egypt with Israel and that Israel was allowed to leave because of Christ is not based on imagination or conjecture; it is taught by Scripture itself. When Matthew wrote his gospel, he applied the text from Hosea directly to Christ. After the story of Jesus' return from Egypt with Joseph and Mary, he noted: "This was to fulfill what the Lord had spoken by the prophet, 'Out of Egypt have I called my son'" (Matt. 2:15). According to Matthew, then, the Son called out of Egypt was really Christ. It was because of this Son that God accepted Israel as a son and prepared a glorious exodus for him.

It was because of this Son! The redemption of all His people could only become a fact when Christ came to earth to suffer in our place. That's when it was all fulfilled.

His exodus from Egypt was only the beginning of His vicarious suffering. It was not a glorification but a humiliation. There was no host of armed men carrying the spoils; there were only three people–Joseph, Mary, and their child. It was more like a desperate flight than a triumphant exodus.

But this exodus, on the part of the child Jesus, took place in order to make the exodus of all God's people possible. That beautiful exodus with music and song is the right fruit of this humble, unpretentious exodus. Because God called His son out of Egypt, death can become a royal departure in which the angels play a role as they carry God's children to Abraham's bosom. Death, then, becomes a passageway to eternal life, a departure from the world of sin to enter the blessed light of eternity.

At the same time, the exodus meant *freedom* for Israel. The slaves had now escaped their yoke for good. They no longer had to build beautiful cities in which the Egyptians would put up notices to the effect that no Egyptian had helped in the construction. The hard labor that embittered them was finally behind them.

In the same way, all who are free through the Lord Jesus Christ are delivered from the service of satan. Satan is a tyrant, and sinners are his slaves—but the sinners don't know it or believe it. What they believe, instead, is that they enjoy a glorious freedom. They believe they don't have to take orders from anyone; they believe they are their own lord and master. There is no more tragic mistake, for anyone who sins becomes a *slave* to sin. Making bricks and gathering straw in Egypt is nothing compared to that kind of slavery.

From this, the children of God are delivered; they are led out of the house of bondage. All of God's sons and daughters were called out of Egypt. They don't feel at home there any longer. They never want to go back. The memory of what happened in Egypt frightens them, and they can well understand why God's prophets always condemn Egypt.

It's not that they never sin anymore or that satan no longer disturbs them. Being delivered from satan's *dominance* does not yet mean being shielded from all his attacks and influence. No one ever promised us the latter in this life. What we are promised is that the gates of hell will not *prevail* against us.

As far as sin is concerned, we know that the evil lusts of the flesh will no longer *govern* us. But that doesn't mean that those evil lusts are entirely absent. In fact, they are often very noticeable, even if they no longer have the reins of control in their hands.

It is a great benefit for a country when Communist government is removed from power. Yet, that removal does not mean that the communists are no longer a factor in politics and no longer form cells and hatch plots. On the contrary, they can still be a headache for lawful government.

Likewise, there are a lot of revolutionary elements still to be found in our lives. But those elements are no longer in control; they no longer dominate us. They may rear their heads from time to time and make things very difficult for us, but in the final analysis, they must bow before Christ.

The more Christ lives and works within us, the freer we will be. That's the secret of true freedom. Just as Israel could leave the house of bondage because it contained Christ in its loins, everyone who lets the Lord work in him through the Holy Spirit will gain more independence and freedom from outside control every day.

Every day will mean a new, triumphant exodus in which we leave the evil lusts of the flesh further behind us and come closer to entering the heavenly Canaan. All the sons that God has *called* out of Egypt, He has also glorified.

# 39

# Paying Attention

*But they did not know that I healed them (11:3).*

WE WOULD DO WELL TO PAY attention not only to God's *judgments* but also to the *grounds* on which they are based. Otherwise, we are in danger of assuming that the judgment is only for *the world* and the hopeless sinners in it, while *we* will surely get off scot-free.

This danger will be reduced to a minimum if we consider the lesson which the eleventh chapter of Hosea teaches, namely, that even a sin like failing to pay proper attention is sufficient reason for the Lord to condemn the nation of Israel to destruction. Let's take a look.

Hosea does not leave us in the dark about the content of the judgment: Israel is to return to Egypt (11:5). In the King James Version, we read: "He shall *not* return to the land of

Egypt," but this translation is surely a mistake, for Hosea has already declared three times that Israel will indeed return to Egypt (8:13; 9:3, 6).

The mention of both Egypt and Assyria in 11:5 suggests that the return to Egypt is not to be taken literally but must be understood in a more general way, as meaning that Israel would be driven out of its own land into exile. Thus, in the next verse, we read:

> The sword shall rage against their cities,
> consume the bars of the gates,
> and devour them in their fortresses.

If we now ask what this frightening announcement of judgment is based on, it turns out that its ground is the *negative* sin of *inattentiveness*. That's an evil that we normally don't regard as overly serious, an evil that doesn't create much of a sense of guilt in us. We would have expected something much more dramatic and consequential–perhaps murder or adultery. But the Lord apparently regarded the failure to pay attention as a serious enough offense. The Israelites' failure to take note of God's *goodness* is enough of a reason for God to send them into exile. Just listen to His complaint: "But they did not know that I healed them."

This charge is more a complaint than an accusation. The entire book of Hosea is really one great complaint on the part of the

Lord, a complaint about His ungrateful, unfaithful people. Here, God's reproach is particularly heart-rending.

God called His own son out of Egypt, but there were also other voices calling this liberated child. Appealing voices whispered to him to follow them to the shining altars of Baal. Ephraim listened gladly to those voices. He always had an ear open for them.

> The more they called him,
> the more they went from me;
> they kept sacrificing to the Baals,
> and burnt incense to idols (11:2).

The Israelites did not want to listen to God's voice. They abandoned the Lord and His commands to follow gods of their own choosing. It's the old, old story we hear so often: they were deaf to God's Word, but they had an open ear for the chorus of voices made up of the devil, the world, and their own flesh.

It's not that we don't hear the Word. We certainly do hear it, Sunday after Sunday. Who is it to say how many sermons we have weighed in the balance and found wanting? Sometimes we even enjoy the sermons. But when we hear that we must deny ourselves and that the first shall be last, we decide that we shouldn't get too heavily involved. God called us to church to repent, but once we're out of church again, it's the same old story: "The more they called them, the more they went from me."

This offense cries out to heaven. Let's look carefully at how the Lord continues His complaint. He contrasts the gross ingratitude of His people with His own goodness. Never has so much good been repaid with so much evil.

> It was I who taught Ephraim to walk,
> I who had taken them in my arms;
> but they did not know that I harnessed them in leading-strings
> and led them with bonds of love—
> that I had lifted them like a little child to my cheek,
> that I had bent down to feed them (11:3–4 NEB).

This is a moving sketch of God's motherly love. Here, as in many other places in the Scriptures, the Lord presents Himself as a mother.

We know that God protects and watches over His children like a concerned father. Now we also know that no mother can say in such a heartfelt way that she will wipe all the tears from her children's eyes. No mother could ask in such a loving way: "Can a woman forget about her own baby? Can she be unmerciful to the fruit of her womb?"

That's how the Lord treated His children in the wilderness. He was like a mother who pampers the child, holds him in her arms, and bends down lovingly to feed him. He taught the inexperienced child to walk, and when he could go no further, He carried him in His arms. When the child fell and hurt himself, the Lord "healed" him. Here is the light. No other love can come close to this love or is as great as this love.

What other response could one expect from this beloved and favored child than words of praise? Wouldn't such a child praise God to the skies and swear never to forget His benefits? But that's not what Ephraim did. Ephraim forgot all about those benefits. "They did not know that I healed them."

No, they hadn't even noticed it, just as a sleeper notices nothing of what goes on around him. Eagerly they laid hands on the gifts which the Lord showered upon them, but that was the end of it. God's goodness left them cold. They didn't even take the trouble to say thank you—never mind repaying that love with their love.

*Because* they did not recognize God's love in and behind those gifts, there was no change in them. They remained just as cold as ever. The nation God had freed did not devote itself to Him.

That's the dark and somber thought behind our text. It's an example of the great evil of failing to pay attention. Not paying attention, not noticing whose liberal hand is behind all those benefits, amounts to *scorning* the Giver. In his sinful failure to understand, Ephraim scorned the land long promised by God.

Thus, we see that failing to understand, failing to pay careful attention, is sin for which we can be *punished*, just as that other seemingly small offense of calling our brother a fool is punishable by hellfire. We could no doubt argue that there are much more serious sins for which we could be punished. We would be inclined to regard the sin of which the Lord, here, accuses Israel as a minor offense, a forgivable shortcoming about which we need not get too disturbed.

But what we think isn't important–not at all! If we bask in God's blessing without being aware that those gifts come from *His* hand, if we receive answers to our prayers even though we have already forgotten that we prayed for success, for health, for strength to right our examinations, for a happy celebration of an anniversary, if we do this sort of thing and think we can satisfy God with a song of praise on Sunday morning plus a dollar in the collection plate–then we're guilty of the sin of failing to pay attention. Let's not forget that God regards this sin as punishable.

God's determination to punish those who are guilty of this sin is not unjust. When we hear Ephraim simply did not know who healed him, we see that there is a *lack of love* here. Love is not being returned. There is also a *lack of faith,* for it is impossible for anyone rooted in Christ in true faith *not* to see God's hand at work everywhere in his life. It is impossible for such a person *not* to be thankful and *not* to devote his life to Christ.

Once we realize this, we will no longer be caught in the trap in which so many are stuck, namely, regarding the failure to recognize God's hand at work in our lives as a difficulty that afflicts only the children of the world. The "world," we sometimes complain, doesn't recognize God, and take Him into account. In its foolishness, the world goes its own way, blind to the fact that it is being chastened by the Lord and equally unaware that it is the Lord who makes the sun shine on the evil and the good. I couldn't possibly list all the misguided things we say about the wicked world. We are not moved by the plight of the degenerate world, and we feel no mercy toward it in our hearts as we sit in our comfortable pews.

Is there any justification for this attitude? Can we thank God calmly that we are not like the wicked people of the world? Doesn't such an attitude testify to the presence of the world in the church and in our hearts? When we receive blow after blow, are we aware of being struck and then healed by the Lord? Are we aware that the Lord is both blessing and chastising us? Do we fly in the face of the beloved, well-known doctrines by assuming in our daily lives that health and sickness, rain and drought, wealth and poverty come to us by chance rather than from God's fatherly hand?

There are so many people who live their lives without recognizing God behind health, sickness, and many evidences of His providence. And there are also many who do recognize

God's hand behind those things but still do not *repent* and turn to Him. Let's not deny it, for it really is so.

Memorizing the church's doctrines just isn't enough. When Jesus tells us that we must confess His name before men, He doesn't just mean that we must memorize and recite the church's official teachings. Only those who learn what is involved in confessing Christ's name before men will be confessed by Christ before His Father in heaven.

Let's think about this carefully as faithful members of the covenant. Failing to pay attention to God's mercies is a sin. Anyone who "forgets" one of God's benefits is in danger of the punishment of death. All you have to do is *forget!*

The Israelites forgot time and again who it was that brought them out of Egypt. God did not take their forgetfulness lightly. He threatened Israel with death, and it was only the intercession of Moses in prayer that saved Israel.

We're not so much different from Israel. But the one who intercedes for us is not Moses but *Jesus*. Let's not forget that He had to pay the price for our forgetfulness. The sin of failing to pay attention is one of the sins for which He suffered. In communion with the One who paid careful attention, we must seek a renewal of our lives so that we may be conformed to His image.

# 40

# Like Doves

*"They shall come trembling like birds from*
*Egypt,*
*and like doves from the land of Assyria" (11:11).*

WHEN WE READ THE 11TH CHAPTER of Hosea through to the end, we might feel inclined to ask whether God is perhaps saying yes and no at the same time. It certainly looks that way. Hardly has God uttered dire threats about sending Ephraim back to Egypt, leading Israel to Assyria, and turning the sword loose in the cities (11:5–6) than the judgment is apparently canceled by a promise of deliverance:

Ephraim, how could I part with you?
Israel, how could I give you up?

> How could I treat you like Admah,
> or deal with you like Zeboiim?
> My heart recoils from it,
> my whole being trembles at the thought.
> I will not give rein to my fierce anger,
> I will not destroy Ephraim again,
> for I am God, not man:
> I am the Holy One in your midst
> And have no wish to destroy (11:8–9 JB).

Thus, the picture doesn't look so grim for Ephraim after all. Those threats must have been expressions of an angry father's frustrations, like the harsh words we sometimes utter but do not act on.

I'm afraid it's not as simple as that. "I am God, not man," the Lord declares, thereby cutting off any such reasoning. The words that proceed from *His* mouth are not subject to recall. Both judgment and reward, threat, and promise, stand firm and unchanged. We must not try to make the Lord say less than He actually did say.

But we must not put words in the Lord's mouth either. After the falsely optimistic conclusion that the Lord really didn't mean those threats, there is a pessimistic conclusion possible: surely, it's all over for God's people. But that's not what the Lord intended to say either. There was nothing whatsoever left of Admah and Zeboiim: these towns in the vicinity of Sodom and Gomorrah were destroyed with them. But such a *total* annihilation was completely out of the question when it came to the covenant people!

In God's name, Hosea rejected this possibility with holy indignation. How could God deal with Israel as He had dealt with those godless cities? It's not that Israel didn't deserve similar punishment: Israel was doubly deserving of Sodom's fate. It's not that Ephraim's godlessness was not equal to that of Sodom and Gomorrah; it was even greater (see Lam. 4:6).

Neither should we suppose that the Lord loved the children of Israel too much to punish them as He had punished Sodom and Gomorrah–that's not it at all. But He did love *Himself* too much to destroy Israel completely. He did not want a conflict within Himself. Didn't corrupt Israel bear the promised Messiah in its loins? Wasn't the Savior of the world to arise out of Israel? That's why a total destruction of Israel was out of the question. God had to spare Israel for *Christ's* sake, for the sake of the Remnant. This meant that a remnant, chosen by God in His grace, had to be preserved.

God's merciful change of heart reflected in 11:8–9 finds its sole ground in Christ, the one to whom the Father showed no mercy, the one who had to feel the unmitigated force of God's wrath. Anyone who had no time for the cross of Christ should not accept any better treatment than Admah and Zeboiim received, but those who fall at the feet of Christ receive the promise:

> My compassion grows warm and tender.
> I will not execute my fierce anger,
> I will not again destroy Ephraim (11:8–9).

God's love for His people for Christ's sake will be answered with love. At the end of the chapter, we are given a striking picture of the "remnant" humbled in exile by the chastising hand of God. This picture shows us what true conversion is. "They shall go after the Lord," we read, whereas they had once "gone after" idols. For the nation sent into exile, there will come a time when the Lord will "roar like a lion" (11:10).

This roaring of the lion is not a sign of doom, as it is in the book of Amos, where the prophet reports that he heard the Lord roar like a lion because of His people at ease in Zion. In Hosea, the roaring of the lion is like the sound of music. Israel's God will rise up like a majestic lion to strike fear and awe into the hearts of Israel's oppressors and force them to let the exiles go.

This repentant people will "come trembling"–not out of fear but out of a deep respect for God's glory. They will come from all sides–from the sea (the west), from Egypt (the south), and from Assyria (the north). They will listen to the Lord's voice and return without hesitation. They will come back in great haste. They will *fly* home like birds from Egypt and doves from the land of Assyria. In this great haste to flee the "land of the shadow of death" with the speed of a dove and "go after the Lord," we see what true conversion means—not just for the "remnant" that returned from exile but for all true Israelites in whose hearts there is no deceit, Israelites who live in humble fear of the Lord.

The first characteristic of this conversion is the burning desire to get away from the "foreign land." Egypt and Assyria, those masters of oppression, had long been Israel's tormentors. But there were many Israelites who didn't seem to recognize oppression for what it was, just as someone mired in sin is not aware that he has become a slave to sin: he regards the tyrant as his friend instead. Thus, many Israelites enjoyed living among the fleshpots of Egypt, and in the days of exile, thousands of them accommodated themselves to life there. In the branches of the great tree Assyria (Ezek. 31), they built a nest. When the tree finally fell, so did they.

The "remnant" was never at home in the land of exile. "If I forget you, O Jerusalem, let my right-hand wither!" (Ps. 137:5). In their hearts, they felt a burning desire to return home. Just as birds feel an irresistible urge to fly south at a certain time of the year, driven on by an inner voice, as it were, Zion's captives left in great haste when the God-appointed time for the return finally arrived. They flew back like birds from Egypt and doves from the land of Assyria.

The instinct that guides birds is present in regenerate man in the form of intuition. The reborn sinner senses intuitively that he can no longer dwell in sin's neighborhood. He feels that he must get away. He must make his escape—not at a snail's pace but with the speed of a dove.

Whenever sin eyes them, these doves fly as though all of Satan's henchmen were pursuing them. And as they fly, they pray to God for a safe journey and for protection from birds of prey that might intercept them on the way.

Thus, genuine conversion involves more than a heartfelt sorrow *about* sin. It also involves a headlong *flight* out of sin's presence. This flight from sin is a sign not of weakness but of strength.

Conversion brings about a change in how we live. We no longer seek sin out but run away from it. But in the second place—perhaps it should have been my first point—conversion brings about a fundamental change in our attitude and outlook. We undergo a complete change not only outwardly (in our behavior) but also inwardly (in our thoughts and feelings). All the changes in us stem from the inner change in the heart.

No doubt Hosea had good reason to compare Israel to a *dove* when he spoke of its repentance and return to God. His use of the dove as an image is not unique or original. David had already seen the people of the Lord as a dove when he spoke of "the wings of a dove covered with silver, its pinions with green gold" (Ps. 68:13).

Israel did not always act as though it possessed the nature and beauty of the dove. On the contrary, in Hosea's days, the Israelites acted more like devils than doves. Perhaps we could compare them to vicious birds of prey. Both the great and small stole shamelessly. The innocence of the dove gave way to the cunning of the serpent.

That's why Hosea's words are so beautiful, for he now tells us that the converted Israelites will return like doves. The bird of prey has been sanctified and has assumed the gentle nature of the dove.

This is the most important element in conversion. Those whose nature and character have not been transformed by the work of the Holy Spirit, who continue to hide behind lame excuses that people should accept them for what they are, have little understanding of conversion. The child of God asks for forgiveness for the shameful nature against which he must struggle all his life long.

The *Holy Spirit* once assumed the form of a dove. It is this same Spirit that wants to renew us in the image of the Son who was compared to a lamb:

> Like a lamb that is led to the slaughter,
> and like a sheep that before its shearers is dumb,
> so he opened not his mouth (Is. 53:7).

There's not much difference between a dove and a lamb in this respect. The lamb is to the four-footed animals what the dove is to the birds. That's what God's Son wants us to be like. We are to have the patience of a lamb and the innocence of a dove. Above all, we must have peace in our hearts. Isn't the dove a symbol of peace?

Let's be honest about it. How far has the renewing work of the Spirit gone in our lives? How far have we advanced in the task of conversion? In the church, we don't always get the feeling of being in the company of guileless, innocent doves and peaceful lambs.

Let's be honest enough to admit that others don't always have that feeling about us either. Asaph confessed that he acted like a beast (Ps. 73:22), and it's not likely that he had a dove in mind. We are left with the distinct impression that he was thinking of some other animal. Asaph meant it when he wrote: "I was like a beast toward thee."

It is certainly painful to discover that there has been so little change in our lives, that we have hardly become different at all. The failure to change can become fatal if we don't do something about it.

But what are we supposed to do about it? If we truly wish to change, we can only do so through the power of Christ's sacrifice. Christ was sacrificed just as a *lamb* is sacrificed and young *doves* are offered as sacrifices. (The lamb and doves were favorite animals for sacrifice.)

We, who are called to be like lambs and doves, must be willing to sacrifice ourselves because of the power of Christ at work in our lives. How do we *benefit* from Christ's sacrificial death on the cross? Through His power, our old nature is crucified and buried with Him.

When we bury that old nature, we'll stop acting like birds of prey. Then, the dove will again parade its beauty–the beauty of the church–before God's appreciative eyes.

# 41

## Our Forefathers

*In the womb he took his brother by the heel,*
*and in his manhood he strove with God (12:3).*

IN THE MIDDLE OF THE complaints Hosea makes about his contemporaries, he calls attention to the life of one of the patriarchs–Jacob. He brings up two incidents. First, he reminds the Israelites what Jacob did at his birth: he held on to the heel of the brother with whom he shared the womb, as we can read in more detail in Genesis 25. Secondly, he reminds them about something Jacob did when he was a full-grown man: he wrestled with God at Peniel, as we read in Genesis 32. What was the outcome of this struggle?

He strove with the angel and prevailed,
he wept and sought his favor.

He met God at Bethel,
and there God spoke with him (12:4).

Naturally, we would not be justified in tearing these observations about the life of the patriarch Jacob out of their context, namely, the admonitions directed towards the children of Israel. Hosea's intent is not to get us to meditate about Esau's fate or Israel's struggle at Peniel. Hosea had a particular purpose in mind in bringing up these historical incidents. Keeping an eye on the situation in his own time, he comes up with an application that someone who simply read the story of the heel as we find in Genesis would not be likely to hit upon.

Hosea's purpose becomes clear when we look at the texts that introduce this chapter. He means to say: "That's what Jacob did, and that's what *you* should do too. Return to God!"

The Israelites liked to talk about their forefathers, the patriarchs, in glorious terms, but Hosea showed that there was still a lot of difference between the "fathers" and their "children." The children of Jacob did not act as their father had done–or perhaps it would be better to say that Jacob did not act as his descendants later acted.

It is a good question whether Jacob, if he could rise from his grave, would recognize those children as his spiritual offspring–despite all their talk about their "forefathers." That's why they would do well to compare themselves once with their father Jacob. *His* faith formed a sharp contrast with their politics of unbelief. *Jacob* held fast to God, but his children covenanted with Assyria and shipped oil to Egypt. Jacob acted in a princely way in God's presence, but his children "multiplied" falsehood (12:1).

The Bethel of long ago where Jacob "met" God was a lot different from the Bethel of Hosea's time, where people worshipped the golden calf. Therefore, children of Jacob, *talk* a little less about your forefathers and make more of an effort to *act* like them. Think especially of *Jacob*, who held onto his brother's heel while they were still in their mother's womb and wrestled with God when he became a man.

Let's take a careful look at what Jacob did, and what his descendants did, and what *we* do. Hosea's lesson about father Jacob may apply just as much to us as it did to the Israelites of his own time.

The Israelites like to talk about "father Jacob." The church teaches that even the holiest among us make only a small beginning in obedience while they are in this life. The story of Jacob illustrates this very well. Jacob cheated and schemed and stumbled his way through life. His garments were covered with dark stains. Nevertheless, the Lord took special delight in being called "the God of Jacob."

This thought should give us encouragement. He is also the God of Abraham and the God of Isaac, but He likes to be called the God of *Jacob*. Why? Jacob was outstanding because he believed. He held fast to God as though he could see the unseen world! His wayward feet always turned back to God in the end.

This faith is the one element that gives continuity to his life. By virtue of this faith, he can claim a place among the "holiest" of God's elect and belongs in the company of the heroes of faith. Despite his sins, Jacob was a magnificent person–through God's grace.

Jacob was not one of those who show great promise in their youth and later turn out to be a bitter disappointment. His faith always came through at the decisive moment, as the Bible shows by pointing to three highlights in his life, highlights drawn from the beginning, the midpoint, and the end. At the beginning of his life, he grabbed hold of Esau's heel. At the zenith of his life, he held on to God. At the end of his life, Jacob blessed each of his sons, "bowing and worshipping over the head of his staff." Hosea brings up the first two incidents; the third is mentioned elsewhere (Heb. 11:21). In all three instances, we see the *power of faith* at work, which is something completely different from physical strength.

The unbeliever relies on his mental abilities or his sheer brawn or some other earthly power, but the believer is strong when he is weak, for his strength is in God. What creature is more helpless than a baby? Yet, the baby Jacob held onto the heel of the brother with whom he shared the womb. The first cry that came from the throat of this screaming child was the cry of faith. The little hand reached out and tried to grab the *birthright* belonging to the firstborn: "In the very womb he supplanted his brother" (12:3 JB).

Jacob's first act was to reach out to God. His first deed–even though it was unconscious–was a deed of faith. He cried out for a blessing, in a prayer without words. Jacob was already saying: "I will not let You go unless You give me a blessing."

This faith dominated his entire life. It's true that he sought the blessing of the birthright, the promised blessing, the blessing of Christ by sinful means. Nevertheless, it was the one passion of Jacob's life. He coveted the Lord's blessing. He sought God's presence earnestly in prayer.

At Peniel, the baby who grabbed his brother's heel showed that he had become a man. His unconscious hold on Esau's heel had become a conscious and deliberate effort to wrest a blessing from the Angel. Here, too, Jacob did not rely on his physical strength, for what can men do against the divine strength that puts a hip out of joint at one touch? Jacob was successful because of the spiritual strength of his prayer as a believer. Finally, what creature is weaker than an old man about to die? But once more, the hero of faith rises up in the power of faith to bless his sons prophetically and await what God has in store for him.

From the cradle to the grave, his life was a life of faith. Therefore, it was a successful and victorious life. Jacob became Israel; He became a prince in God's eyes!

In the day of Hosea, the sons of Jacob had fallen away from this faith–even faithful Judah. Instead of seeking strength from God–as Jacob had done–they sought security from such world powers as Assyria and Egypt. This was a deceitful foreign policy, for at the same time that Israel was receiving support from Assyria, it was trying to buy the friendship of the Egyptians. That's what Hosea means when he talks about carrying oil to Egypt (12:1).

He characterizes such activities as "pursuing the east wind" (12:1), by which he means two things. First, such help will do Israel no good. It can't possibly work, for what is more elusive and unreliable than the wind? Second, seeking such help is like allowing a Trojan horse into the city: it will hasten the day of destruction. There was nothing more destructive to plants than a fierce east wind.

The Israelites had forgotten about the unseen world and reckoned only with the visible world. Instead of building on the Rock of eternity, they sought comfort in the wind rushing by them. Thus, there was a tremendous distance between the patriarchs and their descendants.

Of course, the Israelites were well acquainted with the glorious history of the patriarchs. Their graves were still carefully tended. The places where they had walked, where they had built their altars, where they had dug wells were now honored as holy places. But the image of the patriarchs as a brave and pious generation had little appeal for the Israelites of Hosea's time. The faith of the patriarchs no longer lived in the hearts of their descendants. The struggles with God in which the patriarchs engaged in prayer were foreign to their descendants. The passionate yearning for the coming of Christ that dominated Jacob's life had died down in the nation that bore his name. Things had certainly changed!

In our time, we also like to talk about our forefathers. We hold differing views about the value of their scholarly work. Some of us maintain that their scholarship was primitive, while others argue that much of it hit the nail on the head. But on one point, virtually all of us are agreed: our forefathers were a brave and pious generation of people who excelled in *prayer*. The church of our day is concrete evidence of this. It exists as a fruit of their prayers.

Sometimes we maintain–without trying to blow our own horn too loudly–that we find the image of our forefathers appealing. That may be. Of course, this does not mean that we find it sufficiently appealing to adopt it as a model and live by it–or at least, take a few steps in that direction. Some people look at those appealing forefathers and think, "Long may their glory shine—but we don't pay much attention. They're only figures from the past."

Whatever you and I may think, our faith life doesn't seem to match our extravagant praise of our forefathers, and in this sense, we have not made their faith our own. Where they prayed, we get involved in quarrels; where they built, we tear down. We learn that it's not so easy to emulate our heroic ancestors. Backbone is in short supply!

I can already hear your objection. "We've heard enough of that talk about the good old days. We know all about those days. Let's not forget that there were a lot of things wrong then too, for the people who lived in that era did more than their share of fighting. Furthermore, we've made great advances in doctrinal matters and other intellectual questions. We live in a time of true reformation. Not even our forefathers were able to accomplish as much."

Hosea must have heard objections like this. I'm sure of it. When the prophet pointed to Jacob and told his contemporaries that they should learn to pray and believe and struggle and repent as Jacob did, the Israelites rejected his words with complacent boast about their own riches. Ephraim declared: "How rich I have become! I have amassed a fortune" (12:8 JB) and proudly maintained that his wealth was not in any way a fruit of sin. And that's exactly what we hear from today's Ephraim.

# 42

# Sins on Record

*Ephraim's guilt is tied up in a scroll,*
*his sins are kept on record (13:12 NEB)*

HERE WE ARE TOLD IN NO uncertain terms that God keeps careful track of our sins. Ephraim's iniquity is not forgotten by the Lord; it is written down, sin by sin.

Hosea does not speak here of a *book* as such. What he has in mind is a group of papers bound together somehow. Just as one takes a series of letters or papers and binds them together in a folder to preserve them and make them readily available for future reference, the Lord has recorded Ephraim's sins and bound them together. There is not one that escapes His attention. Israel's recorded sins are carefully *put away*, the prophet assures us, so that they may be introduced as evidence when the hour of reckoning comes on the day of judgment.

The church teaches that God will forgive us our sins and not hold them against us. This doctrine is based on scripture: "Thou wilt cast our sins into the depths of the sea" (Mic. 7:19). Doesn't that contradict what Hosea says here? What is the truth of the matter, then? Is Hosea right, or is Micah right?

Both are right, of course. God certainly remembers all our sins, but He does not hold them against us. He forgets nothing. Yet, in a way, He forgets everything. The one truth seems to cancel the other, but that's only how it *looks*. (I'll come back to this later.)

We are often inclined to play off one doctrine against the other. In this case, we would like to be on the safe side and say that God does forget all our sins, for this would give us a bit more elbow room. But that doesn't work! Those who feel the desire in their hearts not to worry too much about the sins they commit now receive a message from Hosea. The prophet gives us the frightening news that Ephraim's sins are tied up in a scroll and kept on record. This applies not just to Ephraim but to you and me as well. What is sauce for the goose is sauce for the gander!

It has gradually become clear to us what these sins of Ephraim are. Hosea does not beat around the bush when it comes to exposing the sins of the people to public view; he says exactly what's on his mind. Israel's prophets simply were not interested in assuring themselves and others what a faithful and obedient nation Israel was—or that Israel was a much better nation than the surrounding heathen nations.

The prophets came not to sing Israel's praises but to call her to repentance. Therefore, they did not tell their hearers that they were gentle lambs, lovable creatures that could safely be fed by hand. The prophets knew they were called to go after Israel's lost sheep, and therefore, they made no attempt to hide the sinfulness and godlessness of the covenant people. They were right, of course, for a physician who shrinks from taking the drastic measures necessary leaves his patient even worse off.

In the final chapters of his book, the prophet gives us another short résumé of those sins. Despite Hosea's brevity, it turns out to be quite a bundle that God has bound together. Listing the sins of one day alone is already quite a job.

In the first place, Israel followed a foreign policy based on unbelief, as we saw earlier. Then, there are the commercial sins (12:7–8), e.g., the deceitful use of weights and measures, which the Israelites even tried to justify. Hosea never tires of denouncing such sins. Those sins are bound up; they are kept on record. Don't forget that! Finally, there is the great sin on Hosea's mind when he goes to sleep at night and when he wakes up in the morning, a sin that usually doesn't concern us very much—ingratitude.

Earlier, we saw Hosea point to Jacob as an example (12:2–6). The Israelites of Hosea's day could well take a page from Jacob's book when it comes to living by faith.

The prophet now comes back to Jacob and points out that Jacob clung to God despite the fact that he lived in much less fortunate circumstances. *Jacob* had to *flee* to Syria to *serve* there–but *Israel* was *led* by the Lord out of bondage in Egypt. Jacob had to "do service" for a wife, but Israel was "preserved" by a prophet (12:12–13).

But this nation that had arisen from Abraham's loins and had enjoyed so many favors from God's hand, this nation of people descended from Jacob and chosen by God, was not interested in honoring God. Instead, the Israelites serve Baal and kiss the golden calf. But those who kiss the calf rather than the Son will perish!

So angry is the Lord that he even calls on the pestilential powers of death and the destructive forces of hell to consume the godless nation:

O death, where is your plague?
O Sheol, where is your destruction? (13:14).[1*]

Do your worst to this degenerate nation!

---

1 * The context precludes us from regarding these well-known words, which are also quoted in I Corinthians 15, as a promise. These words are preceded and followed by threats, and therefore, Hosea must also mean them as a threat. When Paul quotes these words, he gives them a different meaning; He turns them into a cry of triumph. But we would not be justified in projecting Paul's meaning backed into Hosea.

In church, we confess bravely that our guilt grows day by day. We wouldn't do that so blithely if we were not accustomed to repeating phrases and formulas, for this confession is quite a mouthful when you stop to think about it. We are confessing that the record of our sins fills a thick file bound together and preserved by God.

This idea did not suddenly occur to Hosea at some point. It also finds support in other parts of the scriptures, for we read that the books will be opened someday. When this happens, we will have to render account not just of our gross transgressions, but also of our many idle and useless words.

If we were honest about it, we would admit that we would prefer it if God did not keep such a precise and accurate record of our sins. We would like it even better if he entrusted the task of binding together and preserving those sins to us, for then, the file would look much different.

First of all, there are many sins that we would *forget* to record. We commit so many trivial sins that aren't even worth writing down and repeating. Sometimes we're in a bad mood and speak to someone in anger; at other times, we fail in our duty in some small way.

Now, we know from the Bible that anyone who calls his brother a fool is liable to hellfire and that anyone who hates his brother is a murderer, but we do wonder whether it's necessary to include all the minor and inconsequential sins in our file. Given our inclination to cover up our own sins and to defend ourselves against all criticism, we would probably wind up overlooking a great deal. There's a definite danger, then, that we would overlook many of our sins.

In the second place, I would be so afraid that my neighbor might forget to record some of his sins that I would soon be doing it for him. And that would keep me so busy that I would never get around to writing down my own.

In the third place, we know that people are much more interested in writing bills than in confessing their sins. Thus, I would be too busy trying to squeeze a few pennies out of my neighbor because he owes me money to worry about the ten thousand talents I owe to God. I might even come to the conclusion that God owes me more than I owe him. That happens too!

Finally, there's a distinct possibility that we might wind up listing our liabilities as assets, for we often regard our vices as virtues. If we are greedy, for example, we tell others that we are careful stewards of what God has given us. Although we may *know* that even our best works are stained with sin and declare in church that our righteousness is a filthy garment that should be thrown away, we're not so quick to practice what we preach. Instead of actually throwing that filthy garment away, we parade around in it proudly and even go so far as to bill God for our good works and our prayers–instead of asking him to forgive us for our shortcomings.

Yes, we would certainly like it if God left it to us to record our sins. But he doesn't! Remembering and punishing every sin, no matter how trivial it might seem, is a matter of God's honor. To make sure that not one sin is forgotten, He assigns the task of keeping the records to no one other than Himself.

> Ephraim's guilt is tied up in a scroll,
> his sins are kept on record.

When the judge of heaven and earth unrolls these scrolls on the day of judgment to see what the record contains, the sins that have long been hidden will be exposed to the light of day. When our secret sins are subjected to the light of His presence, each sinner will have to bow his head and confess: "You are just in Your judgments and holy in all that You do."

But when we consider all those sins of ours that God has on record, we wonder who can ever be sanctified. How is it possible that Hosea rightly calls upon death, which is a consequence of sin, to come from the underworld and strike this sinful nation, while Paul laughs at death and asks what becomes of its sting? How can Hosea call on the pestilential powers of hell while Paul commands them to go away? How can Hosea's threat be transformed into Paul's shout of triumph?

This is possible only because the cross of Christ stands between Hosea and Paul. Hosea called upon his great namesake Jesus when he complained about all the sins recorded and rolled up on a scroll, and his prayer did not go unanswered. But *how* are we to interpret Hosea's words as an appeal to Jesus?

In Christ, who was humiliated for our sakes, all our sins were bound together. All the evil was saved for *Him:* the Lord burdened Him with the iniquities of us all. He was not spared in the slightest. God forgot none of our sins; Jesus had to suffer for them all.

Through the wonder of the cross, the amazing contradiction between Hosea and Paul is resolved. For the sake of Christ, God, who forgets nothing, can forget, and forgive everything. The One who keeps a record of all my misdeeds will no longer hold them against me. The One who wrote down my sins and kept them on file can now throw the file away.

It is impossible to be rooted in Christ in *upright* faith without bringing forth fruits of gratitude. What are those fruits? First, that we no longer act so nonchalant about our sins (the sins for which Christ had to suffer so much) but bind them together every evening in our prayers and confess them before God one by one as we ask for forgiveness. Second, that we learn to let go of those sins we cling to stubbornly and even try to hide from God. It is our faith in Christ that gives us the power to do so.

# 42

# The Lily and the Poplar

*EI shall be the dew to Israel,*
*he shall blossom as the lily,*
*he shall strike root as the poplar (14:5)*

IN THE FINAL CHAPTER, we encounter the same Hosea we met at the very beginning–the prophet of love, the man with a warm heart full of love. But the language of love is not always uniform. Sometimes love speaks in tones of wrath, and sometimes it speaks in a gentle whisper. Sometimes it curses, and sometimes it prays. We have heard Hosea utter many threats, but now we hear him pray, or–to be more precise–we hear him teach his people to pray, just as fathers and mothers teach their children to pray.

Hosea had appealed to Israel earnestly to repent. He pointed out that the Israelites could demonstrate the sincerity of their repentance by no longer coming to the Lord with sacrifices and gifts but coming instead with words, with a prayer of penitence. They had already offered the Lord so many sacrifices, and Hosea let them know what the Lord thought of those sacrifices. Like a child seated on its mother's knee, Israel must learn to pray again. The Israelites must learn to say to the Lord:

> Take all iniquity away
> so that we may have happiness again
> and offer you our words of praise.
> Assyria cannot save us,
> we will not ride horses anymore,
> or say, 'Our God!' to what our own hands have made,
> for you are the one in whom orphans find compassion
> (14:3–4 JB)

As you can see, this is truly the prayer of a believer, a prayer in which the old sins of seeking help from Assyria and worshipping idols are finally given up. The people now take refuge in Israel's protector, just as a helpless orphan looks for shelter.

If only it would come to that! If only Israel would sink to her knees! Then the Lord would not leave Israel's prayer unanswered. He would hasten to the side of His chosen people crying out to Him night and day.

Hosea is so deeply convinced of this that his threats automatically give way to promises. He prophesies that blessing after blessing will rain down on Israel. The prophecy of Beeri's son ends in a resounding chorus of deliverance and redemption, a chorus that should long echo in the hearts and homes of believers.

The most beautiful promise is that the Lord will be "as the dew to Israel." Because of where we live, we can hardly imagine what dew means in a land such as Palestine. It makes little difference there whether it rains or not, as long as there is plenty of dew on the land each morning. (Gideon was able to squeeze an entire bowl of water out of a piece of wool left on the ground overnight.) That's why the judgment of Elijah was so frightening when he told Ahab: "There shall be neither rain nor dew these years except by my word." Dew is what refreshes the land at night after a scorching day of sunshine.

"I shall be as dew to Israel." That was a promise of life and abundance for a miserable people consumed by its own sin and guilt.

Of course, the Israelites were not to attain this new life and health through their own power. Dew comes not from below but from above. The blessing would rest on spiritual Israel as a whole–but also on each individual, just as there is dew even on the smallest blade of grass. The blessing of the Lord would not come every now and then but *regularly*, just as the dew appears on the ground *every* morning during Palestine's dry season. God is faithful in blessing us, and therefore we sing that he showers his favors on us day after day.

Thus, Hosea gives us a rich promise when he speaks of dew. In the final analysis, it is a promise of the outpouring of the Holy Spirit, an outpouring through which Israel is born not of the flesh but of the Spirit. Because of this dew, Israel will bloom like the lily and strike root like the poplar.

Hosea uses lovely comparisons to tell us about the fruits of grace. First of all, he tells us of the beauty which grace brings about. The Savior used the same metaphor when he pointed to the lilies of the field and declared that even Solomon in all his glory was not arrayed like one of them. Who gave the lilies of the field their beauty? Who gave them their incomparable appearance?

We could–and should–ask this question of every Christian, for when the dew of the Spirit forms upon him, he will blossom just as the lily does. The beauty of the lily is not obtrusive; it is not dependent on makeup or cosmetics, and it does not seek admiration. The lily blossoms in hidden, unseen places. Its beauty is the inner beauty of the heart, a beauty that pervades the whole of a Christian life.

When we are reborn and enjoy the dew from heaven, our callousness and insensitivity naturally start to give way to nobler traits. Grace makes us gentle in our judgments, careful in our speech, and holy in our way of life. We remove the ashes from our head and adorn ourselves festively as our anxieties give way to praise.

We must always remember that we are not only *justified* through Christ but also *sanctified*. If we rest content with justification and care nothing for sanctification, we're settling for *half* of Christ.

It is the purpose of grace that we be conformed to the beautiful image of Christ, that the ugliness of sin be driven away by the beauty of grace. Israel shall blossom as the lily, we're told. It is no accident that the parable of the treasure in the field is followed by the parable of the pearl of great value: through Christ, we lay up in heaven treasures that glisten like pearls.

The citizens of the Kingdom of heaven are not rich in that they own many jewels. In fact, they normally don't wear jewels, for few of them are wealthy or belong to the aristocracy here on earth. It is their good fortune to *become* jewels instead–gems of people. Their minds are always on good and beautiful things.

We like to speak of the jewels in Christ's crown–but this requires that we do something to become like jewels. We like to dream of a heavenly paradise with exquisite flowers–but we are the ones who must blossom like lilies. After all, we feel the *beginning* of eternal joy in our hearts.

Perhaps the beauty of the lily is seen most of all in the quiet *faith* and *trust* that often arouses the world's jealousy. The Savior also pointed to this aspect of the flower's beauty when He spoke of the lilies as examples for us: they neither spin nor weave, but God takes care of them all the same.

There is something majestic about this faith and trust that rises above anxiety. It contains an element of true nobility. It is no wonder that aristocrats have often chosen the lily to form part of the family coat of arms, for it is a fine symbol of nobility. There was even lily work on top of the pillars in Solomon's temple.

Hosea adds something to this. Not only will Israel blossom under the dew of the Spirit as a lily blossoms in the field, he will also strike root like a poplar. The comparison that the prophet suddenly introduces here is completely different. First, he speaks of the tender lily, and then of the mighty poplar, whose "roots" or foundations extend far into the depths of the earth. He speaks first of the frail flower, whose place we cannot even find after a fierce wind has swept across the field, and then of the majestic poplar, which does not budge an inch from its place even in the face of the storm's fury. The poplar shows us what it means to be unshakable and unwavering.

The metaphor of the lily needs to be complemented by the beautiful metaphor of the poplar. The lily is indeed beautiful, but it is also frail and transitory. The church of the Lord, however, is not a frail, temporary phenomenon! It has the beauty of the lily, but it also has the strength and permanence of the poplar. Actually, even the metaphor of the poplar is too weak. The Lord our protector assures us that mountains will move and hills shake without affecting His covenant. The church has its roots in that firm covenant with God.

The pairing of the lily and the poplar also shows us that in the life of the Christian, feminine beauty and masculine strength should be combined. Often, we are too one-sided. Some people put all emphasis on beauty. They are the attractive, winning flower-Christians who do not take firmness in matters of principle and doctrine very seriously. On the other hand, there are also rigid battlers, the poplar-Christians whose immovability can often make them seem hard and cold.

Hosea now declares that these two do not exclude each other but belong together. Grace works in such a wonderful way that each of us shares in both, becoming as tender as the lily and as steadfast as the poplar.

It cannot be denied that we could do with more beauty as well as more strength. Do you see much evidence that we possess the beauty of flowers and the majesty of mountains?

After we ask ourselves this question, which cannot help but make us feel ashamed, we can close the book of Hosea and ponder his concluding words–words so clear that they need no commentary:

Whoever is wise, let him understand these things;
whoever is discerning, let him know them;
for the ways of the Lord are right,
and the upright walk in them,
but transgressors stumble in them.

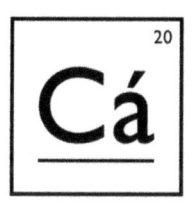

**ABOUT THE CÁNTARO INSTITUTE**

*Inheriting, Informing, Inspiring*

The Cántaro Institute is a reformed evangelical organization committed to the advancement of the Christian worldview for the reformation and renewal of the church and culture.

We believe that as the Christian church returns to the fount of Scripture as her ultimate authority for all knowing and living, and wisely applies God's truth to every aspect of life, her missiological activity will result in not only the renewal of the human person but also the reformation of culture, an inevitable result when the true scope and nature of the gospel is made known and applied.

Milton Keynes UK
Ingram Content Group UK Ltd.
UKHW030149051224
452010UK00001B/1